TENDING TO THE PAST

Children's Literature Association Series

TENDING TO THE PAST

Selfhood and Culture in Children's Narratives about Slavery and Freedom

Karen Michele Chandler

University Press of Mississippi / Jackson

The University Press of Mississippi is the scholarly publishing agency of the Mississippi Institutions of Higher Learning: Alcorn State University, Delta State University, Jackson State University, Mississippi State University, Mississippi University for Women, Mississippi Valley State University, University of Mississippi, and University of Southern Mississippi.

www.upress.state.ms.us

The University Press of Mississippi is a member of the Association of University Presses.

Any discriminatory or derogatory language or hate speech regarding race, ethnicity, religion, sex, gender, class, national origin, age, or disability that has been retained or appears in elided form is in no way an endorsement of the use of such language outside a scholarly context.

Copyright © 2024 by University Press of Mississippi
All rights reserved

∞

An earlier version of chapter 2 appeared in *Children's Literature Association Quarterly*, vol. 31, no. 1, Spring 2006. Published with permission by Johns Hopkins University Press. Copyright © 2006 Children's Literature Association.

An earlier version of chapter 4 appeared in *Children's Literature in Education*, vol. 47, no. 1, 2016, pp. 77–92. Reproduced with permission from Springer Nature.

Library of Congress Cataloging-in-Publication Data

Names: Chandler, Karen Michele, author.
Title: Tending to the past : selfhood and culture in children's narratives about slavery and freedom / Karen Michele Chandler.
Other titles: Children's Literature Association series.
Description: Jackson : University Press of Mississippi, 2024. | Series: Children's literature association series | Includes bibliographical references and index.
Identifiers: LCCN 2023040991 (print) | LCCN 2023040992 (ebook) | ISBN 9781496845931 (hardback) | ISBN 9781496845948 (trade paperback) | ISBN 9781496845955 (epub) | ISBN 9781496845962 (epub) | ISBN 9781496845979 (pdf) | ISBN 9781496845986 (pdf)
Subjects: LCSH: Slavery—United States—History—Juvenile literature. | American literature—African American authors—History and criticism. | Children's literature, American—History and criticism. | African Americans in literature. | African American children in literature. | African American children—Books and reading. | African American authors. | African Americans—Social conditions—History—Juvenile literature.
Classification: LCC E441 .C45 2024 (print) | LCC E441 (ebook) | DDC 810.9/9282—dc23/eng/20231002
LC record available at https://lccn.loc.gov/2023040991
LC ebook record available at https://lccn.loc.gov/2023040992

British Library Cataloging-in-Publication Data available

In loving memory of
Irene Chandler and Ben Chandler

CONTENTS

Acknowledgments ix

Introduction 3

Chapter 1. Freedom Narratives, History, and Black Agency 22

Chapter 2. Retaining African Selfhood and Culture in
American Slavery 51

Chapter 3. Tending to Memory and African American Culture 71

Chapter 4. Stealing Letters: Freedom Narratives, Literacy, and
Black Vernacular Traditions 100

Chapter 5. Let's Play: Black Children's Agency and the
Pursuit of Fun 126

Chapter 6. Tending to the Land: Challenges of Black Financial
Agency and Community in Youth Freedom Narratives 160

Afterword 200

Notes 203

Works Cited 219

Index 233

ACKNOWLEDGMENTS

I am very grateful to friends, family members, and colleagues who have helped me during the many years I worked on this book. Their help has taken so many forms and proved indispensable.

I would be remiss not to acknowledge early professional allies: Betsy Erkkila and David McWhirter. Betsy not only provided regular encouragement but also offered an inspiring model of a scholar and teacher whose interests encompassed film, literature, culture, and theory. David read my writing carefully and encouraged me to write a book, providing detailed guidelines for how I might do so. His constructive, discerning commentary about an earlier project greatly aided my work on this book.

I thank the College of Arts and Sciences at the University of Louisville for its generous support for my scholarship through its professional development fund. I used some of the fund for children's books and films, which helped as I concentrated more on writing about children's texts. I also very much appreciate the support of the late Dean J. Blaine Hudson as I expanded the focus of my work to include children's literature and cultures. I benefited from his two visits to my classes where he spoke about the history of Black resistance and misconceptions about Black history.

I am grateful to Lisa Sizemore Valenzuela and Linda Wilson for sharing their knowledge of diverse children's books. I also thank the staff at the Jaffrey Public Library, particularly the former director Joan Knight, who accommodated my visit to explore the Amos Fortune papers.

I also thank past and current colleagues, including Susan Griffin, Carol Mattingly, Beth Willey, Mary Makris, Susan Ryan, Benjamin Hufbauer, and Frank Kelderman, for reading various parts of this book when it was still very much in process. Their comments helped me sharpen my ideas and confront important questions. Mary, Susan Ryan, Carol, and Benjamin were especially helpful when I shifted the focus of my writing and research to children's literature. I am grateful to Sena Naslund for her friendship and encouragement. I thank Nancy Theriot for inviting me to give my first public lecture on children's literature. That lecture was one of the starting points for this book.

I am profoundly grateful to scholars of children's literature, who helped me think in complicated ways about culturally responsive children's literature. These scholars include Leona Fisher, Susan C. Griffith, Michelle Pagni Stewart, Lois Rauch Gibson, Yvonne Atkinson, Lisa Rowe Fraustino, Andrea Wei-Ying, Meena Khorana, Naomi Lesley, Paula Connolly, Althea Tait, Richard Flynn, Katharine (Kate) Capshaw, Michelle Martin, Claudia Nelson, Jesus Montaño, Dawn Heinecken, and the late June Cummins. I thank the organizers of Children's Literature Association panels for accepting my work and giving me opportunities to try out my ideas and gain feedback. I am grateful to those who attended the panels and shared questions or feedback about my papers. I thank Richard, Kate, and Annette Wannamaker for accepting earlier versions of two chapters that appear here for publication in *Children's Literature Association Quarterly* and *Children's Literature in Education*.

I thank Roxanne Harde, Katie Keene, Katie Turner, and the staff at the University Press of Mississippi for their kind support.

I am grateful to Naomi, Kate Capshaw, Jane Gangi, and KaaVonia Hinton for having read and commented on drafts of the book's chapters. I thank Kaa, too, for her dedication to our writing support group. I am also grateful to Carol Cummings and my husband David Anderson for inviting me to join their weekly writing sessions.

My family have inspired me as I have worked on this project. My children Maya and Ben Anderson, now adults, led me back to children's literature years ago and guided me to interesting questions about it. My sister Joyce Patterson has offered support by expressing sincere interest in everything I write. James, Patrice, and Parker Anderson provided space as I was finishing my revisions on the book. My dear husband David has been supportive and encouraging throughout the long process of writing.

TENDING TO THE PAST

INTRODUCTION

My fascination with children's historical fiction was sparked by Charles Burnett's film adaptation of Gary Paulsen's novel *Nightjohn*. I had long taught antebellum and postbellum literature about slavery and neo-slave narratives such as Toni Morrison's *Beloved* and Octavia Butler's *Kindred*, which informed my interest in the adaptation.[1] Burnett is best known for arthouse films such as *Killers of Sheep* (1978) and *To Sleep with Anger* (1990) and is a central figure in the L.A. Rebellion, a collective of independent, UCLA-affiliated African and African American cinematic artists who began making films in the 1960s. As a director, writer, and cinematographer, Burnett has translated an aesthetic attuned to the nuances of the Black vernacular into inventive, provocative representations of everyday African American experiences. Although more commercial than his independent films, *Nightjohn*, which aired on the Disney Channel in 1996, was strikingly different from many other representations of slavery, especially in its portrayal of the relationship between literacy and vernacular culture. Unlike Gary Paulsen's novel and many antebellum slave narratives, the film does not valorize reading and writing over orality. Burnett's film portrays enslaved and fugitive African Americans who rely on both Black and non-Black ways of communicating, without one way being valued as better.[2] The film's Black characters, within the constraints of slavery, claim and creatively transform the dominant culture's tools, such as alphabetic literacy, to express themselves, resist domination, and gain freedoms. The characters demonstrate the nurturing and ingenious powers of Black culture through storytelling, religious practice, and modes of leadership, caretaking, learning, and other interpersonal connections.

I wondered how common this emphasis on Black cultural supports for survival was in texts for children, and started a search that led to my discovery of the representational patterns in many fictional narratives about African Americans' enslavement and freedom in eighteenth- and nineteenth-century America. My search led me to formulate the questions that shape this book: How have twentieth- and twenty-first-century Black authors reimagined African American personal and cultural survival during the eras of slavery and Reconstruction? And, what is the significance of these narratives' historical reconstructions for young audiences in our own neoliberal era? In other words, what ideological work are these texts performing through their focus on Black culture and its strategies for surviving oppression?

Tending to the Past argues that the narratives under discussion in this book, along with ideologically similar texts, comprise the freedom narrative genre, which challenges longstanding stereotypes of Blackness and fills in significant gaps and silences that inform many popular accounts of Black history. They perform this cultural work by recreating Black historical experiences through the perspectives and actions of young Black persons and rooting these perspectives and actions in distinctly Black cultures. In doing so, these children's texts resist, and provide alternatives to, abiding cultural myths about African American identity and status, such as the lingering condition of "group victimization" (C. Johnson), the persistence of personal and group inadequacy, and the incapacity to realize the promise of American life.[3] As Christopher Myers has pointed out, historical writing about the era of slavery and twentieth-century civil rights struggles has been one of the few areas in which publishers have allowed Black lives to be central ("The Apartheid"). Yet much of the modern literature and film set in the era of slavery or Reconstruction explores African Americans' group subjection, and presents Black resistance and empowerment as exceptions that only a small number of heroic Black individuals have achieved. By contrast, many authors, including those I explore in this study, have been instrumental in using this focus to normalize African American individuals', particularly African American children's, agency. Freedom narratives contribute a distinctly pro-Black message that counters popular dominant culture assumptions about African Americans' "group victimization," waywardness, pathology, and other conditions and behaviors commonly understood as misaligned with American opportunity. These historical texts acknowledge and evoke the horrors of slavery, even as they highlight representations of Black communal resourcefulness and group and individual creativity. In offering this balance and correction, these culturally informed narratives not only address the expectation that children's literature should offer hope and reassurance to child readers, but also reflect historical evidence of African American individual and communal resilience that is not widely acknowledged in the popular imagination (Berlin xvi).

My book's title, which I borrow from Lucille Clifton's poem "I am accused of tending to the past," reflects her speaker's need to go beyond the dominant culture's inadequate attention to Black history. The poem's speaker is "accused of" shaping Black history in a way that suits her rather than offering an objective, balanced account (Clifton, "I am"). Similarly, freedom narratives might arguably be called attempts to shape Black history into something that is palatable, celebratory, and partial to Black political agendas. The texts are partial because they emphasize Black perspectives, but these perspectives are legitimate, informing interpretations that are sensitive to a range of lived and felt experience that is too often ignored. Like Clifton's speaker, freedom narratives maintain and encourage a connection to history that is complex and that discourages complacency. Whereas the poem's speaker envisions herself as a mother figure who helps a personified history grow and express itself, freedom narratives rely on a blend of researched and imagined constructions of Black experience to encourage their audiences to see what may be very unfamiliar, not only because the representations are historical, but also because they depart from dominant culture standards and approved or official ideas about Blackness and American history. The narratives, for instance, complicate and even subvert polarities, fostering readers' capacity to develop various resources in envisioning the past and seeing its relationship to the present. In tending to the past, the films and fiction encourage critical thinking about it, about the relationship between past and present systemic oppression, and about the prevalence of ideas about Black history that simplify and distort Black American experiences and identities.

Tending to the Past concentrates on children's historical fiction and film created by Black authors from the 1980s onward. I argue that these freedom narratives are radical in exploring Black persons' lives within and outside American slavery in the eighteenth and nineteenth centuries. The texts, as my book shows, portray the creativity and power of ordinary Black people who were enslaved or lived in circumscribed freedom during the era of slavery or Reconstruction. In offering important revisionist histories that challenge stereotypes of African American identity, culture, and history, the narratives counter silences about Black lives that have long been standard in mainstream accounts of American history, especially school textbooks and children's literature. The freedom narratives I examine do not focus, for the most part, on epic heroics, such as those detailed in many antebellum slave narrative accounts of escapes from slavery, which continue to serve as the basis for many children's books about Black history. Enslaved persons' autobiographies are significant parts of the African American literary heritage, and contemporary children's narratives about fugitives from slavery are essential, too, because they acknowledge ways in which African Americans—albeit a minority of African Americans—resisted enslavement.[4] Yet escape narratives are disproportionate in literary and cinematic representations of slavery. The primary sources central to this book, by contrast, portray the everyday struggle of Black children and youth (and their biological and adopted families) to think and act in ways that preserve themselves and their networks of support. These texts focus on the ways Black children and adults created sustainable lives in spite of enslavement, racism, and socioeconomic oppression. I use the term *freedom narratives*, because although they were crafted to explore experiences that were shaped by enslavement, they insist on the power of ordinary African Americans to assert their freedom to resist a dominant culture's circumscriptions and violent denials of Black selfhood and community.

Freedom narratives I discuss in this book encompass the experience of enslavement and freedom; they show the continuities between what are often thought to be sharply different conditions. I would never equate freedom and slavery, but by including narratives about characters who are not enslaved, along with texts that focus on slavery, I show how eighteenth- and nineteenth-century Black freedom was informed and limited by the practice of slavery and the racism that justified it. Whether legalized or illicit, freedom for Black persons, as Joyce Hansen's *Home Is With Our Family*, Marilyn Nelson's *My Seneca Village*, Mildred Pitts Walter's *Second Daughter*, Christopher Paul Curtis's *Elijah of Buxton*, and other narratives pointedly demonstrate, was precarious. It depended on both white persons' and institutions' acknowledgment of Black civil rights and humanity and a Black person's and community's ingenuity and persistence in claiming rights. Whether Black characters are free during or after the antebellum era, they are often judged by the status of the enslaved, but they also operate with self-conceptions that transcend legal definitions and the dominant culture's diminishment of Blackness. Yet this is true to a great extent in the narratives that concentrate on characters who are enslaved: They see or aim to see themselves as free, in spite of their legal status. *Tending to the Past* explores these complex reckonings with social identity and with the private sense of selfhood that Black communities nourished. Thus, the protagonists in the freedom narratives I discuss here and the larger body of texts to which they belong are varied: children and youth who are enslaved in the South or North, who have gained legal freedom through the US justice system, a state's legislative action, federal law (i.e., the Emancipation Proclamation), or flight. In some narratives, characters are free while family members remain enslaved; others are part of families that emerged from slavery before they were born. These are just some of the conditions that define characters' social positions and identities. Yet in spite of this variety, the freedom to resist inscribed in the narratives calls on readers to see beyond abiding stereotypes that associate Black people with subjection, pathology, incompetence, and victimhood. The narratives not only portray Black agency, but also foster readers' awareness of their own power to interpret the past and present, to resist social injustice and to be creative interpreters of American experience amid dominant cultural protocols that push them to conform to a status quo that discounts and distorts Black experience and perspectives.

In selecting texts for this book, I have concentrated on literature and film by Black writers and directors that reflect the influence of the Black Arts Movement (BAM) of the 1960s and 1970s. The BAM, the artistic extension of the Black Power Movement, centered Black perspectives and cultural values and rejected integration and dominant cultural standards as indicators of Black success. I argue that the roots of the freedom narratives of the late twentieth and early twenty-first century are largely in the BAM, which fostered a commitment to representing Black lives in their complexity and to acknowledging the generative powers of Black people, communities, and cultures. The BAM's emphasis on foregrounding Black expressive traditions and worldviews is evident in the freedom narratives' reconstructions of Black history, which give weight and dimension to ordinary African Americans' fight for freedom and dignity within and outside the bounds of legal slavery. The freedom narratives are also shaped by Black feminist critiques and revisions of BAM's often masculinist tendencies. This feminist influence is evident in many texts' portrayal of girls' agentic action and leadership, often within the contexts of home and community, rather than in white-dominated spaces. Yet the feminist influence extends to textual representations of voice, intergenerational respect, and the creativity possible in ordinary persons' lives. Moreover, the narratives represent the interiority, social struggles, and achievement of children, youth, and adults through Black perspectives that often depart from and critique the emphases in dominant culture stories. The narratives' emphases thus call on audiences to read and understand history, selfhood, achievement, and freedom differently—indeed to free themselves from the stereotypes of Black personhood and culture that have long persisted in American culture. As my examination of various freedom narratives reveals, the influence of Black 1960s and 1970s social change movements is instrumental to the genre's representations of Black agency, community, and freedom.

I call the texts *freedom narratives* because of their focus on characters' insistence on thinking and acting freely within the constraints of slavery and circumscribed legal freedom. The words "free" and "freedom" are common in the texts, resonating with the revolutionary spirit of the 1960s and 1970s.

Within the civil rights movements of the period, ideas of Black freedom proliferated through events, actions, and words that referenced liberation: The Freedom Riders, the Freedom Now Party, Freedom Schools, Freedom Summer, and freedom songs are examples. Although the term *freedom narrative* has served as a synonym for enslaved African Americans' autobiographies, or slave narratives, I borrow and adapt the term, because it refers to storytelling and can be understood as alluding to Black persons' fight for freedom in the eighteenth and nineteenth centuries and in the civil rights and Black Power movements of the twentieth century. As historical texts about the struggle to be free, freedom narratives also evoke Virginia Hamilton's conception of "liberation literature," a range of her historical writing that foregrounds the pursuit of freedom. In describing the contents of *Her Stories*, a collection of folktales and biographical sketches that she classifies as liberation literature, she explains that they are drawn from tales "told by mostly girls who lived on plantations" that were a means "to free themselves through their imagination"; in adapting these stories for her book, she sought to evoke this claiming of freedom and "to show the empowerment they gave themselves" (Clark 29). In other discussions of her "liberation literature," Hamilton also explains that the freedom extends to the reader, who by identifying with a Black protagonist, "bears witness to the character's trials and suffering and triumphs. To the extent that the protagonist finds liberty, so, too, does the reader, as the witness who understands the struggle as a personal one and responds within with a spiritual sense of freedom" ("Reflections" 285). As Hamilton asserts, historical literature provides opportunities for readers to recognize and understand experiences that may be outside their frames of reference; the process can be profound, transformative, and empowering.

Tending to the Past explores middle-grade historical narratives from the early 1980s through the mid-2010s. The primary texts include a diverse set of middle-grade novels such as Virginia Hamilton's *The Magical Adventures of Pretty Pearl*, Sharon Draper's *Copper Sun*, Joyce Hansen's *The Captive* and *Home Is With Our Family*, Julius Lester's *Time's Memory*, Walter Dean Myers's *The Glory Field*, Christopher Paul Curtis's *Elijah of Buxton*, and Jewell Parker Rhodes's *Sugar*. In addition to these stand-alone novels, my list includes a few series books: Hansen's *I Thought My Soul Would Rise and Fly: The Diary of Patsy, a Freed Girl* and Patricia McKissack's *A Picture of Freedom: The Diary of Clotee, a Slave Girl*, both part of Scholastic's Dear America series; Hansen's *Out From This Place*, the second book in a trilogy that begins with *Which Way Freedom?*; and Mildred Taylor's *The Land*, an installment in the Logan family series. I do not classify Paulsen's *Nightjohn* as a freedom narrative, because the novel lacks the attention to Black culture that enriches the film adaptation, but I discuss both. In addition to Burnett's *Nightjohn*, *Tending to the Past* examines another children's film, Zeinabu irene Davis's *Mother of the River*. The primary sources also include Marilyn Nelson's *My Seneca Village*, a book of poems that chronicles a Black community's history and resonates in interesting ways with Hansen's *Home Is With Our Family*, which dramatizes the last year of the community's existence.

This formal variety suggests some of the versatility Black authors have brought to answering the call for recovering Black history for young audiences, but I could have ranged much more broadly to include picture books, biography, graphic narratives, additional verse novels, and even young adult literature.[5] I decided to focus on middle-grade narratives because they follow child protagonists over time, focusing in considerable detail on the dynamics of interpersonal relationships, the effects of societal shifts on individuals and families, and the ways in which children and youth embraced and used culturally specific survival methods (Brooks and McNair 130). Long-form narrative is well-equipped both to show the personal and cultural processes that enable creativity and survival: As my analysis shows, the texts' uses of narrative allow audiences to see Black children and youth grow, explore, and create within and outside the contexts of nurturing family, friendships, and/or community, giving detailed attention both to characters' interior and external realities. The decision to focus on middle-grade novels also facilitates exploring how the generic elements of freedom narratives work across formally similar texts. This is not to dispute the power of other literary modes, such as the compression and evocativeness of lyrical poetry. Yet the novels I discuss here are so varied and rich that I found it useful to keep to a relatively narrow focus in order to dig deeper to illuminate the significance of recurring narrative patterns and motifs in the genre's centering of Black worldviews.

Yet my parameters do hint at broader possibilities. *Tending to the Past* argues that children's films by Burnett and Davis, such as *Nightjohn* and *Mother of the River* (1995), respectively, also serve as important, if often overlooked, Black alternatives to mainstream entertainments for young audiences. With their children's films, Burnett and Davis, much lauded independent filmmakers, are specifically concerned with offering young viewers empowering portrayals of young Black protagonists within the fold of Black communities. The films relate thematically to the novels I discuss, using cinematic means to explore the child protagonists' Black cultural values, communicative power, and resistance. While filmmaking is a collaborative art that involves input from dozens of technicians and artists, *Tending to the*

Past relies on the auteur theory's conception of the director-artist who is able to use the contributions of a film's cast and crew in the service of distinct, identifiable visual styles and, perhaps more importantly, thematic emphases (B. Nichols 222; Sarris 662–63).[6] As artists who largely have worked outside the Hollywood film industry, Burnett and Davis, another member of the L.A. Rebellion, arguably exercise considerable control over the process of shaping their films as lead authors ("The Story").

Certainly, *Nightjohn* and *Mother of the River* parallel the other freedom narratives' use of sustained storytelling to portray young Black characters' agency. Another text central to my analysis, Nelson's *My Seneca Village* (2015), as a book of lyrical persona poems, would seem to be more of an outlier. Nelson's book departs from other texts under discussion here in not focusing on a single protagonist and in not presenting a sustained period of any particular character's childhood or youth. Instead, *My Seneca Village* offers the story of a Black community through highlighting personal moments, exchanges, and epiphanies of various characters. This approach provides a collective insiders' account of the community's history as both a predominantly Black village and an inclusive, tolerant mecca that drew European immigrants, working class persons, and fugitive and newly emancipated enslaved persons. In spite of its formal difference from other freedom narratives I examine in *Tending to the Past*, *My Seneca Village* highlights Black interiority, supportive interpersonal networks, and Black cultural emphases in ways that resonate with Hansen's more documentary-like narrative interpretation of Seneca Village, *Home Is With Our Family* (2010), and other place-based novels about Black survival.[7] In bringing *My Seneca Village* into conversation with Hansen's novel, I suggest that freedom narratives are not only long-form novels. And I encourage others to investigate how the forms and modes of other young people's literature and media shape the freedom narratives' representations of Black agency and community.

In organizing my argument about the freedom narrative genre, *Tending to the Past* takes a comparative and thematic, rather than a strict chronological, approach. I found that a thematic approach aided my efforts to consider the continuities between the texts I discuss and the freedom narratives' relative consistency in sharing radical pro-Black perspectives on history. My approach does permit me, however, to consider how neoliberalism's increasing entrenchment in American society in the 1990s and afterward has affected the development of diverse literature. The genre continues to evolve, and it will be interesting to see how the Black Lives Matter movement and the widespread protests against anti-Black policing influence historical writing and how the reactionary moves to ban culturally sensitive literatures affect authors' ability to promote radical thinking about Black history and racial difference.

While centering on close textual analysis of the freedom narratives, *Tending to the Past* also reckons with their cultural work: They provided audiences with culturally specific frameworks for understanding a range of eighteenth- and nineteenth-century Black experiences (Brooks and McNair 130). Central to my discussion of the various freedom narratives is a concern with the texts' representations of Black struggle and survival in the past and with their concern with empowering audiences in the present by fostering intellectual engagement. As my argument shows, Black history is never done; the freedom narratives encourage audiences to see continuities between past and present structures of racism and economic injustice and to recognize and lay claim to the creative means by which many African Americans navigated and survived these challenges. Julius Lester's *Time's Memory* (2006), for instance, is emphatic about the need for later generations of African Americans to understand and empathize with those who preceded them and to memorialize Black lives in their complexity. The novel follows a West African (Dogon) spirit's transformation into an enslaved Black youth who discovers a viable way of preserving the memory of enslaved persons who have died. As a collector and recorder of their stories, he relies both on oral testimony from the dead and his own written "as-told-to" accounts that honor their lives and share their memory. In the process, Lester models ways of understandings that resist the common reduction of enslaved persons to the condition imposed by enslavers and legalized by society. This lesson has applications beyond the novel's concern with slavery, for Lester charges his readers with seeking out the stories of older generations more generally, not only to honor ancestors, but also to have a fuller understanding of society.

In recognizing freedom narratives as an important current in the larger tradition of African American children's literature, *Tending to the Past* contributes to a substantial body of scholarship that illuminates the literature's necessary correctives to the omissions and misrepresentations in much of children's literature and popular culture. As Violet Harris, Wanda Brooks, and Jonda C. McNair have argued, Black children's literature challenges dominant cultural myopia, amnesia, and simplifications that shape much of children's literature (V. Harris 547, 555; Brooks and McNair 129). As Brooks and McNair explain, Black children's literature "emerged, in large part, as an oppositional and creative endeavor that challenged the selective tradition in children's literature" that dominates publishers' catalogues and curricular plans (130). The "selective tradition" excludes "culturally specific" perspectives and experiences of minoritized racial and ethnic groups (130). By contrast, Black children's books and media that are attuned to Black culture and history, engage, as Harris avers, in "'a storied tradition of resistance'; that is, while accurately portraying historical facts, they do so in ways that highlight African American resistance" (V. Harris 555).[8] As I argue in *Tending to the Past*, this opposition or resistance is manifest in freedom narratives not primarily through portraying dominant culture practices, rituals, or values, but rather through focusing on Black characters' perspectives, actions, and networks of support in contact with or beyond the dominant culture.

This contrast between literature in the selective tradition and an African American tradition that resists its protocols is central to Paula Connolly's research on the history of representations of slavery in children's literature created from the late eighteenth century to the early 2000s. In examining a variety of categories of child- and family-friendly reading, Connolly found genres throughout this time span that conveyed white supremacist values and thus perpetuated the selective tradition, as described by V. Harris, Brooks, McNair, and others. In exploring antebellum abolitionist literature, for instance, Connolly found that many representations of the fight against slavery foregrounded white children's and youth's potential and agency and assumed Black dependency, discounting Black agency and denying Black persons' interiority. Black children's and youth's agency was more evident in the literature created for literacy projects involving Black children and youth after the Emancipation Proclamation. Yet according to Connolly, Black children's agency in this instructional context was circumscribed to emphasize racial conciliation and personal sacrifice as model behaviors, with more activist, even violent, means of confronting slavery and racism ignored in *The Freedman's Third Reader* (1865), a popular anthology for young Black readers (98–99). The earlier children's literature Connolly has studied remains important because its models of white and Black childhood continue to influence representations and understandings of slavery and enslaved people. The freedom narratives reconstruct a fuller array of Black subject positions that challenge this cultural inheritance and encourage readers to see Black identities and cultures in greater complexity.

Tending to the Past builds on Connolly's research on late twentieth- and early twenty-first-century children's literature about slavery, including her analysis of neo-slave and neo-abolitionist literature. Connolly has pointed out that the latter continues to reflect white cultural norms and to foreground white children's and youth's power at the expense of Black agency. As she has observed, the "neo-abolitionist" genre for young readers usually foregrounds free, white protagonists' growing awareness of the injustice of slavery, often through friendship with an enslaved person (173). One motif in this genre is having the free character play an integral role in securing an enslaved person's freedom. Because the free character is usually white, this dynamic reinforces conceptions of Black history that magnify white activism and obscure Black persons' and organizations' contributions to freedom struggles. By contrast, the neo-slave narrative is a form that usually explores the nature of slavery and freedom from Black characters' frames of reference. Mostly discussed as an adult genre, the neo-slave narrative relies on the conventions of nineteenth-century antebellum slave narratives but plays with them, as Connolly has noted, to do "something new" (200). *Tending to the Past* examines the ways freedom narratives, including neo-slave narratives like *Second Daughter* and *The Captive*, confront earlier writings' silences about or neglect of Black children's agency and the communal supports that foster it. My book is also indebted to Angelyn Mitchell's *The Freedom to Remember*, a study of Black women's historical fiction about slavery, which examines how Black women's historical fiction confronts gaps in earlier Black autobiographical writing and mainstream histories that obscure Black women's agency (7). Concentrating on Octavia Butler's *Kindred*, Sherley Anne Williams's *Dessa Rose*, J. California Cooper's *Family*, Lorene Cary's *The Price of a Child*, along with the "ur-text," Harriet Jacobs's *Incidents in the Life of a Slave Girl*, Mitchell argues that they undermine common ideas about US slavery through their focus on female protagonists who realize self-possession and power in their struggles against social oppression (9, 12). In similar ways, freedom narratives address the need to reconstruct for young readers the means by which Black children and youth expressed their creativity in navigating and surviving systemic injustice.

AGENCY, CREATIVITY, AND FREEDOM

Freedom narratives come from an especially fertile period for African American children's literature, the 1980s through the present, when many Black writers of culturally sensitive children's literature emerged and came to prominence. As Rudine Sims Bishop has noted, Arna Bontemps, starting in the early 1930s, contributed in substantial ways to the body of culturally sensitive Black children's literature, with fiction and nonfiction about Black children's contemporary and historical experiences (*Free Within Ourselves* xv). Moreover, scholars such as Katharine Capshaw and Anna Mae Duane have made important efforts to reconstruct a fuller history of Black children's literature. Yet, starting in the last decades of the twentieth century, the field of Black children's literature expanded, with the continuing productivity of writers like Hamilton and W. D. Myers, whose first books appeared in the late 1960s, and the first publications by Hansen, Walter, Sharon Dennis Wyeth, Vaunda Micheaux Nelson, Andrea Davis Pinkney, Sharon Flake, Rita Williams-Garcia, and others (Bishop, *Free Within Ourselves* 221–22). One distinctive contribution of freedom narratives within this field is their insistence on Black children's and youth's agency in past circumstances that were so limiting and dire that thinking and acting freely was virtually impossible. Enslaved persons had to comply with enslavers' demands or suffer severe punishment. Free African Americans' mobility, civil rights, and socioeconomic status were often severely restricted. The freedom narratives reckon with these limitations and their psychological effects. Yet, as Hamilton has observed, these unjust conditions did not prevent many African Americans from surviving and at times overcoming challenges. Just as it was imperative for Hamilton to create fiction and nonfiction for young readers that featured "strong stories and memorable characters living the best that they know" ("Regina Medal" 192), freedom narratives in general operate on the assumption that Black individuals have historically relied on and shared reserves of "culturally specific" knowledge that enabled survival (Brooks and McNair 130). My book examines some of the ways, to invoke Hamilton's conception of historical writing for children, that freedom narratives portray "a people's range of unique capacity for living" ("Ah, Sweet Rememory" 101) to foster young audiences' imaginations and historical awareness.[9] Hamilton's children's books balance her portrayal of her protagonists' precarious circumstances and the resulting emotional and psychological costs, with the characters' persistence, ingenuity, and openness to learning. Similarly, in freedom narratives, young persons draw on various resources to confront difficult challenges, in the process showing both an abiding creativity and the importance of familial, communal, and cultural supports. These emphases are aligned with the BAM's commitment to supporting Black children's development, along with other aims, and defining Black achievement through a Black perspective.

Tending to the Past brings a child-centered critical approach to interpreting the texts' representations of everyday resistance. Especially relevant is Marah Gubar's kinship theory, which recognizes that like adults, children have particular powers and limitations and continue to develop during their lives, and should thus not be defined at any one time exclusively by what they cannot do ("Hermeneutics" 300). Yet in applying this theory to freedom narratives, it is necessary to consider Black children and adults' positions in the American popular imagination. The dominant culture denied Black children opportunities to be innocent and to be understood as embodying innocence in the ways white children did (Bernstein, ch. 1). As Robin Bernstein has argued, popular ideas about Black childhood allowed the dominant culture to subject Black children to various kinds of exploitation and violence (Bernstein, ch. 1). In other words, the status of youth did not protect Black children, but neither did their state of noninnocence associate them with proficiency, ingenuity, and maturity (Bernstein, ch. 1). As freedom narratives pointedly acknowledge, Black adults were defined by the dominant society as children, lacking the cognitive and moral abilities of white middle-class men. Yet pushing against these cultural conceptions are freedom narratives' portrayals of the diverse ways in which Black adults and children were capable and still growing. Gubar's kinship model can help elucidate these texts' representations of Black communal foundations for Black children's and youth's creativity, inspired education, and mentoring relationships with peers and elders.

My book argues that one of the ways in which freedom narratives counter stereotypes is by foregrounding and reinventing characters' attributes and situations, such as being playful, not being able to read, and lacking parents, that are often wielded as evidence of Black insufficiency, delinquency, and pathology and that thereby feed stereotypes. If in other texts, such depictions serve popular anti-Black stereotypes, freedom narratives complicate their representations of Black inner and external experience by contextualizing it within an intricate web of personal, communal, and historical conditions. Being playful in freedom narratives like Burnett's *Nightjohn* and Rhodes's *Sugar*, for instance, does not affirm the equation of African American children with the Sambo minstrel character whose laughter obscures the anti-Black violence of slavery and Reconstruction. Instead, being playful is a freedom exercised by Black children in spite of expectations that they submit to work demands and prioritize enslavers' or employers' desires. Similarly, freedom narratives reject the idea that needing to learn is evidence of incapacity. In some texts, the child depends on the adult or larger Black community to learn how to navigate the world's injustices; in other texts, the child reminds an adult community inured to the demands of subordination and self-suppression how to express their agency. This creative process is freeing, even if the characters' outer circumstances do not appreciably change. And, of course, some texts present both scenarios, in sum, indicating that children and adults use their varying stores of knowledge and navigate their unknowing in their struggle to maintain integrity and self-respect, honor community, and survive.

Tending to the Past thus shows how the texts present a creative synergy that allows children to learn from other children (*The Captive*), children to learn from adults (*Sugar*), and adults to learn from children (*Sugar, Nightjohn*). These processes manifest the generative powers of Black culture, which fosters individual initiative and innovation that may be visible only to cultural insiders, though freedom narratives invite all readers into the process to see Black agency at work and to foster confidence in their own powers. In freedom narratives' portrayal of characters' intellectual growth, for instance, learning is not simply receiving information or acquiring skills, such as literacy: Learning, like many achievements, involves creative interaction with Black cultural practices and values in ways that elevate the individual without making them exceptional or better. This is evident in *Sugar*, for instance, when the protagonist uses her insights into the trickster tales shared by an elder to take some control over the pace of labor. In this and many other instances, freedom narratives portray agency as a way of using the resources of one's community to facilitate survival.

The freedom narratives' reckoning with the characters' power in reduced, oppressive, and violent circumstances also functions to promote readers' agency. *Tending to the Past* shows how the texts encourage readers to experience a sense of kinship with fictional Black characters who live in a past West African or American society quite different from the present. Hamilton describes this identification as freeing, a use of the imagination that forges connection, inspires empathy, and yields insight ("Reflections" 285). Lester also expresses optimism about young readers' ability to see past the differences posed by history, socioeconomic class, race and nation and to develop a communion with Black protagonists. His stated purpose in writing *To Be a Slave* was to encourage child readers to "experience slaves as human beings," which might enable "that same child to look at the descendants of slaves and also see another human being, no more, no less" ("Thirty Years" 8). In seeking to foster readers' sense of kinship with enslaved persons, Lester alludes to and updates a key purpose of the slave narratives: to develop a sense of relatedness with enslaved persons. Lester is not advocating to a largely white readership in the nineteenth century who defined Black people as things; he is writing to a diverse, post-World War II US readership about the need to reckon with divisions and hierarchies rooted in the past that continued to hamper Americans' awareness. Lester believed that in reading culturally sensitive historical texts, contemporary young readers could establish a complex connection to their forbearers, and see aspects of past life in dimension and depth, as they would have themselves seen.

The texts I consider in this study repeatedly portray Black children's and adolescents' agency as power to use the resources available to them to counteract racism, poverty, rigid social structures that hamper Black mobility and achievement, and other destructive social forces. The resources may take the form of family connections and the culture of home (including memory of lost family and home), the insights and models of Black vernacular culture, or even aspects of print culture and elementary education. What is powerful is the child and youth protagonists' use and transformation of these resources to facilitate their own and often their community members' survival. Child and youth agency, rather than indoctrination, victimization, and deficiency, are the lingua franca of the narratives, which define freedom as the often difficult achievement and expression of this power. Freedom is self-realization that is grounded in a history marked by oppression but also by a Black culture of survival that makes a way out of no way, that insists on growth and being, rather than giving in.

Keeping sight of one's selfhood and working to secure freedom are the guiding goals that a mentoring character accentuates in speaking with the younger newly enslaved protagonist in Kwame Alexander's *The Door of No Return* (2022): "And you will believe in / your freedom, yes?"[10] The teen mentor explains:

> It is your right, Kofi. No one can give it. No one can
> take it. It will not be easy to survive that which
> you are not meant to, but you must know your
> worth, fight to maintain it. . . . (378)

The will to survive in Alexander's book and other freedom narratives is a will to power that depends on being perceptive and creative and on using personal abilities, cultural traditions, and other resources to challenge injustice.

SURVIVING THE HORRORS OF THE PAST

As Ebony Elizabeth Thomas has observed, representations of slavery in children's literature often obscure its horror and fit within a category of the "literature of triumph" that reflects American progress and fosters a sense of complacency about the injustices of the past and present (Thomas). With their reassuring messages about Black survival, the freedom narratives might seem, at least on the surface, to conform to this category. Yet their messages about individual and group creativity and survival coexist with representations of Black suffering, loss, alienation, and uncertainty. Their complicated messaging presupposes young readers' capacity to see historical complexity, including the paradox that recognizes the difficulties of Black lived experience and the inventive ways many Black persons navigated these difficulties. If many of the texts end with some sense that protagonists have not been completely undone by racism and socioeconomic oppression, freedom narratives balance these suggestions with portrayals of Black vulnerability and precarity. In these texts, all problems are not resolved, achievements are contingent on how circumstances develop, and young protagonists must remain vigilant to maintain their powers.

In texts that focus on slavery, its horror is evident through the displacements and deprivations that protagonists endure and that affect their conscious and unconscious experiences. Significantly, the horror is evoked through the persistence of protagonists' and other characters' grief, fear, confusion, and related emotions. Hansen's *The Captive*, Lester's *Time's Memory*, and Draper's *Copper Sun*, which are set partly in West Africa, convey this complex lived experience: Child and adolescent characters see enslavers kill family members, neighbors, and servants and then live with the resulting trauma. In *The Captive*, the twelve-year-old protagonist Kofi sees his father and brother killed, is taken, along with a surviving brother, as a prisoner, and, after being enslaved and escaping, he is recaptured and endures the Middle Passage, which involves physical confinement, forced feedings, and witnessing the death of other captives. In Draper's *Copper Sun*, the fifteen-year-old Amari's experience of the Middle Passage includes her own and other girls' and women's rape. Although Kofi and Amari survive these circumstances, their survival is marked by trauma and by continuing efforts to heal, efforts that often depend on their ability to remain open to the benefits of mentorship, friendship, and remembering what has apparently been lost—family, ancestors, and culture. These and other representations of slavery call on readers to engage with the confusion and uncertainty characters feel and to empathize with their suffering and efforts at self-protection and self-care.

Children who live in freedom may not experience the same level of trauma, but they also bear a heavy burden that does not equate easily to ideas of American triumph. Freedom exists on a spectrum that is informed by the dominant culture's systematic denial of Black agency and by Black individuals' and communities' challenges to this limitation. Whereas Rhodes's *Sugar*, for example, presents Black persons, including its ten-year-old eponymous protagonist, living in a Reconstruction-era Louisiana in conditions close to slavery, Taylor's *The Land*, another Reconstruction-era novel, portrays its teenage protagonist, Paul-Edward, navigating racism as he tries to build wealth as a free laborer and prospective landowner. Unlike Taylor's Paul-Edward, Sugar has little sense of having attained freedom, for she is being socialized to fill the role of laborer and supply the same body- and mind-depleting labor that killed her beloved mother after slavery officially ended. Admittedly, other protagonists in the freedom narratives have lives cushioned from the racism and economic exploitation so present in Sugar's and Paul-Edward's lives, but awareness of these problems becomes central to their psychological and moral development. In Hansen's *Home Is With Our Family*, the protagonist Maria, who lives in a village within New York City, attends school, plays with friends, and has a comfortable middle-class life, but her friendship with a classmate who has escaped slavery makes her attuned to the precariousness of Black experience. Whether enslaved or free, they are children or youth who are witnessing and having to reckon with horror, incorporating it within their frames of reference, and their understanding of the world and their places within it. Freedom narratives explore the psychical and social consequences of this reckoning and invite readers to participate in this process, which includes not simply being resigned to history's and the present's injustices but recognizing the power Black individuals and communities wielded.

BLACK HISTORY TODAY

Indeed, freedom narratives challenge popular understandings of Black history that emphasize African Americans' deficiency and pathology, stereotypes that help to perpetuate the social divisions that privilege the white middle-class and those who reinforce its dominance. These Black freedom narratives counter the cultural myths that maintain that as enslaved persons, Black people had only the identity imposed by their enslavers: The enslaved were supposedly lesser humans, their African identities were destroyed, and they only gained autonomy and agency after slavery and subsequent Jim Crow oppression ended. These assumptions were exposed in a public debate in 2018, when Kanyé West asserted that enslaved African Americans were complicit in their enslavement, stating "When you hear about slavery for 400 years . . . for 400 years? That sounds like a choice" (Burton). Many commentators, including other artists and entertainers like Ava DuVernay, Trevor Noah, and John Legend, objected to West's assertion, while media reported that white supremacist organizations applauded it (O'Connor). The fact that West's assumptions about Black complicity gained traction with at least some Americans is a sign of how conceptions of Black history, particularly slavery, lack logical coherence and can be used to shape an ideological or personal agenda, whether it be an entertainer's or hate-group's aggrandizement. A study conducted by the Southern Poverty Law Center found that teachers and history textbooks relied on outdated concepts in units focusing on slavery, which led to a lack of nuanced historical understanding—a systemic problem in US education (M. Anderson). The *New York Times* is one of many media organs that has sought to bridge this gap between professional history and popular understanding. The introductory essay for its 1619 Project commemorating the arrival in North America of enslaved African laborers addresses this disjunction and its implications, affirming the need to right largescale distortions of the American past and take needed steps to "reframe the country's history" (Silverstein).[11] Freedom narratives remain an important resource for building historical understanding.

CHAPTER SUMMARIES

Tending to the Past continues with chapter 1, which focuses on freedom narratives' origins and proceeds to explore the literature in detail. The chapter identifies the genesis of the narratives in the Black Arts Movement and outlines their importance as activist writing in the late twentieth and early twenty-first centuries. To underscore their distinction, the chapter also compares the genre to a body of historical writing created during the New Negro (or Harlem) Renaissance. Chapter 2 focuses on Draper's *Copper Sun* and Hansen's *The Captive*, arguing that the protagonists' upbringing in Ewe and Ashanti cultures orients them during their enslavement in America and facilitates their survival. These two novels, which are thematically related to several other freedom narratives that give attention to protagonists' birth and enculturation in African communities, challenge long-standing assumptions about cultural erasure. This is the idea that the trauma and displacement of the Middle Passage and resettlement in America erased enslaved captives' cultural knowledge.[12] The chapter's comparative analysis also shows that freedom narratives' pro-Black messaging reflects a spectrum of radicalism.

Chapter 3, "Tending to Memory," examines Virginia Hamilton's *The Magical Adventures of Pretty Pearl* and Julius Lester's *Time's Memory*, which rely on the fantastic to represent the ongoing relationship between African and African American practices and beliefs. Both novels portray the importance of oral storytelling in Black communities and relate the practice to African traditions. The novels emphasize that Black cultures developed art and communication to maintain connections to tradition and to negotiate conditions of life in America. The novels variously portray roots of Black American cultures and their function as repositories and processes that exercise the imagination and encourage personal and communal growth and survival. Chapter 4 explores more commercial texts that revise a myth conveyed in many antebellum slave narratives and much subsequent African American literature: the myth of literacy's predominance as a path to freedom. The focal narratives in this chapter—two Dear America novels, McKissack's *A Picture of Freedom: The Diary of Clotee, a Slave Girl* and Joyce Hansen's *I Thought My Soul Would Rise and Fly*, and Burnett's adaptation of Gary Paulsen's *Nightjohn*—demonstrate the power of the Black vernacular as a framework that shapes Black girl protagonists' uses of literacy. Chapter 5 refocuses the discussion of Black children's self-expression, arguing that in Rhodes's novel *Sugar* and Davis's film *Mother of the River*, Black girls' play and command of their time transform unjust social and economic relations. The chapter also considers the alternative treatment of play in Curtis's *Elijah of Buxton*. In chapter 6, I argue that texts portraying the relationship between African American labor and socioeconomic success are also informed by Black cultural imperatives that counter dominant American values. A brief afterword considers freedom narratives in light of the backlash in the 2020s against diverse children's literature.

Chapter 1

FREEDOM NARRATIVES, HISTORY, AND BLACK AGENCY

Although at some temporal remove from the energies of the civil rights and Black Power movements, freedom narratives bear their influence, in particular the imprint of the Black aesthetic principles forged in the 1960s and 1970s and associated with the radical activism of the period.[1] The narratives, which reconstruct young Black persons' struggles to assert their agency during the eras of slavery and Reconstruction, attest to the continuing influence of the Black Arts Movement and its call for astute cultural awareness. Aligned with the aesthetic commitment to portraying the nuances of Black experience from a perspective attuned to Black culture and history, these books and films represent not only the oppression and circumscription of eighteenth- and nineteenth-century African American life, but also Black agency, autonomy, and creativity (Bishop, *Free Within Ourselves* 89). The texts, whether openly or subtly Afrocentric, were conceived and released at a time when racial oppression continued to inform African American lives, in spite of the gains of the long civil rights movement (C. Anderson 106; Hall 1235, 1237–1238). Freedom narratives propel pro-Black values rooted in 1960s social change activism into a more recent cultural climate in which consequences of racial difference are often denied, obscured, or simplified. These historical narratives are part of a tradition of African American writing for children shaped, as scholar Rudine Sims Bishop has noted, by attention to specifically Black cultures (*Free Within Ourselves* 89). These cultures should not be taken as simple constructs, for, as Bishop notes, they encompass diverse populations of African Americans and various time periods, even though, as she observes, "All Blacks are touched by or participate in . . . shared collective memories and frames of reference" (*Free Within Ourselves* 10). In reconstructing historical experiences of Black enslavement and freedom through African American "frames of reference," freedom narratives encourage their child audiences to engage critically with the actualities of the world and to see young and older Black persons' creative means of surviving systemic injustice: Though the world portrayed is part of the past, readers are urged to consider how this history, including expressions of Black agency, remains important within their own lives and communities.

The concern with making the past present and meaningful is central to the historical writing of Mildred Pitts Walter, one of several Black authors of children's literature who has contributed to the freedom narrative genre. Walter has had a long, distinguished career as a writer, educator, and social activist, and in 1967, she joined other African American intellectuals to protest William Styron's popular novel, *The Confessions of Nat Turner*. The novel's success angered Walter because she thought it deflated the heroic, revolutionary Turner and his African American partners in resistance and recycled stereotypes of Black self-hatred and insufficiency (*Something* 104). Although Styron's novel is for adults, and it would take Walter more than twenty years to write her own historical novel about slavery, her protests in the 1960s are relevant to her conception of the freedom narrative as a culturally specific reconstruction of Black experience. What was missing from Styron's novel, according to Walter and many other African American critics, was a sensitive accounting of African Americans' psychological experience and interpersonal dynamics (Rushdy 82; Walter, *Something Inside* 104). Walter's novel *Second Daughter: The Story of a Slave Girl* (1996) supplies this Black interiority and cultural nuance.[2] The novel acknowledges both the hardships of her protagonists' enslavement and their creativity in expressing themselves and living with some autonomy as they survived potentially dehumanizing conditions. Like Styron's novel, *Second Daughter* is inspired by actual historical figures, in this case, Elizabeth Freeman and her sister Lizzy. In the 1780s, Elizabeth Freeman successfully used the judicial system to challenge legalized slavery in Massachusetts. Walter uses the sisters' story to do several things: to reconstruct the obscured experience of Lizzy and a larger Black community, to explore slavery and Black freedom in the Northeast, to show the relationship between Black lives in America and African cultures of origin, and to engage with ideas of cultural loss and retention and of culturally grounded agency. Unlike Styron's novel, *Second Daughter* demonstrates the ongoing influence of the Black aesthetic and feminist insistence on recognizing Black power in both overt confrontations with racism and the patterns of everyday African American life (Neal, "The Black Arts Movement" 56; Walker 242).

Representative of freedom narratives in its culturally informed characterizations, *Second Daughter* highlights the dynamics and values of African American life that were largely invisible to the protagonists' white contemporaries. In doing so, Walter is also making public an alternative to dominant culture portrayals of Black history that rarely acknowledge Black historical agency or its relationship to the behaviors expected of and imposed on African Americans. Namely, Walter shows her Black protagonists' apparent compliance with the imposed role of slave and their various, often inventive ways of complicating this role by asserting Black selfhood and community. Her portrayals, like those in other freedom narratives, underscore the powers of Black children and youth, even as they acknowledge young characters' personal and circumstantial vulnerabilities and limitations. In *Second Daughter*, for instance, Elizabeth and her sister Lizzie routinely resist their enslaver's dictates by using their given names, Fatou and Aissa, in their private conversations with each other and with Elizabeth's husband. The names are traditional within Fulani culture, and thus are a link to this culture and the sisters' position within their family of birth—Aissa, for instance, means "second daughter." In emphasizing the importance of kinship and Fulani tradition, the sisters are resisting the forces of "natal alienation" that slavery depended on and reinforced (Patterson, *Slavery* 5). In numerous ways, the experience of enslavement was designed to estrange an enslaved individual from their communal and familial heritage and obviate personhood in order to secure the enslaver's authority (Patterson, *Slavery* 5). Through their naming practices, however, Elizabeth and Lizzie resist this process of effacement, which sociologist Orlando Patterson has called "social death" (*Slavery* 38). Also manifesting resistance to white domination is Elizabeth's work as a healer and midwife within a community of enslaved and free African Americans, work that results from her training with a Yoruban elder and reflects her concern for Black community members' well-being. Moreover, Walter shows the persistence of her protagonists' West African enculturation in a scene in which Elizabeth tells Lizzie of their father's efforts to navigate the devastations of enslavement by drawing on the Fulani worldview of his upbringing (Walter 72). *Second Daughter* thus envisions Black supports, such as affective relations and epistemological frameworks, for personal understanding and public action. Its portrayal of personal freedom includes the freedom of self-invention that is rooted in past processes of Black African cultural formation. By presenting Elizabeth and Lizzie's experiences through a culturally specific perspective, Walter shows an attention to cultural and psychological nuance that is missing from many historical novels for young readers.

Second Daughter epitomizes the genre that I delineate and begin to interpret in this book and invite other scholars to examine and theorize further. Like other freedom narratives, Walter's novel encourages readers to see Black historical experience as more than the power to escape slavery or the noble achievement of celebrated heroic figures, which were of great importance, but were not representative of most African Americans' personal experience. Although Elizabeth Freeman was a celebrated public figure, *Second Daughter* is about her participation in a Black world that includes her sister and a larger, diverse community of enslaved and free Black persons. Rather than being an exception who deserves rewards and attention unavailable to others, Elizabeth represents the generative possibilities of belonging to and benefiting from community: She counters understandings of youth that emphasize their deficiency or difference and conducts her life within a spectrum of Black achievement that includes the young and old (Gubar, "The Hermeneutics" 454). This emphasis on a Black collective helps readers see an alternative to the individual-oriented, progress- and triumph-trajectory common in historical writing for children (Thomas). Freedom narratives' emphasis demands that readers think about Black power, and children's power, in new and more complicated ways, and to think about freedom differently. Freedom is not just about relocating to the North but instead entails thinking deliberately and productively in a society that discouraged and vilified Black autonomy and the Black communities and cultures that promoted it. Freedom involves mapping out and acting on one's creative powers, on one's ability to make something positive out of often constrained, oppressive situations and material lack, to mine alternatives to the protocols of a racist status quo, or to use these protocols subversively to act to satisfy personal and Black communal needs.

Many of the writers of the earliest freedom narratives, such as Walter, were active in civil rights and social reform efforts and their writing for children showed their commitment to social change and African American empowerment. Walter, for instance, balanced her commitments as an elementary school teacher and dedicated member of the Congress of Racial Equality (CORE). In this latter role, she helped stage protests demanding fair employment and housing practices and worked with businesses to implement them (Walter, Interview). Walter also expressed empathy for youthful protesters in Los Angeles's Watts neighborhood who used violence to protest racism and poverty (*Something Inside*). On the contrary, Virginia Hamilton, another early crafter of freedom narratives, or "liberation literature," as she called it, did not engage in marches and other such protests. Yet Hamilton's literary aesthetic, like that of the more obviously political Walter, is informed by her profound understanding of Black experiences and perspectives. Hamilton's insistence that her writing be attuned to "the essence of a people who are a parallel culture in America" resonates with the Black Arts Movement artists who valorized Blackness and centered their representations on a Black world ("Regina Medal" 192; Sims 2; Austin 263). This focus did not always yield a story of celebration, for as Hamilton acknowledges, the specifics of

Black experience can be grim; the "precarious" M.C. Higgins and many other Hamilton characters "know that at any moment of time and in any place the American dream can become a bad dream and may well turn into a nightmare. This, then, is their reality" ("Regina Medal" 200). Hamilton's, Walter's, and other African American authors' concern with Black realities is influenced by a societal context in which African Americans and their allies fought racist institutions in multiple public ways, from marching to writing.

Walter's commitments as an activist reflect the integrationist orientation of the civil rights movement; when CORE's focus shifted in the mid-1960s away from nonviolent strategies to achieve racial integration to Black nationalism and self-determination, she stepped away from the organization, though her activism continued (*Something Inside*). She and other creators of freedom narratives, however, were influenced by the more radical energies of Black Power and its artistic branch, the Black Arts Movement (BAM). Adherents of Black Power rejected the pacifism and integrationist goals of the national civil rights movement represented by the Reverend Martin Luther King Jr. and many other church-affiliated leaders. Although Black Power and BAM are associated in the popular media with antiwhite pronouncements and Black separatism, it is important not to reduce them to a few simplistic principles some deemed extremist. As theorist Margo Natalie Crawford has averred, for instance, "the Black Arts movement attacked the ideology of whiteness as opposed to biological whiteness" (124), a distinction that informs freedom narratives' critiques of the dominant culture and complements their foregrounding of Black perspectives that are often silenced or pathologized in mainstream media and cultural outlets. Walter's and other authors' freedom narratives show the influence of the BAM through the texts' commitment, on the one hand, to showing the generative interplay between Black individual and group autonomy, between Black self and culture, and, on the other hand, facilitating attention to the systemic nature of oppression.

In providing some context for freedom narratives' emphases, this chapter engages several questions: Why did "tending to the past" become a concern among African American writers in the 1980s, 1990s, and early 2000s? How did the Black Arts Movement, and other, related intellectual and artistic developments, facilitate freedom narratives' particular approaches to "tending to history" for young audiences? How do the narratives compare to earlier periods' Black historical writing for young audiences, such as the historical literature that appeared during the New Negro (or Harlem) Renaissance? What do freedom narratives' concern with eighteenth- and nineteenth-century struggles against inequality, discrimination, and racism contribute to discourses about the continuing inequities in American society, particularly those that most affect African Americans? Admittedly, these questions can apply to the larger body of historical narratives exploring Black experience, including historical fiction about the twentieth-century civil rights movement and biographies. Many of these texts are also about Black persons' struggles for freedom and autonomy and deserve careful analysis. Yet freedom narratives' focus on the direct effects of slavery and its immediate contexts demands special attention. Representations of Black life during and immediately after the era of slavery, though related to depictions of later Black experiences under Jim Crow, with urban discrimination, and in civil rights protests, emerge from a legacy of radical thinking about slavery and Black agency. This critical legacy has confronted and challenged longstanding stereotypes that discount past and current Black humanity, dismiss the legitimacy of past and current Black cultures, and neglect the nuances of African American historical experience. Focusing on narratives about eighteenth- and nineteenth-century Black history illuminates the ways Black authors have countered these imaginative failures.

FREEDOM NARRATIVES AS ANTIDOTES TO CULTURAL AMNESIA

Second Daughter and other freedom narratives provide an alternative, for instance, to William Armstrong's controversial, prize-winning *Sounder* (1970), which represents the focal family's reliance on Black cultural practices but ultimately suggests that they lack the efficacy to orient and sustain the family in its struggles against racism (Schwebel 112). The need for Walter's and other African American historical writers' recovery and reconstruction of Black history has persisted because of the prevalence of a white conservative perspective on Black life and identity in school curricula and avenues of US popular culture (Givens). Advances in the field of historiography since the 1960s that brought attention to Black persons' agency have long bypassed social science textbooks for children and youth (Loewen, *Lies* 390 note 13). And recently efforts to address these gaps, such as The 1619 Project and the Zinn Education Project, have led to censorship and legislation targeting "woke" books that challenge or complicate white-centered narratives about American historical achievement and progress. This anti-intellectual movement promises to perpetuate gaps in historical awareness that educational researchers see in elementary- and secondary-school curricular materials.

Education researcher LaGarrett King, drawing on a 2017 study conducted by the Southern Poverty Law Center (SPLC), explains, "At the moment,

Black history knowledge required by the curriculum is often additive and superficial. In many ways, we teach about Black history and not through it. The voices and experiences of Black people have often been silenced in favor of the dominant Eurocentric history curriculum" ("The Status of Black History in U.S. Schools and Society" 17). What King describes is a process of objectifying African Americans rather than seeing from their perspectives in order to understand the world Black forbearers saw and navigated. The result, according to journalist Melinda Anderson, also commenting on the SPLC study, is "that slavery is mistaught, is mischaracterized, sanitized, and sentimentalized—leaving students poorly educated, and contemporary issues of race and racism misunderstood" (M. Anderson). The SPLC report explores recent data on the teaching of history, but the problems of ignoring and simplifying Black history are longstanding (Simmons 43; L. King, "'A Narrative to the Colored Children'"). According to Anthony L. Brown, gaps in historical knowledge have perpetuated a white supremacist perspective about African American experiences (54–55). Brown, among others, has traced a history of Black intellectuals' critiques of this pedagogical tendency (55). And scholar Jarvis Givens has found that for many decades Black teachers were indispensable in addressing these gaps to ensure that Black students in segregated schools benefited from less biased instruction in the social sciences (Givens).

Freedom narratives, though often written with a concern for Black children's need for positive representations of Black experience, target a diverse audience to confront and remedy these gaps in historical understanding; they foster young audiences' critical thinking about the prescribed roles Black people historically filled, the lives they created beyond these roles, and the ways Black identity was negotiated in certain socioeconomic contexts. Freedom narratives emerged in the 1980s, authored by writers like Walter and Julius Lester, who had taken public roles in antiracist protests during the 1960s, and by writers like Hamilton, who embraced the Black artistic principles associated with the civil rights and Black Power movements of the 1960s and 1970s.[3] Writers and filmmakers who have produced children's narratives since the 1980s, such as Jewell Parker Rhodes, Brenda Woods, Christopher Paul Curtis, Charles Burnett, and Zeinabu irene Davis, have carried on a legacy of crafting culturally informed historical narratives for young readers. Burnett and Davis, for instance, were members of the L.A. Rebellion, a group of Black filmmakers trained at UCLA starting in the late 1960s, whose work is defined by "their utopian vision of a better society, their sensitivity to children and gender issues, their willingness to question any and all received wisdom, their identification with the liberation movements in the Third World, and their expression of Black pride and dignity" ("The Story of"). Davis's, Burnett's, and other authors' post-civil rights era narratives demonstrate how the influence of the 1960s and 1970s social change moments persisted into the 1980s and beyond. They are also responses to the promise and precariousness of the movements' achievements.

The freedom narratives began to appear at a time when racial inequality was both manifest in the United States and more subtly working in its many institutions. Yet the problems of racial inequity and discrimination were often obscured in official public discourse, and when they were recognized, they were treated not as evidence of systemic bias, but as incidents of anomalous racism or of African American failures. Young African Americans were (and are) disproportionately imprisoned; urban public school systems, which were often associated with African Americans, were (and are) routinely called "failing," with standardized testing indicating that many Black students were significantly behind their white peers in academic achievement. The gaps between African American families' income, financial savings, and inherited wealth, and those of white Americans remained (and remain) considerable (Hacker 111–15). Close attention to these social conditions suggest entrenched, structural imbalances that were obscured but perpetuated by legislative and judicial processes in the 1970s and afterward and by an ongoing misunderstanding of African Americans' complex historical experience.

Landmark antiracist legislative and judicial achievements such as the Civil Rights Act of 1964 were proving effective by the early 1970s, positively impacting African Americans' standing in American society. One obvious example was increased access to higher education, which might have positioned African Americans for a greater range of salaried work.[4] Yet Ronald Reagan's presidency issued in a "'new era of stagnation and decline' for the 'vast majority of average black Americans.' Reagan's job cuts, retooling of student financial aid to eliminate those most in need, and decimation of antipoverty and social welfare programs 'virtually ensured that the goal of the African American community for economic stability and progress would crumble and fade'" (C. Anderson 123). Rather than providing a logical analysis that clarified the processes and benefactors of this regression, American popular culture discounted and obscured them, redirecting attention away from the political, economic, and social systems that cemented racial bias. Mainstream America's answer to the question of why many African Americans were not fitting into the American mainstream and living the American dream focused less on systems that denied equal or equitable access, but rather on African American personal and cultural deficiencies (C. Anderson 3–6, 100).

In the realms of primary and secondary public education, for instance, the signal achievement of *Brown v. Topeka Board of Education* was under assault, impacting African Americans and other persons of color in complicated ways. This legal decision was designed not only to redress racial segregation in school systems but also to facilitate access to equal education. Yet subsequent decisions by the Supreme Court in *San Antonio Independent School District v. Rodriguez* (1973) and *Milliken v. Bradley* (1974) denied the reality of systemic racial discrimination in public education (C. Anderson 114–15). The courts did not acknowledge how the long history of housing segregation had created advantages for white Americans, including location-based funding for public education. School districts depended on real estate taxes rather than other forms of funding, which means that often the richest areas had significantly higher per student funding, even if the tax-base was lower. By contrast, as Carol Anderson explains, many urban schools served African American (as well as Latino, Indigenous, and immigrant) persons who had higher tax rates, but whose property was appraised at lower levels, with the result that per-student funding was significantly lower (115–16). These funding discrepancies have correlated to higher achievement in better-funded schools (Owens). Legal decisions have authorized this inequity, glossing over systemic economic differences. In sum, schools serving students of color lacked the financial support that those in high-income areas, whose populations were largely white, received. Advocates' demand for more equitable distribution of resources was dismissed, with attention shifted to African American students' failure to thrive in a supposedly fair, colorblind society (C. Anderson 114). Similarly, the demand for racially integrated schools was often recast in language emphasizing white students' subjection to "forced" busing or desegregation (C. Anderson 100). Such obfuscation was common in the national discourse about African Americans, often emphasizing African Americans' deficiencies rather than American dominant culture's entrenched inequities.

In exploring the antiracist literature of the 1980s and 1990s, Jodi Melamed has found patterns of concealment that enable rather than expose systemic injustices: "Liberal multiculturalism created a fatal detachment. It produced the possibility for multiple disassociations: of cultural production from people of color, of representation from context, and of antiracist intentions and desire for interracial exchange from activism for racial equality" (92). In her analysis of this late twentieth-century literature (and a literature anthology's selection and framing of texts), Melamed shows how presenting the experiences and perspectives of under-represented minoritized writers can serve dominant culture obfuscations about the roots and realities of historical and current social inequities (112–15). This kind of multiculturalism fosters readers' complacency about social difference, prioritizing "cultural recognition" rather than deeper interracial understanding and cogent analysis of systemic racism (May and Sleeter 3; Melamed 115). Although Melamed's focus differs from mine, her and other scholars' critiques of liberal multiculturalism are useful in exploring children's literature in the same period. As Sara Schwebel has observed, canonized Black children's books, such as Curtis's *The Watsons Go to Birmingham-1963* (1995), a historical novel that provides a devastating portrayal of mid-twentieth-century southern racism, can simplify, and thus obscure, the historical forces that have shaped African American life (127). Curtis's novel, which is partly set in Flint, Michigan, does not offer its target youthful readership a clear accounting of the racist and classist oppression of northern urban life, focusing instead on a Black Michigan family's confrontation with southern racism. Schwebel speculates that "It is in part the novel's silence on federal failures in regard to racial equality [as opposed to southern failures] that facilitated its entry into the classroom canon" (128). She sees the book as a "consummate text of a multicultural, capitalist moment," in which representations of Black experience ultimately encourage complacency about interracial matters (128). Although one region, institution, or villain may be exposed and attacked, the exclusionary multiculturalism that Melamed and Schwebel critique does not sufficiently attend to the larger structures that perpetuate inequity.[5]

As a means of social critique and enlightenment, however, antiracist literature and film, such as freedom narratives, play a significant role in challenging these obfuscating tendencies. Melamed, for instance, acknowledges that some literature carries forward the radicalism of 1960s antiracist activism, which modeled rigorous analysis and debate about social structures (xvii, 94). While catering to young audiences' cognitive abilities, freedom narratives' portrayals of eighteenth- and nineteenth-century Black enslavement and freedom counter the tendency to conceal the intricate workings of socioeconomic realities and African American strategies for countering the resulting oppressions. The texts resonate with Stephen May and Christine E. Sleeter's definition of critical multiculturalism, which acknowledges the ways "Individuals live within multiple collectivities that share existence: families, communities, gender groups, and so forth"; going far beyond a simple "recognition" of difference from a standardized group, this kind of text portrays how self-definition is "refracted through multiple communal experiences, such as social class, religion, and ethnicity" (5). Davis's *Mother of the River* (1995), Lester's *Time's Memory*, Hansen's *The Captive*, and other freedom narratives portray such layers of identity and resist the enforced protocols in the American dominant culture designed to simplify African American vulnerability and to cloud and distort issues of African American autonomy. These books and films provide alternatives to dominant cultural protocols of forgetting and stereotyping that perpetuate racism and faulty assumptions about the American present and past.

ROOTS IN THE BAM

In challenging what scholar Ebony Elizabeth Thomas and others have called the pervasive racism of children's literature, freedom narratives use and remake the conventions of children's literature and film in carrying on the legacy of the Black Arts Movement and earlier freedom movements that fostered cultural awareness and critical thinking (Thomas; Bishop, *Free Within Ourselves* 23–24). As a Black Nationalist movement, the BAM, which began in the early 1960s, encompassed writers and artists in various regions of the country who debated conceptions of art and history and strategies for Black empowerment. A full-scale description of the movement and of radical Black activism more generally is beyond the scope of this study. Yet identifying currents in the Black Arts Movement that have had integral roles in shaping the freedom narratives can sharpen our sense of the latter's contributions. In particular, freedom narratives have been influenced by the BAM's emphasis on Black collective power, intergenerational supports, creativity, and communication; the narratives are also defined by their significant revisions to the movement's conceptions of history, personhood, and audience. The movement brought to the fore Black anger over systemic racism and an emphatic call for revolution in politics and art. Rejecting assimilation to white American political, social, and artistic standards, the BAM attacked mainstream stereotypes of Black persons, foregrounded alternatives that emphasized Black courage and autonomy, and stressed the necessity of a Black world divorced from white culture and its racist, exploitative, and obfuscating structures and assumptions. Communicating the marriage of politics and art was central to BAM artists' interventions, and scholars of the BAM agree that conveying pro-Black principles and values through art, including literature, was "an absolute political priority" that was inextricably connected to Black persons' self-actualization (Smethurst 16).[6]

The process of disentangling Black thought from a web of white cultural influences was a necessary endeavor for BAM leaders and all Black Americans, as author Jean Smith asserts in her essay, "I Learned to Feel Black."

"Negroes must turn away from the preachings, assertions and principles of the larger white society and must turn inward to find the means whereby black people can lead full, meaningful lives.... We must become conscious that our blackness calls for another set of principles derived from our own experiences" (quoted in Rushdy 49). Affirming Blackness was central to the process of re-education within a white supremacist society that fostered in African Americans "racial self-hatred, the internalization of anti-black ways of seeing and thinking" (Collins and Crawford 70). The process also entailed seeing oppressions in American society that touched Black people and acknowledging the distinct Black worldviews and cultural practices that helped Black people survive. As children's literature scholar Nancy Tolson explains, "A Black consciousness became visible across America as Black people chose to wear African clothing, and natural hairstyles, and to create music once more that sent out messages of freedom, telling Blacks to 'Say It Loud, I'm Black and I'm proud'" ("The Black Aesthetic" 70). BAM literature conveys this affirmation of Black culture, identity, and appearance, delineating Black ways of being, acting, thinking, talking, and making art unapologetically in a distinctly Black style (Collins and Crawford 11). The BAM was an artistic and intellectual force that charged this spirit of Black pride: it not only offered a revolutionary, Afrocentric orientation in the 1960s, but also has had a profound effect on Black art, politics, philosophy, and many other cultural interventions since (Crawford, *Black Post-Blackness* 4). One important influence was the emergence of freedom narratives, which are infused with key BAM principles and which negotiated and revised several others.[7]

Some of the BAM's values and inclinations were especially instrumental in shaping the freedom narratives. Perhaps the most important legacy was the BAM's concern with delineating an authentic Black epistemology and culture, that is, centering Black thoughts and feelings and their roots in Africa. This entailed rendering the achievements of ordinary Black people, showing the resourcefulness of Black vernacular expression, and promoting Black self-determination, which was understood as combining individual and collective responsibility and power. As Crawford mentions, BAM literature enables engaging with or connecting to a "black interior" that is little rarely portrayed within texts concerned with placating white audiences (*What Is African American Literature?* 3). The BAM insisted on centering texts on Black experiences in ways that reflected, reinforced, and revealed Black thoughts, feelings, gestures, and behavior.[8] This was the experience behind the veil that W. E. B. Du Bois associated with the Black experience in America and within the mask Paul Laurence Dunbar wrote about in "We

Wear the Mask": recognizable and understandable experience to cultural insiders, but protected from or overlooked by the hostile, uncaring, or disrespectful gaze of outsiders. Black interior life was often left out, minimized, or displaced in white American literature because it did not fit with white middle-class standards.

In presenting first-person accounts of experience and adapting genres associated with interiority, such as diaries, autobiography, letters, and persona poems, freedom narratives foreground Black interiority and often thematize the process of translating its energies to print culture (Connolly 200). Thus, the narratives bear an obvious debt to BAM artists and theorists conceiving the "black book" as a possible "entrance into a black interior" and as a kind of Black public space, facilitating "Black thinking" (Crawford, *What Is Black Literature?* 9; Crawford, *Black Post-Blackness* 89). The "black interior" is not only the contents of the book, but also Black readers' intellectual, emotional, and bodily responses to it. Examples of this focus are plentiful, but Hamilton offers an especially eloquent articulation in discussing her historical nonfiction. She points to her work's close attention to the personhood of enslaved Black persons, to "how human beings, who were considered property belonging to someone else, felt inside their suffering, inside themselves" ("Together: Virginia Hamilton and Arnold Adoff" 214). Hamilton's comments here refer to biographical portraits in her collection, *Many Thousand Gone*, about African Americans who had been enslaved. Yet a focus on African American interiority, particularly Black children's inner feelings and perspectives and the processes through which they recognize and understand others', is central to the body of fictional and film narratives under consideration here. This focus on Black interiority counters the neglect or discounting of Black perspectives in official versions of American history and in much of children's literature and popular culture.

The BAM's conception of Black interiority also depends on frank Black modes of self-expression, including Black speech, tones, and communicative devices, to convey Black experiences, and this emphasis has also influenced freedom narratives' form and content. Rejecting the formal conventions and aesthetic standards associated with white American literature and mainstream American English, BAM writers argued for the richness and legitimacy of Black modes of communication. Describing one influential Chicago group's effort to articulate a Black-centric aesthetic, critic Hoyt Fuller observes that the Organization of Black American Culture's "writers [were] deliberately striving to invest their work with the distinctive styles and rhythms and colors of the ghetto, with those peculiar qualities which, for example, characterize the music of a John Coltrane or a Charlie Parker or a Ray Charles" (135). Fuller is focusing here on twentieth-century urban musicians, but his conflation of everyday Black talk, gestures, and style with the musical achievement of Coltrane, Parker, and Charles is relevant to freedom narratives' focus on the creativity of everyday Black life, even within sites of oppression. Fuller, like other BAM theorists and practitioners, insisted on the importance of seeing and theorizing the creativity of Black self-expression, whether it took the form of music, formal or casual speech, writing, or graphic art. Music and oral expression were understood as bases for other Black art, including literature, because they were divorced from European artistic conventions and thus more authentically Black (Dubey 24). In invoking Charles's soul music and Parker's and Coltrane's jazz, Fuller is characteristic of the BAM theorists who acknowledge the collaboration, improvisation, and innovative play with form and content that are defining features of Black communication. Freedom narratives portray this creativity in characters' use of song, speech, and play, as well as their practices as thinkers, neighbors, mentors and mentees, artists, laborers, and money-makers.

As Fuller's statement suggests, writing played a major role in the BAM's articulation of a Black worldview, including the generative power of Black methods of communication. The BAM's conception of literature's importance deserves particular attention, because writing is both a medium and major theme in many freedom narratives. As literary scholar James Edward Smethurst asserts, although the BAM is often associated with live performance, in the form of theater, improvisational spoken-word events, and poetry readings, the printed text was central, as evidenced by the founding of many independent Black presses and journals in various regions of the United States (92–93). According to Smethurst, BAM writers articulated their critiques of Euro-American conceptions of textuality through their own written texts (92). Their use of Black-owned presses and Black-edited journals was a testament to the importance of alphabetic literacy in developing and maintaining an engaged Black nation and fostering awareness of current Black experience. Like many BAM theorists, the authors of freedom narratives reject opposing print and oral expression or suggesting that the oral is premodern and less advanced than the written (Nielsen 34; Smethurst 99). The BAM's influence on freedom narratives is evident in their thematic concern with literacy and print culture as means of communication that Black people adopted and transformed for their own purposes. And freedom narratives portray the ways Black people use the tools of print culture creatively to satisfy their needs and pursue their own interests. The film *Nightjohn*, for instance, envisions a Black-centered world in which Black characters use alphabetic literacy, along with orality, visual literacy, and other means, strategically and ingeniously to express their will. In Lester's *Time's Memory*, the act of creating autobiographical books from oral sources honors individual voices and experiences and both reveals and facilitates intergenerational understanding and historical awareness. By claiming writing and reading as viable and authentic modes of Black cultural action, freedom narratives echo the BAM's insistence on the legitimacy of literature that is attuned to Black perspectives, feelings, lived experiences, and aspirations.

In spite of these substantial influences, the freedom narratives significantly depart from the BAM in defining audience. A quintessential feature of BAM literature is its refusal to cater to white readers' tastes, standards, and assumptions; BAM literature did not coddle white readers but instead focused on its connection to a Black audience, in the process possibly alienating white readers and Black readers who opted for assimilation to white cultural standards. In this conception of the Black book, explanation was not central, because Black cultural knowledge was assumed; Crawford, for instance, uses the word "is-ness" to describe a defining quality of Black literature that involves representing and evoking experiences that Black readers can recognize and understand without needing definitions, directions, and other prompts: It is "above the level of plain narrative" or simply airing surface facts, but instead comprises "the shared atmosphere of unapologetic black existence," summoning an array of experience that may not be visible (*What Is Black Literature?* 29). Freedom narratives carry forth a similar commitment to engage a specifically Black audience, for they, like many other Black-authored children's texts, were created with a special attention to the cultural needs of a young Black audience in a racist world. These needs entail providing alternatives to the stereotypes that dominate popular culture and that fixate on Black victimization, deficiency, or unthinking compliance with and fulfillment of white norms. Thus, creators of freedom narratives have insisted that engaging Black audiences is imperative, but many also have striven to reach non-Black children and foster interracial understanding and an empathetic perspective on Black history.[9] Walter, for instance, has explained that she sees her books as supports for all children's moral and political agency: "I hope that [my writing] tells children, black and white, all children, that they can make a difference. And all of my books point that out, that you do what you feel is right" (Interview). Walter is characteristic in her concern with providing, to draw on Bishop's metaphors for children's reading, both mirrors through which Black children can see people like themselves as historical actors and windows through which non-Black children can understand the nuances of Black historical experience ("Mirrors, Windows, and Sliding Doors").

Compared to BAM writers' emphases, this purpose involves taking a different approach to writing: As is characteristic of historical writing for young audiences, freedom narratives introduce and explain worlds of the past that are likely foreign to most young audiences, including African American children. Indeed, as Dianne Johnson stresses, through challenging racist stereotypes and providing alternatives, Black children's literature is fundamentally instructive (2). The texts are full of information and explanations designed to support Black and non-Black audiences' connection to and empathy for characters and situations from an earlier time. Yet, while inviting a diverse audience to learn how to read about and process Black experiences, freedom narratives adhere to BAM principles of foregrounding Black interiority. This sense of inclusivity suggests the authors' and filmmakers' faith in both the power of storytelling and actual children to bridge social differences. To further adapt Bishop's metaphor, these historical texts serve as windows to the past that support young readers' and viewers' understanding of the specific challenges that Black Americans faced and some of the specific ways that members of this group, in particular Black children and youth, navigated those challenges. Thus, the texts offer mirrors for Black children and youth through which they can recognize Black characters' racial likeness and negotiate the historical differences and distances the texts illuminate. The texts suggest that knowledge is power and signal that young readers have the ability to use this power in generative ways.

Central to this project of building and reinforcing historical awareness is freedom narratives' conception of Black agency, which also departs from many BAM authors' thinking about Black identity. The freedom narratives' specificity about historical oppression and the ways African Americans resisted and survived it must be distinguished from the BAM aversion to representing Black subjection and victimization. As Crawford has noted, "The BAM's ethos of black cultural nationalism needed too much space for agency and resistance to let slavery become the all-determining air of black experience" (*What Is African American Literature?* 157). This refusal to have slavery be the foundation of Black life shapes freedom narratives' portrayal of slavery, which acknowledges its power to limit action and thought for both enslaved and free Black persons, but the texts also portray the struggle against this circumscription and the processes African Americans used to act and think on their own authority. Thus, the freedom narratives do not follow the direction of some key BAM representations of Black history that replace a detailed portrayal of enslavement with representations of mythical, heroic Black feats that occurred in a time before the trans-Atlantic slave trade and Europe's colonization of Africa (Smethurst 79; Dubey 25–26). This kind of writing often focused on heroic Black masculinity set against a vague "essentially ahistorical" Africa that served "as an alternative to history, a return to cultural wholeness before the fall" (Smethurst 82). Although this focus allowed for ennobling and inspiring pictures of Black identity, it opposes the freedom narratives' concern with reconstructing specific Black geographies, social dynamics, and cultural behaviors in African and, more commonly, African diasporic communities. The common BAM focus on a mythical Africa also contrasts with freedom narratives' concern with showing the creativity within everyday life. Freedom narratives instead resonate with the achievement Alice Walker, a BAM-era feminist writer who criticized many BAM tenets, sees in the hard life of her mother, whose commitment to beauty, self-expression, and integrity were manifest in her storytelling and gardening. In portraying her mother, Walker acknowledges both the hardship and constraints of life as a working-class Black woman in the Jim Crow rural South and the power her mother claimed and expressed in giving shape to her life, creating order and beauty, and inspiring others to be creative (238–42).

In reconceiving and appreciating the creative power of African Americans, freedom narratives are indebted to writings by Walker and other BAM-era Black feminists, who provided important alternatives to prominent BAM's conceptions of historical agency. Black feminist writers such as Walker, June Jordan, Lucille Clifton, Ntozake Shange, and Toni Morrison brought attention to Black women and girls and the diversity within Black communities, as well as a range of relationships between Black persons that aided Black self-expression and self-development. Although different in subject matter, tone and theme and targeting an adult readership, historical writing by Black women, such Gayl Jones's *Corregidora* and Alice Walker's *The Third Life of Grange Copeland*, resisted the BAM concentration on transcending recorded history and foregrounding masculine heroism, instead exploring the dynamics of Black intraracial and intergenerational life. These examinations are not celebratory or triumphal. As Madhu Dubey has maintained, the women writers often relied on a conception of history that emphasized its circularity and the recurrence or continuity of problems of economic injustice, racism, and sexism, rather than their resolution.[10] And scholar Angelyn Mitchell has argued that Black women authors helped to establish a distinct genre of historical narratives that interrogates the nature of Black freedom and fosters readers' critical thinking about the legacies of slavery in the present (3). This literature, influenced by the intellectual energies of the BAM and by Black feminism, parallels the freedom narratives in many regards.

The Black feminist focus on family, friendship, domestic economics, class, and other interpersonal relations, as well as the persistent constraints on Black agency, shape the work of a radical Black male author who participated in the BAM: Lester, whose fiction explores a range of Black experiences in history. His writing for children, including *To Be a Slave*, the collection *This Strange New Feeling*, and the novels *Day of Tears* and *Time's Memory*, often balances a concern with Black interiority and culture, and the complicated ways Black cultural values are expressed through individual choices and actions. The texts take a comprehensive view of individual lives that shows the BAM concern with agency and cultural integrity, as well as the feminist concern with how gender, age, and other aspects of identity factor into characters' experience, particularly in claiming a life of one's own. In his nonfiction book *To Be a Slave*, Lester's comprehensive examination also informs the questions that guide his fiction, which explores the lives Black people made for themselves, often in defiance of slavery, and if characters were free, in defiance of the ever present impact of racism and economic oppression. Lester and other authors of freedom narratives strike this balance through their careful, culturally informed mining of historical sources, insistently reimagining the specificity of Black historical experiences—specific oppressions, specific ways of surviving—to counter stereotypes, apathy, and misunderstanding.

MAKING BLACK HISTORICAL TESTIMONY AVAILABLE

Tailored to the cognitive needs of young readers, *To Be a Slave* appeared the same year as Lester's *Look Out, Whitey! Black Power's Gon' Get Your Mama* (1968), a long essay targeting adult readers and exploring Black radicalism within the United States. The latter's title obviously signals its radicalism, but the contemporaneous children's book is also revolutionary, for as Nick Batho asserts, "Lester was an activist closely tied to the black power movement" whose writing needs to be considered in light of its values (25).[11] Batho argues that "Black power ideas of pride and resistance to white hegemony permeated *To Be a Slave*, as Lester emphasizes slaves' pride in their culture and the work was filled with admiration for how slaves retained their humanity in the face of such brutality" (37). The title of *To Be a Slave* is also radical, indicating a departure from what was standard in American popular culture—representations of Blackness "distilled" through white values and perspectives (Batho 37). By contrast, the title and the book itself focus on Black interiority, and provide insight into the questions of how being was affected by the condition of slavery, how people thought and felt when enslaved, how they regretted, remembered, planned, and hoped, and how they responded to their own and other enslaved persons' power and disempowerment. *To Be a Slave* foregrounds enslaved persons' testimony and Lester's thoughtful commentary provides pictures of enslavement from inside the experience, thereby honoring the perspective of people too often reduced to stereotypes of limitation and victimization. The book is an important model for freedom narratives, which as fictional texts, creatively portray the distinction between enslaved persons' sense of personal being and their social designation—the ways they thought of themselves and the ways the enslaving class thought of and treated them ("Thirty Years" 8). Freedom narratives explore these dynamics by drawing on the resources of fiction, as well as documented history and cultural knowledge, to show African American characters surviving and resisting the dehumanizing powers of slavery. The fictional narratives mine the gaps and silences that are common in the antebellum sources that appear in *To Be a Slave*. These gaps and silences about personhood, feelings, memory, family, and community, as well as the contours of free African American lives, become central in fictional re-creations of early Black experience.

Stereotypes in a prominent study of African American slavery inspired Lester to write *To Be a Slave*. He was moved to conduct his own research on enslaved persons' identities and lives after reading B. A. Botkin's *Lay My Burden Down*, a collection of interviews with former enslaved persons that Lester thought perpetuated stereotypes of the complacent slave: "I was curious," Lester explains, "about what he had left out" ("Thirty Years" 5; Batho 36). This research led him to nineteenth-century slave narratives, which helped him view enslaved persons not only through their position in a racialized, oppressive hierarchy, but also through their complex psychological and spiritual identities. According to Lester, he wanted *To Be a Slave* to show a paradox of enslavement that Botkin's book overlooked: "To be a slave was to be a human being under conditions in which that humanity was denied. They were not slaves. They were people. Their condition was slavery" ("Thirty Years" 8). Lester's commitment to exploring the physical, psychological, and social damage of slavery and African Americans' ways of withstanding and surviving, as well as suffering, this damage has fueled much of his writing for young readers.

Lester's reliance on slave narratives as a rich source for nonfiction writing for young readers parallels many historians' reckoning with the genre in the 1960s and 1970s: These historians questioned and rejected longstanding bias against the narratives as abolitionist propaganda (Connolly 171). Since the mid-twentieth century, historians have drawn on the testimony of enslaved persons to provide accounts of slavery that are more balanced than earlier studies that omitted or minimized enslaved persons' perspectives (Loewen "Slave Narratives" 381).[12] With some caveats, historians, literary artists, and other creatives came to see the narratives as valid sources of information about enslaved persons' external and internal experiences and a much-needed means of engaging with Black voices (Rushdy 4). Although one might argue that this is part of the sugarcoating that is requisite for a representation of slavery in children's literature, acknowledging African Americans' agency within the condition of enslavement has become commonplace within historical treatments of slavery produced since the 1960s. Of course, depriving enslaved persons of their sense of self-possession and power was a strategic part of the enslaving class's domination. The perpetrators of American slavery, according to Patterson, sought to suppress and destroy Black persons' sense of personal and communal history, to dissociate them from their past, and to destroy their sense of personhood, enacting "social death" (*Slavery* 38). This figurative death was designed to render the enslaved person an object or tool of the enslaver. Yet, as James Loewen noted in a review of studies of slavery, many historians acknowledge that this process of domination was met with forms of resistance that made enslavers' control incomplete (Loewen, "Slave Narratives" 382).

To Be a Slave was one of several collections of first-person testimony to appear in the 1960s and 1970s that highlighted enslaved persons' perspectives: William Loren Katz's *Five Slave Narratives* (1968), Arna Bontemps's *The Great Slave Narratives* (1969), Gilbert Osofsky's *Puttin' On Ole Massa: The Slave Narratives of Henry Bibb, William Wells Brown, and Solomon Northup* (1969), and Norman Yetman's *Voices from Slavery* (1970) are others.[13] Several antebellum and postbellum slave narratives were reprinted by mainstream publishers in the 1960s and early 1970s as stand-alone texts.[14] This wave of publications demonstrates that interest in Black history not only energized professional historiography, but also influenced popular renderings of history. E. James West observes this trend in his study of editor and popular historian Lerone Bennett Jr.'s role in making *Ebony* magazine an instrument for presenting Afrocentric perspectives on history. According to West, in the 1960s and 1970s, the Black-owned monthly magazine, edited largely by Black writers and aimed toward a middle-class Black readership, exercised great influence in shaping public discourse about Black history:

> *Ebony*'s historical content was catalyzed by, contributed to and served to complement the struggle for black-centered education and the black independent school movement, the institutionalization of black studies within American higher education, the growth of black

history programming on commercial television, the embrace of black history by corporate advertisers, the federal recognition of Black History Month, and the movement to establish a national holiday for Dr. Martin Luther King, Jr.—all important parts of black history's 'coming of age' and its transition from the margins to the center of American cultural, historical, and political representation. (6)

This legitimating of African American voices and experience in education and popular culture is an important context for understanding the freedom narratives' historical reconstructions and antiracist activism.

African American children's book authors and illustrators, as D. Johnson notes, participated in this broadening of the publishing industry to include Black experiences, including Black history (5).[15] Their literary contributions suggested the multifarious nature of Black experience and identity, resisting the pat assumptions that all early African Americans were slaves, that enslaved African Americans had only the identity imposed by their enslavers, that African Americans, whether free or enslaved, were lesser humans, lacking culture with their African identities destroyed, and that they only gained autonomy and agency after enslavement and subsequent Jim Crow oppression ended.[16] The Black-centered reconstructions also foregrounded Black networks of support, displacing the role of white saviors prominent in popular understandings of the Underground Railroad. Although this reconstructed history often acknowledged the important role of white American and British activists in the struggle for African American freedom, the history emphasized African American agency and the contributions of Black cultural institutions. Freedom narratives countered the messages of what literary historian Paula Connolly has called "neo-abolitionist literature," a popular genre of historical writing for young readers that often foregrounds white persons' subjectivity and roles within civil rights struggles (173).[17] By contrast, notable writers, such as Lester, Hamilton, Hansen, and Patricia McKissack, wrote freedom narratives that conveyed alternative messages about Black historical conditions and encouraged readers to see the versatile powers of Black persons.

Before turning to historical fiction, many of these authors, like Lester, published nonfiction historical books or biographies that investigated Black subjectivities and cultural frameworks. Patricia McKissack's and her husband Fredrick McKissack's careers as writers are illustrative. In writing about more than a century of African American life, the McKissacks sought to help create a body of historical writing that was informed by responsible research on African Americans and responsive to children's needs for cultural supports for navigating a complex world (Bishop "Mirrors, Windows, and Sliding

Doors;" C. Myers). In a video interview, they explain that "our niche was that time period between 1800 and 1900—that's pre-Civil War, Civil War, post-Civil War, up through and until the Harlem Renaissance. And we just carved that out as our niche and we worked very, very hard to try to tell that story. And I hope that what we've done is to make our history a little bit clearer" (McKissack and McKissack). Through their collaboration, the McKissacks produced nonfiction books on early African American sailors, rebellions against slavery, plantation life for enslaved persons and enslavers, and early Black American freedom. These books, including collaborations on historical fiction like *Let My People Go: Bible Stories Told by a Freeman of Color* (1998) and Patricia McKissack's picture books and novels, challenge the popular understanding of Black history promulgated in textbooks, classrooms, political speeches, and celebrity commentary. Although other writers may not have marked out a particular historical period as the McKissacks did, they also responded to the call to reconceive Black history and foreground Black consciousness and culture.[18]

The rediscovery of slave narratives helped to guide this participation, providing a reserve of knowledge about the past that many writers drew upon for their nonfictional and fictional treatments of history. Yet many writers of children's texts did more than reproduce the plots and characters from the earlier narratives. As Connolly observes, the antebellum slave narrative inspired experimentation with themes and forms: "By definition, a 'neo-slave narrative' does something new with the antebellum slave narrative as a genre and focus" (200). Examples of this experimentation are plentiful among freedom narratives. Some play with the conventions of diary and letter writing, using the epistolary forms as structures to convey Black feeling and vision, as in Hansen's *I Thought My Soul Would Rise and Fly: The Diary of Patsy, a Freed Girl* and *The Heart Calls Home*, respectively. Others play with the conventions of the bildungsroman, centering Black youth's awakening and growth, as in Mildred Taylor's *The Land*. The antebellum narratives routinely foregrounded and authorized African American perspectives, and presented Black authority and ingenuity (Connolly 200). But they are informed, even limited, by their abolitionist mission and are reticent about many experiences, whether psychological, familial, and social, which do not clearly align with the fight against slavery. Also, as Toni Morrison has observed, these autobiographical texts omit aspects of enslaved persons' lives that would have been too hard for genteel readers to confront ("Sites" 90). In sum, they provide only limited attention to Black persons' interiority.

Such limited sources of information about the past required supplements, which writers offered through their creative reading of silences within the texts and in official histories conveyed in textbooks. Morrison called this process of filling the gaps "literary archeology," the process of making meaningful narratives out of fragments: "On the basis of some information and a little bit of guesswork you journey to a site to see what remains were left behind and to reconstruct the world that these remains imply" ("Sites" 92). According to Morrison, the process entails attending to and building on fragments of Black historical experience by relying on relevant sources and an imaginative use of inherited cultural knowledge, memory, and evidence-based invention (92). The process Walter described for her book *Second Daughter* mirrors Morrison's description. Although she relied on conventional historical research about Elizabeth Freeman's life in Massachusetts in writing *Second Daughter*, Walter found that her travels to Africa and her grappling with questions derived from her own observations of African American identity guided her in "creatively" transforming her sources (*Something Inside* 123–25) and making them reflect a Black perspective. Walter's example of creative reconstruction resonates with the approach of other freedom narrative authors.[19] These authors wrote from their particular positions as African Americans in a society still shaped by structural racism, and the discrimination, social exclusion, and economic and educational gaps that it has fostered.[20]

Using and transforming the stories from eighteenth- and nineteenth-century slave narratives was a creative and political act informed by freedom-narrative authors' commitment to creating art that was attuned to the realities of the Black present and past. One of these realities was African American children and youth's need for alternatives to the narratives about Blackness that cast past and present-day African American personages as deficient. The freedom narratives are designed to address this need in ways that are attuned to an aesthetic affirming African American identities and histories. In writing their "clear" reconstructions of Black history, for instance, the McKissacks also were concerned with providing "something that doesn't make the children feel ashamed or hurt" (McKissack and McKissack). This involved providing inspiration and hope, as well as reckoning with a trauma-filled past. Moreover, freedom narratives do not present history as over or finalized. Hansen's and Nelson's books about New York City's Seneca Village, for example, represent a Black community's displacement from their longtime home; other freedom narratives end with characters not having fully realized their goals, whether these are reuniting with family, returning home, securing a position or property, or attaining economic independence. The texts instead affirm characters' creativity in defining and pursuing goals, and weathering the challenges imposed by a stratified social system. These texts comprise a functional art that calls a young Black audience and empathetic non-Black readers and viewers to responsible action, in keeping with the activist purpose of the art influenced by the Black Power Movement. As Larry Neal has stressed in describing the role of literature and art in the movement, a knowledge of history is essential for this orientation: "The manner in which we see this history determines how we act. How should we see this history? What should we feel about it? The sense of how that history should be felt is what either unites or separates us" ("And Shine Swam On" 639). The freedom narratives provide young readers with interpretations of Black history that call for active engagement and questioning that urge critical and creative thinking about the relationship between past achievements, limitations, and their current relevance.

COMPARING BLACK AESTHETICS

Certainly, Lester, Hamilton, Walter, and others of their generation helped lay a foundation for subsequent culturally specific historical fiction. Yet representing the hard realities of Black life in ways that respect Black subjectivity was not new to children's literature when these writers emerged in the 1960s and 1970s. Biographical and historical profiles of African Americans, such as those in Ann Plato's *Essays* (1841), William Wells Brown's *The Black Man* (1863), and William Still's *The Underground Railroad* (1872), comprised a significant current in children's, crossover, and family literature directed at Black readers.[21] Nineteenth-century African American periodicals acknowledged and often catered to child readers. The children's literature created during the New Negro Renaissance continued this tradition of curating literature and images designed to counter the practices and effects of a racist American society and provide alternative narratives of African American creative power and resilience (Fielder 160; McNair and Bishop 29–30). And attention to New Negro Renaissance children's literature especially can help illuminate the later freedom narratives' parallels with this past writing and their differences. Like the Afrocentric aesthetic movements of the 1960s and 1970s, the New Negro Renaissance involved often fervent debates among intellectuals, creative writers, artists, and politicians about art's purpose, relationship to current and past events, and significance for children and adults. *The Brownies' Book*, the children's edition of *The Crisis* magazine, epitomized the New Negro effort to present nonfiction, fiction, and poetry that provided perspectives on African American experience. As Katharine Capshaw Smith observes, historical pieces were a common feature in the periodical, part of an imperative among many African American intellectuals to use writing as a technology that would authorize the experience of the past (77). Yet the emphasis and purpose of New Negro historical writing for children and later freedom narratives are distinct, in spite of a parallel commitment to African American children's emotional and intellectual welfare.

The New Negro children's literature is not a thematically unified body of texts, though some of it resonates, at least in part, with the freedom narratives. In her study of Harlem Renaissance children's literature, Smith explains that one of its two dominant aesthetics emphasized portraying the patterns of ordinary African American lives at a time when most Black persons lived in the rural Jim Crow South. This aesthetic, associated with Alain Locke, "advocated realistic depictions of black folkways and rituals, as well as of black individuals' psychological trauma" (56). Although this aesthetic did influence some of the children's literature published during the period, the competing aesthetic associated with W. E. B. Du Bois, held more leverage. Exemplified by *The Brownies' Book*, Du Bois's approach emphasized Black achievement that aligned with white middle-class cultural values; representations of African American history tended to downplay the disabling effects of slavery and racism (Smith 189).[22] As Smith argues, the magazine's integrationist approach and favoring of modern Black identities resulted in mixed messages about Blackness and the experience of the majority of African Americans (26, 56).

For instance, rather than depicting and interpreting the everyday lives of this majority and exploring its diversity, *The Brownies' Book* published biographical essays about celebrated and less well-known Black social achievers who overcame the constraints of slavery and other social injustices. Whether focused on the Haitian leader Toussaint L'Ouverture, the New York City Sunday school founder Katy Ferguson, or the feminist abolitionist Sojourner Truth, these Black historical figures embody a sound work ethic, self-development, and a commitment to community welfare and assertive, reform-oriented action within the public sphere. The essay on L'Ouverture in the May 1920 issue of *The Brownies' Book*, is characteristic of these essays; it describes his dedication to education and intellectual engagement, rise from obscurity to the role of national leader, and ability to work effectively with Black and white persons.

The essay on Ferguson, in the inaugural January 1920 issue, further demonstrates how *The Brownies' Book* filtered history through a New Negro concern with social progress enabled by self-direction and community service. The essay validates Ferguson's self-determination in overcoming slavery—it acknowledges its "horrors," but offers few details about her life as an enslaved person. The essay leaves the experience to readers' imaginations, asking them to "picture the horrors of such a condition [as slavery]," and immediately urges them to use their will and "resolve that in no sense of the word will you allow such a fate to overtake you and yours" (27). Speculating that "Evidently Katy thought something like this, for when she was eighteen, due to her own efforts and the fortunate impressions she had made on some friends, she became free" (27), the essay makes enslavement seem like a condition one can choose to avoid or overcome. Moreover, the essay parallels Ferguson's agency with the assumed power of New Negro child readers to direct the course of their lives. Here, as in many of the biographical profiles, the focus is on an exceptional African American's ability to apply herself to realize her own selfhood and ameliorate the conditions of others. Ferguson's reform efforts involved providing shelter and spiritual support to impoverished and neglected Black and white children, which advances another common theme in *The Brownies' Book*: the generative possibilities of racial amity (Smith 189). As Connolly has observed, in its profiles of Black achievement, the exceptional, heroic African American embodies the ideals of American democracy, underscoring for Black and non-Black readers African Americans' affinity for citizenship (156). Missing, however, is a more balanced treatment of history that acknowledges the Black lives that did not always conform to these particular models of self-actualization. Also missing from the profile of Ferguson and many other historical treatments in *The Brownies Book* is analysis of the systemic social structures that prevented most Black persons from realizing success like hers. Unlike the later freedom narratives, *The Brownies' Book* limited representations of enslaved and working-class free African Americans who did not overcome economic oppression. More important for many writers and editors during this period was inspiring young New Negro readers to see their connections to past heroic achievement and to use these connections as guides for their own potentially fruitful interventions within the dominant culture.

More resonant with the freedom narratives were some contemporaneous New Negro children's historical drama and pageants that reconstructed ordinary Black persons' experience, and textbooks issued by the Associated Publishers, a press founded by historian Carter G. Woodson. One book published by the press, Janet Dabney Shackelford's *The Child's Story of the Negro*, for instance, provided information about enslaved black persons' lives (Smith 65, 72). Yet most theatrical texts concentrated on showing African Americans' heroic transformations of limiting circumstances, rather than the patterns of everyday lives and the ways individuals expressed themselves through these daily rituals (Smith 65, 72). Moreover, Shackelford's book was characteristic of others in providing mixed evaluations of early African

Americans, both affirming their humanity and emphasizing their failure to achieve self-realization. In analyzing the Associated Publishers' textbooks, *Child Story of the Negro* and *Word Pictures of the Great*, for instance, Smith notes that their "depictions of enslavement vacillate between commemorating black individuals and family structures and emphasizing quite adamantly the modern reader's remoteness from slavery, which allows the authors to align black readers with white social structures in order to argue for integration" (189). The exceptions were those early African Americans who freed themselves from societal chains and made something of themselves, usually without the support and influence of a Black community. Through valorizing individualism and exceptionalism, the Associated Publishers' texts and *The Brownies' Book* essays obscure or discount Black cultural values that deviate from white middle-class norms. These earlier texts' shared focus illustrates their key difference from freedom narratives: a concern with integration into a dominant culture that rewards individual achievement, innovation, and productivity. This integration often at least implicitly reinforces a capitalist status quo without sufficiently acknowledging the systemic barriers to African American socioeconomic development. It obscures the distinctions of African American history, as well as the diverse means by which African Americans survived.

BLACK FRAMEWORKS FOR UNDERSTANDING

If New Negro Renaissance historical writing for young readers shows an optimism about racial integration, freedom narratives are more invested in showing that processes that support Black self-development and survival are more of a priority than integration. That is, African American self-expression, survival, and freedom. Even when a freedom narrative represents integration or cross-racial alliance, it facilitates questions about these social configurations, encouraging readers to ponder their stakes and limitations, and to consider ways Black self-determination and culture coexist with assimilation and interracial relations. Taylor's *The Land* exemplifies the turn away from integration and towards Blackness, because it focuses on a biracial young man, Paul-Edward Logan, who has grown up identifying with his white upper-class southern father but who adjusts his perspective to fashion a viable place within Reconstruction-era Mississippi as a Black man. Paul-Edward uses his agency in interracial business relationships that often end to his disadvantage because of his white southerner employers', partners', and customers' racism. These transactions not only comprise a critique of the New South's economic priorities and racism but also encourage readers to see Paul-Edward's and his Black allies' efforts to live with integrity in spite of society's restrictions. Through his hard work and determination and creative problem-solving and through the creative efforts of supportive friends and family, Paul-Edward is able to realize his dream of owning a farm. In *The Land* and other freedom narratives, creating and sustaining a way of life that is enabled by Black communal effort and that allows for individual differences within community counters the white-controlled social structure that demands the Black self-abnegation requisite for assimilation into a white supremacist system. This emphasis on culture and collectivity, rooted in the revolutionary thought of the Black Arts and the Black Power Movements, should not be equated with a rejection of individual agency. Rather than defining individual success as a gateway to assimilation into the dominant culture, freedom narratives focus on characters who, enmeshed in and nourished by Black cultures, express autonomy through their creative, active engagement with their circumstances.

Freedom narratives' Black Nationalist predispositions are also responding to and resisting the cementing and legitimating of neoliberal practices in the 1980s and onward. In these texts, the commitments of the 1960s' Black aesthetic are vivid and adapted to confront the neoliberal tendency to co-opt resistant voices and normalize and legitimate a white-supremacist status quo. As a set of socioeconomic structures, neoliberalism has proven to be nearly all-encompassing in its power to displace or co-opt alternative values (Harvey 12). Melamed has described how the neoliberal imperative absorbed the literature by and about under-represented minorities, by validating conformity to its standards of success and pathologizing divergences (116–17). A common assumption informing the literature is that everyone is the same, a dedication to color-blindness that denies the particular socioeconomic locations and histories of many African Americans, Indigenous persons, and persons of color, as well as many white Americans for whom affluence is elusive. Much children's literature serves neoliberalism's smoothing out of social differences, but freedom narratives are among those texts that foster understanding of difference in ways that promote cultural and historical awareness. They encourage readers to free themselves of narrow and stereotyped conceptions of the past that pervade popular culture. Because their portrayals of the relationship between Black selfhood and culture are often immersive, the texts encourage readers to engage deeply with African American perspectives and to embrace more comprehensive understandings of the world. Culturally specific historical narratives have the power to give audiences interpretive frameworks that refute neoliberal understandings of the world and the destructive values that inform them.[23]

In subsequent chapters, I focus on Black cultural frameworks as tools for understanding Black agency, culture, and community. In the next chapter, I focus on two books, Sharon Draper's *Copper Sun* and Joyce Hansen's *The Captive*, which emphasize their protagonists' cultural distinction as members of Ewe and Ashanti societies who are captured in their homeland and transferred to America as enslaved laborers. The novels demonstrate how two prolific, well-respected African American authors personalize the Black aesthetic in portraying young enslaved African youths' struggle for autonomy and integrity. In reconstructing young Black identities grounded in particular African ethnic cultures, both authors insist on the power of the protagonists' African enculturation to continue to shape their worldviews and provide bases for thought and action. Yet the texts' ideological variances indicate that freedom narratives exist on a spectrum in portraying Black identity in the context of Black community and in countering the influence of neoliberal imperatives.

Chapter 2

RETAINING AFRICAN SELFHOOD AND CULTURE IN AMERICAN SLAVERY

Joyce Hansen's *The Captive* (1994) and Sharon Draper's *Copper Sun* (2006) are freedom narratives that represent the experience of the Middle Passage, the crossing of the Atlantic Ocean that millions of Black African captives endured as part of their captivity and forced migration from coastal West Africa to the Americas. These two middle-grade novels continue the legacy of the ground-breaking *Middle Passage: White Ships/Black Cargo*, Tom Feelings's illustrated book that vividly and movingly represents the human dimension of this devastating, violent journey. A growing number of children's books portray the Middle Passage, including nonfiction picture books such as *The 1619 Project: Born on the Water* and *Your Legacy*, which retell the history of the Black American experience. Books for older children, such as Marilyn Nelson's hybrid verse biography of Venture Smith, *The Freedom Business*, and Kwame Alexander's verse novel *The Door of No Return*, also offer powerful representations of the Middle Passage that acknowledge its devastation. Many of these texts share *The Captive* and *Copper Sun*'s concern with acknowledging the journey's trauma and violence, while showing the ways many Black persons survived them and encouraging young people to engage thoughtfully and empathetically with this difficult history. All these texts underscore the importance of the Middle Passage, but as Alexander has insisted about his book, this harrowing experience was not enslaved Africans' "beginning," nor was it the beginning for their descendants (Hunter). Like many other freedom narratives, Alexander's *The Door of No Return* relies on the premise that the foundations of African American history lie in the patterns of everyday life in West African localities, rather than the Euro-American systems of slavery that disrupted these patterns.

I focus on *Copper Sun* and *The Captive* because of the texts' status as fiction that renders the experience of young protagonists in their African homelands, during the Middle Passage, and in America. Like Alexander, Draper and Hansen illuminate the beginnings of African American history by focusing on young Black persons' lives within their homes and families in West Africa. The novels also portray their protagonists' reliance on their upbringings in particular African ethnic cultures as they survive the Middle Passage and adapt to life in America. By presenting the processes through which African youths become African American, *The Captive* and *Copper Sun* reflect the Black Art Movement's concern with emphasizing African roots of Black selfhood and culture. Hansen's and Draper's novels insist that the Middle Passage and the brutality of slavery did not destroy ethnic African influences, a message that resonates with the emphasis in many other books that explore African Americans' beginnings in Africa. *The Captive* and *Copper Sun* are especially notable, because of their detailed portrayals of how African protagonists' socialization within America was framed by their upbringings in Africa.

Part of the wave of books appearing in the 1990s and 2000s in response to demand for multicultural titles, *The Captive* and *Copper Sun* provide opposing resolutions to the question of how a Black person can fit with dignity and self-possession into a diverse, stratified, and market-driven world dominated by white Americans. As in all historical fiction, the novels' representations of the past comment on aspects of the authors' own era (Schwebel 3). *Copper Sun* ultimately offers assurances about America's cultural pluralism in ways that elide aspects of the historical community that Draper presents as an American home for her protagonist. Draper's integrationist ending fits within the parameters of the neoliberal multiculturalism Jodi Melamed has associated with the early years of the twenty-first century: endorsing business-friendly practices, valuing productivity, and marginalizing persons who cannot contribute (148, 150). The cultural plurality Draper portrays is different from the Black abolitionist network Hansen highlights at the end of *The Captive*. This earlier novel offers a vision of transnational personhood and leadership as means of surviving and continuing to fight against racism and slavery. Hansen brings to *The Captive* the unadulterated, radical vision of Black diasporic activism that suggests her and many other freedom narrative writers' optimism about children's literature as a vehicle for inciting positive social change through changing minds and institutions.

Copper Sun, set in 1738, focuses on the fifteen-year-old Amari, who is taken into slavery after a raid kills her family and destroys their village. She goes on to suffer sexual exploitation during the Middle Passage and later in South Carolina, where she serves as a concubine on the Derby family plantation. Draper alternates aspects of Amari's experience with that of another fifteen-year-old, the white servant Polly, who has been indentured to the Derbys. Although Amari and Polly initially dislike each other, they gradually become friends, escape the plantation, and find refuge in Fort Mose, Florida. *The Captive*, set between 1788 and 1811, begins with its protagonist Kofi as a privileged youth in the Ashanti kingdom, but his family falls victim to the slave trade when an enslaved man who serves the family betrays them. After his father and older brother are killed, Kofi is enslaved in West Africa, endures the Middle Passage with help from two other youths, one of whom is white and indentured, the other, Black and enslaved. When they reach Boston, the three go to work for a harsh Calvinist couple, the Brownes. With the support of the historical figure Paul Cuffe, Kofi gains his freedom and embarks on a career as an abolitionist.

The Captive and *Copper Sun* are part of a long tradition of children's writing by African American authors that explores the importance of Africa to Black Americans and promotes solidarity among persons with African ancestry. The novels thus exemplify the freedom narrative genre's concern with an inclusive understanding of Black community that acknowledges the importance of African traditions and their continuing relevance within the African diaspora. Yet freedom narratives, including Hansen's and Draper's novels, that represent Black protagonists' lives in African communities depart from many other children's texts about Africa. The significance of Africa has varied among writers and in different eras, but for much of the history of African American children's literature, Africa has been portrayed with ambivalence. In exploring the nuances of the pan-Africanism in New Negro literature for children, for instance, Katharine Capshaw Smith finds mixed messages. Only some of the literature encourages African American children to identify with African children. Smith mentions two African American contributors to *The Brownies' Book*, Kathleen Easmon and Sarah Talbert Keelan, whose pieces foster Black children's awareness of racist oppression in the United States and Africa, support the concept of an African diaspora, and emphasize the need for social activism at home and in African nations (32–33). Yet, Smith admits that in encouraging this sense of "solidarity," the writers downplay the particularities of ethnic African groups. Furthermore, often texts for children reinscribe "[d]ifference from Africa" in a way that "establishes New Negro distinctiveness and progress, a pattern that becomes pronounced in some of the Associated Publishers books of the 1930s and 1940s" (35). These children's books from historian Carter G. Woodson's press were shaped by conflicting factors, including contributors' respect for African cultural achievements, acceptance of white American middle-class values, and integrationist orientation, resulting in contradiction (Smith 172).

Child readers of at least some Associated Press books about Africa were invited to see African subjects as exotic and distant, occupying the position of "tourist of Africa," more akin to a white American reader than to a resident of an African country (Smith 176–77).[1]

The freedom narratives' portrayal of African influences and retentions is related to the Black Arts Movement's more positive reconceptions of Africa. In BAM literature, Africa had undisputed value, especially its precolonial history, and particular African ethnicities might be invoked, but in much of the literature, the priority was emphasizing an empowering connection to a generalized sense of an Africa uncorrupted by white Western influence (Smith 179). Virginia Hamilton's first novel *Zeely* (1967) is a good example of a children's book that explores the connection between Black American and African identities: It centers on an imaginative African American girl Elizabeth's fascination with Zeely, a young woman whom she identifies as Watutsi and associates with the beauty, nobility, and fantasy missing from her own life. Zeely teaches Elizabeth she needs to accept people, including herself, for who they are. For Elizabeth, Africa is an alternative to the mundane, but the novel complicates her perspective by having Zeely explain that ties to Africa are common, not extraordinary, and are a reality of the Black African diaspora that one must learn to know and accept. By the 1970s, poets such as Nikki Giovanni and Sonia Sanchez, well-known for their writing for adult readers, published books of poems that echo this sense of a Black selfhood informed by a rich African American and African experience. Giovanni's "Ego-Tripping (there may be a reason why)," for instance, affirms pride in a heritage that lays claim to cultural and geographic features of Africa and that is manifest in the use of the Black vernacular's creative play with language:

> I was born in the congo
> I walked to the fertile crescent and built
>   the sphinx
>   . . .
> I am bad. (42)

The speaker uses exaggeration, a feature of the African American oral tradition, to underscore her confident sense of self that is informed by Africa's excellence and that has the power to transform, travel, and enrich the world. Giovanni's vision of a productive continent and Black female self emphasizes agency, geographic plenty, and even acquisitiveness. And as a celebratory poem, it evokes Africa's great human and geographical resources with no mention of colonialism or slavery.

Still, reconstructing the lines of descent from particular African ethnic groups to an African American character's beliefs and actions has been a rarity in children's historical fiction about slavery until relatively recently. Relatively few literary works for children follow a person's beginnings in Africa to their forced move and experience in America. Two novels that do trace the influence of African culture, Virginia Hamilton's *The Adventures of Pretty Pearl* and Julius Lester's *Time's Memory*, which I discuss at length in chapter 3, rely on folklore and fantasy in rendering African elements of nineteenth-century Black communities during and after slavery, and are not among the most familiar of the celebrated authors' books. One of the most prominent children's historical novels with an African-born, enslaved protagonist in America remains Elizabeth Yates's 1951 Newberry Award-winning *Amos Fortune, Free Man*, though it, as Sara Schwebel and others have observed, presents his slavery in a favorable light (99). The freedom narratives' representations of Black agency and resistance, which include Black characters' refusal to let go of African cultural traditions, challenge an interpretation of Black history that discounts both the violence of slavery and the enduring power of African frameworks of thinking, feeling, and acting.

Amos Fortune, a fixture on lists of recommended books for middle-school readers, continues to be accepted in educational circles, according to Schwebel, because it fulfills a cultural need for assurances about "racial harmony and positive progress toward multicultural ideas" (100). The novel's "racial harmony and positive progress" result from Fortune losing his psychological, linguistic, and physical connection to his homeland during the Middle Passage, accepting his enslavement, and succeeding as a village businessman in New Hampshire. *Amos Fortune* promotes a vision of the American and African American past that is shorn of African influence, allowing the novel to encourage young readers to see ethnic and racial diversity within the colonies and the early United States as superficial. As Schwebel points out, this vision of a multicultural American is not uncommon in books that educators have embraced: such books reflect "not a radical particularist movement but rather a politically moderate assertion of the American Dream, recast in pluralistic terms" (Schwebel 31). In effect, Yates's novel shows Fortune embodying a distinctly American success through his acceptance of dominant culture values. Yet this emphasis normalizes a path that relatively few African Americans realized, even as it ignores or discounts the experience of those who could not or chose not to conform. *Amos Fortune* adheres to the pattern that Melamed has ascribed to mid-twentieth-century race narratives whose "representations of African Americans identified the fitness of some to culturally embody the nation" and "testified to ... their underlying cultural sameness with white Americans" (24–25). Fortune, in Yates's book, manifests his sameness, after buying his freedom, by fitting into a New Hampshire town as a self-supporting landowner.

Hansen's *The Captive* and Draper's *Copper Sun*, to varying extents, challenge this emphasis on social homogeneity by portraying the continuity and evolution of ethnic cultural practices and epistemological frameworks in their protagonists' new geographic and socioeconomic contexts. Both *The Captive* and *Copper Sun* are specific about their protagonists' cultural roots: Kofi, of *The Captive*, is Ashanti and Amari, of *Copper Sun*, is Ewe, encouraging readers to imagine ways these particular ethnic Africans survived geographic displacement and slavery in America. Hansen and Draper have done extensive research on early African American history and are attuned to the nuances of the many ethnic groups that in various periods have shaped the African diaspora. Draper's decision to make Amari a member of the Ewe society, for instance, may be related to her research on her own family history, which indicated she may have Ewe ancestry (Hinton 95). Moreover, she, like several other freedom narrative authors, has traveled to Ghana, the traditional homeland of the Ewe, several times to do site research. Although an African homeplace appears only briefly in the plots of *Copper Sun* and *The Captive*, these sites of origin nevertheless maintain a hold on the protagonists' memories and perspectives on life. These representations of the continuing relevance of an ethnic African home testify to the endurance of those who made it through "the school of slavery," the complex socioeconomic contexts in which captive, enslaved persons lived and were expected to accept and conform to their "social death," and yet in many cases strove to define themselves in other ways (Patterson, *Slavery* 38–39).[2] However, where *Copper Sun* presents its protagonist Amari's emergence from slavery as a triumph of socioeconomic inclusion, *The Captive* suggests that freedom is more than individualist success and participation in a market economy. If *Copper Sun* offers a vision of individual struggle and social achievement that meshes with the dominant culture's myths, *The Captive* points to a more radical alternative.

FREEDOM, CULTURAL RETENTION, CREATIVE TRANSFORMATION

Hansen's *The Captive* is a realist novel that renders its protagonist Kofi's consciousness as it evolves from innocence to experience through captivity, the intra-African slave trade, the Middle Passage, and settlement in New

England. Hansen's Kofi represents the possibility of a person maintaining personal and cultural integrity even as they adapt to dislocation and familial losses. *The Captive* speaks to current cultural needs for a past that demonstrates the persistence, richness, and fruitfulness of African ethnic folkways. Kofi's identity is rooted in tradition and defined by the new, including the need to fight slavery. Kofi's American identity would seem to be a break from his Ashanti past, which included his benefiting from enslaved persons' labor, for out of his own enslavement, he becomes a fervent abolitionist. Yet, Hansen suggests that his acculturation to life in the young United States, including his acquisition of English and literacy, is informed by his identity as an Ashanti boy, particularly his respect for his ancestry and his acknowledgment of the importance and complementarity of all life.

The Captive frames the story of Kofi's kidnapping and enslavement with a scene of his imminent return to Sierra Leone in 1811 as a mate aboard an American cargo ship. At the end of the narrative, he discloses that his home is in Massachusetts, where he is part of a community of activists that includes his wife, who was also taken from an Ashanti village. Kofi explains that "My Ashanti village lives only in my soul," but the novel suggests repeatedly that this village's culture continues to influence his thoughts and actions. He remains connected to this foundation of self, drawing on his past and adjusting traditional values in accordance with the demands of his present (Hansen, *The Captive* 193). Central to Hansen's portrait of Kofi is his awareness about and pride in his status as an Ashanti male. At the beginning of *The Captive*, Kofi is about to accept the role of stool bearer for his chieftain father at an annual festival recognizing former and current Ashanti leaders. As an initiate into Ashanti manhood, Kofi is both grounded in and mindful of his culture. As the novel continues, Hansen presents him as thinking and acting in accordance with his culture's standards and beliefs. Kofi represents the continuity of tradition, and *The Captive* suggests that when he is displaced from his own native world and thrust into other cultures in West Africa and North America, he adapts without losing his foothold in Ashanti culture. Kofi, like Amari, manifests the power to reinvent himself by drawing on his original culture as he tries to make a viable place for himself aboard the ship to America and in the colonies. He also offers contemporary readers a model of adjustment and resourcefulness that challenges the concept of cultural erasure, which has long informed discussions of African Americans' connection to their African ancestry. In portraying Kofi's reliance on Ashanti culture, Hansen is attuned to late twentieth-century historical and folkloric research that indicates the ongoing importance of African cultural retentions (Abrahams xxii).

From the adult Kofi's view of the coast of Sierra Leone, the narrative moves back to Kofi's childhood in the Ashanti kingdom. Traveling with his family to participate in a regional meeting as a ceremonial stool bearer, Kofi is conscious of the nuances of his culture and proud of having reached the point where he can take part more fully. Yet his lack of interest in news of intertribal tensions and the growing slave trade suggests his naiveté.[3] These threats quickly become real for Kofi's family when he, his father, and his brothers are kidnapped, and his father and one brother die. Kofi manages to escape, but cut off from surviving family, he soon is enslaved by a merchant who sells him and an Ashanti girl, Ama (Kofi's future wife), to traders for transfer to America. Aboard ship he suffers greatly, but also befriends Tim, a white indentured servant, and Joseph, an enslaved Black African, both of whom assist the crew. Tim and Joseph help Kofi endure separation from his family and community, weather the abusive ship atmosphere, and begin to understand English. Once the ship reaches Massachusetts, the three become bound servants to the Brownes. With the guidance of his mistress, Kofi acquires some literacy and training in household tasks. Yet eventually, the three boys run away and gain support from Captain Cuffe, who helps get Joseph and Kofi released from bondage and takes charge of their care. Cuffe also has adopted Ama, Kofi's friend from his captivity in Africa, and Kofi and Ama later marry. The narrative returns to its starting point, with Kofi looking forward to returning from Sierra Leone to rejoin Ama and Joseph in the United States, where he will resume his antislavery work.

Hansen insists that this path is determined by multiple, at times conflicting, influences and events in Kofi's life, and that chief among these are his socialization in Ashanti culture and his ability to adapt to the changing American society of the early 1800s. Kofi's insistence that he carries his village within him emphasizes his awareness that in spite of the various experiences that have touched him, his upbringing in West Africa has been his foundation. Kofi's experience represents a process that scholars of African cultural retention have seen as commonplace. Maureen Warner-Lewis explains that "What they [displaced Africans] did bring was contained in their minds and motor skills: the capacity for memory, cogitation, problem solving, adaptation, aesthetic judgment, and spiritual transcendence, together with the kinetic routines which accompanied work, leisure, speech, ritual and artistic creation" (37). Hansen's characterization of Kofi is rich with evidence that his enculturation as Ashanti remains secure. Like Draper's Amari, he expresses his cultural affiliation and personal integrity through his reliance on and affirmation of kinship; for him, concern for family is a constant. Back in his homeland, when Kofi is with family, his actions—including fighting against his captors to protect his father— demonstrate his devotion. Hansen shows that amidst the confusions of his experience aboard the slave ship, Kofi remains unwilling to depart from Ashanti customs of hygiene and diet. He refuses, for instance, to eat without first washing (76). When several captives jump into the ocean to their deaths, Kofi says an Ashanti prayer for their spirits. When sailors carelessly dispose of a crewman's body, Kofi is horrified (86). Although he is from a different ethnic group from the deceased sailor, Kofi says a prayer for the man, whose "spirit had to be appeased," and in this way honors the dead man's ties to living family members and ancestors. Just as he insists on establishing a conscious relation to this man, Kofi is able to maintain some "hope of seeing my family" in these dire circumstances (86), and though at times he suppresses his thoughts of family, they are never far from his consciousness. Later in the novel, on meeting an elderly Ashanti woman in Massachusetts (sometime after his arrival there), he introduces himself by emphasizing his family connections: "'Mother,' I said to her in Ashanti, 'I am Ashanti, son of the Amanhene, Kwame'" (124). Establishing a connection to a person with a similar background, from the same language group and ethnicity, and asserting a fact about his paternal lineage allow him to express the Ashanti orientation that informs his identity.

Hansen indicates that this orientation also affects the ways he adopts Western skills and forms of knowledge under the tutelage of his Massachusetts mistress. Kofi's training in literacy, for example, exemplifies scholar Houston Baker's contention that "At best, acculturation must be viewed as a dynamic process, one in which meanings overlapped, conflicted, vied with one another for ascendancy" (21). This overlapping is evident, for instance, when Kofi explains his inclination to learn the English alphabet, "I liked forming the letters [that Mistress Browne taught me]. They reminded me of the markings the priests made on the temple for Nyame in my village" (130). Here Hansen shows that Kofi frames his learning and practicing of a new skill within his memory of Ashanti spiritual script, an important form of communication that is often overlooked in general discussions of African cultures, which are often seen as simply illiterate.[4] Hansen underscores that a person from a tradition-bound culture may negotiate change by relying on what he already knows. Whereas Kofi's white Christian mistress's lessons are designed to empty Kofi of his supposed savagery and replace it with Calvinist beliefs, he has his own designs. After the mistress explains that "By the grace of God you were taken out of the jungle so that your heathen soul could be saved," Kofi insists that he is acquiring English in order to explain his Ashanti lineage and orientation: "Mistress, I am a captive here. My father was the great Amanhene, Kwame, a great chief. Oppong betrayed us and killed Father and my brother. I was stolen from my home, and my family doesn't know where I am. Can you please tell Master to send me home?" (138). In one sense, Kofi's assertion of his identity and affiliation to his homeland can be seen as ineffectual, for his mistress will not support his desire to return home. Yet that does not discount his perspective for readers, who are encouraged to regard Kofi's acquisition of English as a vehicle for expressing his Ashanti identity and perspective within an Anglo-American environment. Later, he will encounter in Cuffe, a Black, Indigenous mentor who understands and respects this assertion of identity. Acquiring English does not primarily signify a diminishment of Kofi's particular ethnicity, but rather demonstrates the "dynamic process" through which ethnic identity can be translated (Baker 21).

That the process of socialization involves adapting to the pressures and influences of a new environment is obvious, however, when Kofi deviates from Ashanti tradition by renouncing slavery and thus obviously departs from his father's and his native culture's practices. Kofi's acquaintance with the abolitionist Cuffe is especially instrumental to this process—that the name *Cuffe* is an Americanized version of *Kofi* underscores the importance of Cuffe's model of masculine identity, which is self-consciously nonwhite. After escaping from the Brownes, Kofi and his two friends take refuge on a schooner, where Captain Cuffe displays his knowledge of the law to support their efforts to gain freedom. Cuffe stands up to the racist Mr. Browne, commands the respect of a constable, and insists that Kofi, Joseph, and Tim be treated in accordance with the law: "'As a citizen of this state, I insist that the law be followed.' He stared directly at the constable. 'You know, sir, that it is illegal to import slaves into Massachusetts. Also, even though the children are servants or slaves, if they are abused by cruel masters, they have the right to petition the court for removal from the home'" (171). Cuffe's assured, authoritative bearing challenges the would-be hegemony of the white culture of New England that Browne represents.

Cuffe, a man of Ashanti and Wampanoag heritage, also upsets the established racial order. Later, Cuffe explains to Kofi that his work as an activist emerges from his biracial and bicultural heritage:

> Son, my father was brought here from Africa and made a slave. When he became a free man, he married my mother who was from the Wampanoag—the native peoples who were here before the whites." He stared deeply at each of us. "I am a man who is the product of two despised races in this land—the Indian and the African. I hate slavery and mean to fight it whenever I can. (172–73)

Cuffe refuses to accept a second-class position in the new American society, choosing to fight to maintain his own dignity and aid others in their struggles against oppression. He raises his voice in resisting wrong-doing, refusing the invisibility often afforded members of "despised" racial groups. He is a man of Black Indigenous identity who serves as a model of public activism that leads to social reform. He is also an important model of masculinity whose sense of public obligation and commitment to social justice and harmony resonate with Kofi's predispositions.

Kofi's influences also include his Ashanti family, particularly his father, who, like Cuffe, works to benefit others. Hansen complicates the characterization of Kofi's father by making him a benevolent Black African enslaver who grants enslaved persons rights and opportunities that were rare in the American system of slavery. For instance, Kofi's father agreed to allow his favored enslaved servant Oppong to become engaged to his daughter; the family thus has accepted Oppong as one of its members. This inclusiveness prepares for Kofi to change his conception of slavery: He shifts from an innocent acceptance of tradition to a more nuanced concern about different forms of oppression. Kofi comes to realize that his family's mild version of slavery has not kept Oppong from betraying their trust and aiding slave traders. Kofi begins to understand, through his own displacement and disempowerment, enslaved persons' liminal positions. He understands that his former life of privilege has depended on others' enslavement and thus on the precariousness and suppression of their personal authority (as well as their own connections to their birth families). He vows to "fight against slavery and open my home and my heart to unfortunate men and women in bondage" (192). Hansen suggests that this work is an expanded expression of Kofi's father's humanitarianism, as well as his mentor Cuffe's sense of justice, thus suggesting Kofi's rich heritage and complex identity as an African American: "I would be a great chief, too, as my father Kwame had been, and as my new father Paul Cuffe was." (192). In fighting oppression, Kofi embodies what are usually seen as characteristically American ideals of freedom, as well as a complicated inheritance from his father and the outgrowth both of his past privilege and of his enslavement. Through Kofi's example, Hansen illustrates "that Africans came to the 'new world' bringing a rich cultural past with them" and that they continued to express aspects of that influence in adapting to and shaping an emerging American culture (195).

The Captive, moreover, offers a powerful lesson about activism that applies to the systems of oppression against which Kofi works and to those of the late twentieth-century US society in which it was published. The novel, even with its focus on Kofi's consciousness, indicates that the problem of slavery is not a matter of one individual gaining freedom. Instead, *The Captive* emphasizes that his personal struggle is part of a larger, ongoing fight against slavery and racism. In the novel's epilogue, as Kofi looks at the shore of Sierra Leone, he contemplates his past and future, accepting the loss of his homeland but committing himself to his principles: "When I complete this voyage ... and we unload the cargo, I will return to Massachusetts, for that is my home now with my beloved wife, Ama, our children, and Joseph who is like a brother. Joseph, Ama, and I have dedicated our lives to helping fugitives who have escaped from slavery. And there is still much work to do" (193). Hansen acknowledges the challenges that Kofi, Ama, and Joseph are facing as African Americans in 1811, even after they have realized some personal freedoms. This emphasis in the novel, which follows the portrayal of Kofi's many forms of resistance against oppression in West Africa, during the Middle Passage, and in the United States, signals the need to be ever vigilant and active against forces that aim to suppress self and cultural expression and that indoctrinate persons into social systems that enforce self-alienation and subservience. *The Captive* encourages the kind of critical thinking that Stephen May and Christine Sleeter associate with "critical multiculturalism," a discourse that facilitates understanding the causes of social difference and oppression (10). Rather than a happy ending that encourages complacency about Kofi's considerable achievements, the novel underscores the ongoing challenges African Americans encounter in navigating American social norms.

BALANCING RESISTANCE WITH INTEGRATION

Copper Sun parallels Hansen's novel in its serious, though perhaps more subtle, portrayal of its protagonist's ethnic roots. Draper's novel presents her protagonist Amari's resourcefulness in surviving and escaping from slavery as, in part, a testament to her Ewe upbringing in West Africa and to cultural forces that foster her development in America, including a group of mentors, friends, and surrogate family members. Amari's linguistic acculturation, for instance, is an outgrowth of her reliance on this network, which becomes central to her survival.[5] Yet more than *The Captive*, *Copper Sun* frames its protagonist within what Schwebel might call a narrative of "racial harmony and racial progress toward multicultural ideas" that requires alignment with American mainstream values such as individualism and self-invention (100). Draper's novel offers a story of ethnic particularity that works in tandem with textual components that neutralize Amari's ethnic differences, ultimately suggesting that in spite of her roots, she becomes an American to fit within a familiar pattern of achievement.

Copper Sun opens in medias res after Amari's capture and relocation from West Africa to South Carolina. In a short vignette, Draper presents Amari on an auction block, standing naked with other female captives but observing and judging "the sea of pink-skinned people" who withhold the "pity or even understanding" that Amari longs for (n.p.). From this scene, the plot moves back to portray Amari's loving Ewe family and hospitable community in Ziavi (now part of Ghana) just before they are overtaken by white and Ashanti traders. Amari, her fiancé Besa, and other young villagers survive the attack, but during the journey to the coast, Amari and Besa grow apart. He becomes depressed and ashamed by his lack of power; and once Amari is raped, she is too ashamed to acknowledge him. When Amari and other captives reach South Carolina, she is bought by a wealthy planter; she serves as both a concubine to his cruel son Troy and a domestic alongside the indentured Polly. After the enslaver learns that Amari and Polly have tried to conceal his wife's illicit relationship with an enslaved man, the young women, accompanied by the cook's small son, escape the plantation. After a violent confrontation with Troy and a brief reunion with Besa, the fugitives reach Fort Mose, a Spanish fort in Florida that shelters runaway slaves. There, Amari learns she is carrying Troy's child, who she resolves to love, but she vows to forget Troy and face the future with confidence.

Throughout this harrowing narrative, Draper subtly, yet persistently, indicates that Amari's grounding in Ewe culture informs her perspective and behavior. For Amari, memory is a willed bond with her family and culture, an act of resistance that helps her survive the horrors of slavery. In many ways, Amari's capacity to hold on to her family's and culture's traditions parallels that of Polly, who has suffered relocation and social demotion after her parents' deaths. Draper's brief portrait of the Ewe shows them to be a peaceful and productive people partly defined by traditions of oral storytelling and textile work that attest to their culture's highly expressive and social qualities. The Ewe, according to Draper's portrait, are hospitable and tolerant, as Amari's mother explains as she encourages her to prepare to honor their white visitors: "We must welcome our guests. . . . We would never judge people simply by how they looked—that would be uncivilized" (5). This statement implicitly contrasts the Ewe—who are open to others, respectful, and try to bridge differences—and Euro-Americans, who exploit them. Ewe communities traditionally have worked with the Ashanti people, for instance, who, according to the novel, are known for being aggressive. Draper also emphasizes this spirit of friendship through her characterization of Amari, who later demonstrates a tendency to learn from and work with others, such as the cook Teenie and her son Timothy, and to maintain a relationship, albeit a strained one, with Polly.

Draper's representation of Ewe culture as harmonious, sociable, and creative certainly runs a risk identified by Paul Gilroy of idealizing African traditional cultures that were disrupted by slavery (188–89). Vivian Yenika-Agbaw has identified such a tendency in Black American authors' representations of Africa that "glorify their cultural heritage and past traditions" (8). According to her, one strain of such romantic images of Africa celebrates "communal living [in villages] over [the] individualistic quest for material goods" associated with urban modernity (53). This tendency often yields a picture of a pan-African culture that runs on reciprocity, creativity, and wisdom and obscures historical actualities, such as ethnic differences and gender oppression (Yenika-Agbaw 53). Draper complicates her own nostalgic picture of Ziavi by acknowledging the convention of gendered labor whereby women make yarn and men weave. Draper has Amari question this convention: When she is expected to help her mother with yarn, she instead chooses another domestic task, delaying the yarn work until the next day. Draper explains, "Amari had often imagined new patterns for the cloth, and longed to join the men at the long looms, but girls were forbidden to do so" (4). Draper suggests that Amari is drawn to the role of artist or designer, rather than that of facilitator for the artist's creativity. Among the Ewe, weavers can express their creativity through their interpretation of traditional practice, particularly through their choice of pattern and colors (Kraamer 49). Amari's desire to challenge gendered conventions indicates her willingness to bend tradition, though it gains little momentum until the end of the novel: Soon after Amari expresses her desire to weave, the enslavers arrive, and the problem of gendered labor is displaced by slavery's disruption of villagers' lives. The scene, however, shows that Amari has some control over her life, for in this instance, she avoids spinning yarn, suggesting that she can negotiate within culturally determined parameters, if only briefly. Her resistance may also be read as a sign of individualism that runs counter to her community's values, a tendency that is more aligned with American ways, foreshadowing her fitting into the Fort Mose community.

For the most part, however, Amari acts on a faith in tradition and community that shows the ongoing influence of her Ewe world, even as she must adjust to the pressures of new circumstances. Draper's portrayal of the Middle Passage provides several telling examples of Amari's commitment to her ethnic group's traditions. For instance, aboard the ship Amari befriends an older, more knowledgeable woman, Afi, who also speaks the Ewe language, advises her to commit herself to surviving, and offers her understanding and comfort. At one point, Afi explains that Amari must survive "to remember the past and tell those yet unborn" (37). Afi's advice encourages Amari to remain true to their people's rituals of remembrance in order to withstand the trauma of loss and displacement. Later, Afi leads a song of resignation that draws in Amari and other women captives: It is "the lament sung at a funeral—a death song. She sang to the ancestors and to the other slaves. Gradually, even those not of that tribe joined in. Close to a hundred women softly sang with her" (44). The women's song of mourning marks their removal from their past lives, but it also affirms their use of their creative powers to establish a sense of community and to comment on and withstand the horrors of the present. This moment resonates with the emotional and creative expression common in African American musical genres such as spirituals, blues, and jazz.

The scene also strongly challenges earlier treatments of the Middle Passage, including the one in Yates's *Amos Fortune*, which portrays West African captives' cultural loss on being wrested from their homelands as a vacuum that empties them to their past cultural orientation. Trying to address his fellow captives during the journey from Africa, Yates's protagonist finds "They had been made to forget—not only that they were At-mun-shi but that they were men. They made sounds to each other in the darkness of the hold, but they were only sounds, they had no meaning" (26). In *Amos Fortune*, slavery dehumanizes Black persons to the extent that they are largely undifferentiated and capable of only inarticulate utterances. In *Copper Sun*, too, slavery is traumatizing, but by contrast, the enslaved women's song serves as a public, transethnic form of social commentary and support. Moreover, this shared communication underscores how evolving and shifting communal ties may have relied on tradition and expediency and facilitated many captives' survival.

By contrast, Amari's English lessons during the Middle Passage might seem to signal her growing remove from Ewe traditions, but these lessons also paradoxically allow her to maintain her cultural integrity. Most obviously, they offer her comfort amid the sexual exploitation common aboard the slave ship. When sailors take the other women for sexual pleasure, Amari is rescued by a man who begins to teach her English. Rather than marking her subordination to white culture, the new language and the values it carries do not dominate her vision, because she makes the language work for her. This experience reflects the process that Mary Louise Pratt has theorized and that Clare Bradford describes whereby "if Indigenous peoples were obliged to speak the language of the oppressor, they did not necessarily speak as the oppressor spoke but developed strategies of resistance and self-representation whose subversion often went unrecognized by colonizers" (Bradford 20; Pratt 8–10). Enslaved Africans may have experienced the language of the white West in this manner. When Amari later becomes a sexual pawn of the sailors, "she repeated the words and phrases [from her English lessons] to herself as the men made her dance or while she was tied up for hours on the deck of the endlessly rocking ship. It kept her from going mad" (58). Draper suggests that such cognitive exercises point to Amari's strong will, and help her steel herself against the chaos and devastation of the Middle Passage. She learns to use English in ways that express her feelings, thoughts, and questions, and significantly, her English lessons prepare for her emergence late in the book as a preserver of her native culture for her American-born child. At the book's end, Amari vows to use her adopted language to "tell this child of her ancestors and her grandparents and tell her the stories my father told me" (301). Draper emphasizes that Amari's embrace of English is not a succumbing to the demands of a foreign culture, but rather an appropriation of an important cultural tool. Amari's English will be a bridge between her present and past, between the Western world and her Ewe family and culture. In presenting English education as both an escape and a resource, Draper challenges the idea that the process of cultural adaptation eviscerates a person's past affiliations and enforces complete subordination.

Draper balances her detailed representation of Amari's resilience with her reintroduction of Besa, Amari's beloved from Ziavi, who demonstrates "the soul-killing effects of slavery," including his sense of lost connection to his homeland (Douglass 14). When she meets him during her escape, he is a broken man defined by his sense of loss and mistrust. For him, enslavement has led first to resistance, then to a long bitter and nihilistic acceptance of his lack of power. Accordingly, he tells Amari: "I no longer believe in anything" and "Trust no one" (258). Though his marriage to an enslaved woman on the property where he is confined might be taken as a sign of hope, Draper suggests it primarily serves his physical needs: "I have found a woman here— a good woman. She keeps me warm at night, and she carries no dreams in her heart. She is safe" (258). Though still a young man, he has lost the desire for discovery and experiment: " 'My spirit is dead,' he said, his voice empty. 'They beat it out of me with their whips, cut it out of me with their knives, shot it out of me with their guns. I can barely see, and every step causes me pain'" (258). Draper presents Besa as an image of death in life: Beaten down in body and spirit, he has gradually accepted his social status as object and rejected both the idea of beneficial future change and many of the values of the past that shaped his identity.

The novel's portrayal of Besa acknowledges the limitations of Black agency in slavery, alluding to the ways its traumatizing, self-denying force could suppress the spirit of resistance. Yet, juxtaposed to Amari's more empowering experience, Besa's example plays into the limited multiculturalism that suggests that personal, rather than systemic, failings result in disparities of achievement among African Americans. Draper contrasts him with Amari and her friends, including the elderly Cato, who has advised against complete submission to the enslaver's will and risked death to help her, Polly, and Timothy escape the plantation (190). When Amari invites Besa to escape and accompany her party to the fort, he refuses, seeing his enslavement as inevitable. Of course, Besa's choice may be taken as a sign of his loyalty to his wife, but in focalizing the reunion through the daring Amari's perspective and presenting him as foil, Draper equates his decision with stasis and passivity. Through Besa, Draper suggests possible roots for enduring patterns, such as alienation, nihilism, and self-destruction that have endured in African American culture. Orlando Patterson, among others, sees these patterns as legacies of slavery.[6] Besa's alienation and passivity make him unfit for the story of personal development that Amari foregrounds, which reflects the progressive cultural narrative about America that much of the multicultural literature of the 1990s and 2000s reinforces (Melamed 114–15).

Draper's handling of Amari's escape from slavery conforms to long-standing patterns in children's literature: acknowledging but overcoming difficult obstacles to self-actualization and, in the process, reinforcing dominant culture values, particularly those associated with middle-class success. It also underscores Amari's achievement of the American dream, her discovery of a place where she can be free from slavery. On arriving at Fort Mose in 1738, she joins a community of fugitives who are protected by the Spanish monarch, and who in turn guard the Spanish border against English interlopers. Amari's new life encompasses her eminent role as mother and, mindful of her parents, she sees herself as connecting their generation to the child she will bear: "*This spirit carries the spirit of my mother*, Amari realized suddenly, as well as the essence of her father, [her brother] little Kwasi, the murdered people of her village, and the spirits of all of her ancestors" (300; Draper's emphasis). She plans to pass on aspects of her Ewe cultural perspective to her child: "*I shall teach him my native language and tell him of the beauties of my homeland*" (301; Draper's emphasis). And just as her cultural knowledge has kept her committed to freedom, her teaching and storytelling will empower her child: "*I will tell this child of her ancestors and her grandparents and tell her the stories my father told me*" (301; Draper's emphasis). Thus, Draper relates Amari to African American women's traditional roles as preservers of cultural knowledge and as storytellers whose creative expression of memory potentially orients and inspires others. Draper's affirmation of Amari's Ewe heritage, however, can also be understood as "an expansion or correction of normal politics" (Melamed 99), because it manifests a dominant, elite white culture's acceptance of an African-born young woman. The racially mixed community is not a free society that sharply contrasts with the plantation from which she fled. Instead, it is a buffer protecting Spain's interests in Florida from the southern Anglo-American colonies (Landers 30). Although Draper emphasizes Amari's self-actualization and Fort Mose's Black communal orientation, she does not explain the implications of Fort Mose residents' status as enablers of what Jane Landers calls "a vital objective of Spanish imperial policy," nor does she explore the possible costs of the Spanish managers' expectation that residents "be assimilated into 'civilized' society" (31). Fort Mose, historically, was a more complicated place than the haven of freedom and opportunity that Draper represents. Emphasizing some elements in the historical record and obscuring others allows her to highlight Amari's emergence as a free woman who can take care of herself and her baby and contribute to society. This trajectory conforms to the narrative of American progress in which personal hardship and suffering are overcome by personal opportunity and dedication, reassuring developments that may stoke readers' complacency.

Draper transforms the fort, for example, into a place with a commander who allows Amari to realize her old dream of working as a weaver. Through textile work Amari will be able to support herself and fill a public need by making clothes. Of course, weaving is an important link to her father's and Ewe society's creativity. In taking on the job men have done back in her homeland, she asserts an American identity that is founded on meaningful aspects of her past. Yet, in allowing for this specific role in America that was denied Amari in Yoruba-land, Draper seems to be reinforcing the idea of American exceptionalism and economic opportunity, albeit in territory held by Spain.[7] It seems as if Amari will be able to fulfill herself in Fort Mose in ways that she has not elsewhere. What Amari seems poised to achieve is a version of the American dream of material success through free labor, after passing through the dreadful trials of slavery. Although Besa has apparently failed, Amari arrives at a promised land where she will thrive. Amari's story as African-born protagonist fulfilling a quintessential American success story speaks to its accessibility for those with determination and with abilities that support the state.

Copper Sun, like *The Captive*, ends with its African-born protagonist free, and unlike Amos Fortune, not fully estranged from her cultural roots. Yet *Copper Sun* and *The Captive* offer different visions of how Amari and Kofi ultimately fit within white-dominated worlds. Both protagonists survive their enslavement and cultural displacement, but where Kofi occupies an adversarial position to US society, Amari seems to find a world, a colony of Spain, that complements her needs and aspirations. As a resident of Fort Mose, Amari recalls such figures as Booker T. Washington and Elizabeth Keckley, who represent slavery as a crucible from which one emerges with the power to find socioeconomic success and serve society fruitfully as a free person (Keckley 19–20; Washington 37). Perhaps the success of *Copper Sun* owes something to its representation of Amari's Blackness and Africanness as in sync with the dominant culture's priorities: She conforms to and reinforces the system she finds at Fort Mose.[8] Kofi in *The Captive*, by contrast, becomes an activist who works against the status quo in order to free other persons and make society more equitable and fair. Moreover, Hansen suggests that his activism is not a simple expression of his having adopted core Euro-American values, but is instead a sign of his development as an Ashanti American shaped by multiple influences, including Ashanti beliefs and practices that have informed Kofi's life. *The Captive* ends on a less triumphal note than *Copper Sun*, in suggesting that attaining personal freedom does not yield the American dream of success, but rather necessitates Kofi's continued fight against injustice and oppression, which Draper's novel associates with British colonies, eliding the injustices that abounded in New Spain.

In the next chapter, I continue to explore the power of West African values in an American landscape, focusing on Hamilton's *The Magical Adventures of Pretty Pearl* and, to a greater extent, Lester's *Time's Memory*. Both foreground African characters who survive a harsh, destructive American social system through their reliance on their particular cultural beliefs, ingenuity, and community connections. Hamilton's and Lester's novels are more intent than Draper's and Hansen's in portraying the ways African American culture is founded on African beliefs and practices. Chapter 3 will allow me to deepen my exploration of the freedom narrative genre's concern with history, including the ongoing relationship between the living and the dead. I will hone in on the ways Hamilton and Lester confront the problem of cultural loss and amnesia and the role of vernacular African American art in African American survival. Although the Middle Passage has an important role at the beginning of Lester's novel, my analysis focuses more on the ways Hamilton and Lester show Black culture as a repository of meaning relevant to Black people's experience. As the chapter shows, these two novels present African cultural orientations as frameworks that foster Black individuals' creativity not through conforming to the old, but by negotiating and reinventing tradition to address current situations.

Chapter 3

TENDING TO MEMORY AND AFRICAN AMERICAN CULTURE

In a wide-ranging speech about her commitment to telling stories centered on African Americans, Virginia Hamilton explains the importance of her historical narratives, asserting "I have an obligation to pass on what I know to those who may not know" ("The Spirit Spins" 122). She clarifies that "what I know" includes her cultural inheritance as an African American woman who has descended from enslaved persons. Hamilton goes further to identify this inheritance by quoting a passage from novelist John Edgar Wideman's *Sent for You Yesterday* that acknowledges the strong connections between the living and the dead: "Past lives live in us, through us. Each of us harbors the spirits of people who walked the earth before we did, and those spirits depend on us for continuing existence, just as we depend on their presence to live our lives to the fullest" (122). The ongoing, productive relationship between the living and dead that Wideman describes is central to many traditional African cultures, and Hamilton claims this relationship as important to her sense of selfhood.[1] Furthermore, she insists on sharing this part of herself with her readers and promoting the inextricable connections between the living and dead in her folklore collections, in contemporary fiction such as *Sweet Whispers, Brother Rush*, and in historical narratives.

Similarly, Julius Lester, who Paula Connolly has called "one of the most important authors in the development of neo-slave narratives for young audiences" (204), has claimed inspiration from his connection with the dead. In the afterword of his novel, *Time's Memory*, he maintains, "Throughout my life as a writer, I have felt that the spirits of dead slaves were lined up inside me, waiting patiently for me to tell their stories, and I have tried my best to do so. Perhaps I needed to write this novel as a way of understanding myself and why so much of my career has been focused on the past, on the dead" (228–29). Here, Lester defines himself as a medium through whom enslaved persons of an earlier era can speak. And he explains that his life and career have been shaped by his awareness of those who have preceded him, maintaining that he has been possessed by spirits of the dead who depend on him to be recognized and honored. Like Hamilton, Lester identifies his mission as a writer as creating texts that bring the dead to life, or at least into contact with new generations of readers. The writer's role is both to appease and honor the dead by recognizing and transmitting their experience and to foster young readers' epistemological and moral development through an engagement with the past. Being attuned to the past, according to Lester and Hamilton, means being better equipped to understand and engage with a complex reality, including the legacies of American slavery.[2]

This chapter examines Lester's 2006 novel *Time's Memory* in detail, because it provides a sustained portrayal of the psychology of loss, grief, and remembrance among enslaved persons in the antebellum South. Like several other neo-slave narratives from the late twentieth century, the novel combines realism with fantasy to explore a breadth of Black historical experience. Highlighting enslaved African Americans' attempts to remain connected to dead family members and friends, the novel describes their adaptation of traditional Dogon beliefs and other cultural practices to combat the destructive effects of slavery and affirm life and human relationship. *Time's Memory* explores obstacles to remembering and the ways that being attuned to past lives can enrich one's experience, though it also acknowledges that certain ways of keeping the past present can diminish Black selfhood and community. By examining the novel's portrayal of spirit possession and different ways of honoring the past, including sculpture, oral storytelling, writing, and book preservation and distribution, I show how Lester interprets African Americans' ways of asserting agency by holding onto memories of family and friends. The novel defines representational art forms as *lieux de mémoire*, or sites or preservers of memory, which helped enslaved persons withstand the abuses and deprivations of slavery (Dixon 18).[3] The arts of memory, according to *Time's Memory*, are at the root of still relevant, though precarious, African American cultural traditions. Ultimately, the novel settles on storytelling and writing as especially effective means of connecting people and generations and making history present. Through highlighting the substantial power of memory-keeping, *Time's Memory* encourages child readers to resist a culture of forgetting that limits understanding of the world, imperils individual Black agency and community connections, and serves a system of exploitation.[4] The novel also critiques practices of remembrance that are less beneficial.

Time's Memory offers an interpretation of American slavery that challenges the idea that it completely converted enslaved persons into enslavers' tools. Drawing on his historical knowledge, including his reading of enslaved persons' testimony, Lester shows Black characters' struggles to free themselves from a racist American system's reduction of Black selves to objects. Among the recent studies that complement this effort, *Child Slavery before and after Emancipation* signals the importance of addressing the issue of empowerment in slavery through a focus on enslaved Black children. Such scholarly treatments acknowledge that resistance could take the form of escape or riot, but it also involved efforts on the part of enslaved children (and adults) to command their bodies, language, and time as they could (Duane, Introduction 14–15). *Time's Memory*, like Draper's *Copper Sun* and Hansen's *The Captive*, suggests that acts of remembering could mean the difference between a living death of subjection and a life of some personal autonomy and integrity for an enslaved person. As such, the novel contributes to a project that critic Anne Anlin Cheng has described of "rethinking" common understandings of agency to address the multiple but under appreciated ways that racial subjects have expressed their personal power within the constraints of slavery (15).

In advocating for holding on to memories of the Black past and Black ancestors, the novel encourages child readers to see the value of history, and in particular the resources of a Black culture that have too often remained obscure within the larger American culture. Moreover, *Time's Memory* calls on readers to establish a personal connection to this history in light of the larger culture's failure to reckon with the legacy of slavery and the actualities of Black historical experience. In spite of professional historians' acknowledgments of Black persons' efforts to resist complete subjection, for instance, history textbooks for children and teenagers have continued to minimize and exclude enslaved African Americans' perspectives (Loewen, *Lies* 390 note 13). This kind of cultural amnesia facilitates the perpetuation of stereotypes of African American persons and history, and African cultures. *Time's Memory* circumvents these stereotypes by showing Black people in a respectful light, even when they are caught in terrible circumstances. The novel thus indicates that enslaved persons were more than their socially defined roles, and it speaks to the possible shame or embarrassment young readers may have about the condition of slavery, which is out of sync with the dominant US culture's valuing of self-possession, self-control, and material success. The novel also offers the children born after the civil rights era a critical backstory that suggests the continuities of African Americans' fight to affirm their autonomy in US society. Just as important, Lester's novel, like freedom narratives, calls into question official, but partial histories, and encourages young readers to seek out additional, alternative stories that can lend nuance and complexity to their understanding of the past. Young readers influenced by Lester's text might move on to other neo-slave narratives and to antebellum and postbellum autobiographical narratives that collectively tell a fuller story about American history and the many ways in which African Americans' presence has shaped this past.[5] *Time's Memory* encourages young readers to be active in looking for multiple stories and to think carefully and critically about what they find.

HAMILTON, LESTER, AND INTERPRETING BLACK AMERICAN CULTURE

Having started this chapter with a statement from Virginia Hamilton, it would be remiss not to acknowledge that her 1983 novel *The Magical Adventures of Pretty Pearl* is a groundbreaking precursor to *Time's Memory*. The two novels are different in style and tone, but they have many parallels that emanate from their shared interest in portraying African sources for Black American culture. Both novels rely on the fantastic to insist on the importance of remembrance: They present African spirits' or deities' transformation into African American persons as central to the process of establishing and disseminating cultural beliefs and practices. In representing the transfer of African songs, dances, and other folkways to a Black southern American population, *The Magical Adventures of Pretty Pearl* underscores the importance and fragility of cultural memory within a community of free, but sequestered, African Americans in the nineteenth century. This community, whom Hamilton calls "outside people," fits historian Sylviane A. Diouf's definition of maroons who escaped white-dominated society in order to secure freedom and self-government during the antebellum era (2). Maroon societies afforded their residents the ability to express, negotiate, and adapt African cultural influences in response to the particular pressures and necessities of their physical environment (R. Price "Maroons"). Although mostly set in the postbellum era, *The Magical Adventures of Pretty Pearl* focuses on a community that has insisted on living outside of the dominant American culture and is concerned about preserving its values as it prepares to leave its isolation. Like *Time's Memory*, *The Magical Adventures of Pretty Pearl* explores the development of an African American culture, and calls on child readers to be mindful of the rich and diverse founts of cultural knowledge that helped earlier generations of African Americans navigate the challenges of life in (or in proximity to) a white-dominated, racist world.

The novel implies that this knowledge was relevant not only in the past, but can also orient and empower individuals in the present and future.

The novel links Africa and African American society in multiple ways, and makes African cultural inheritance a central thematic current, presenting an allegory that unfolds as a series of fables. In these episodes, encounters between the human and superhuman bear cultural fruit that will continue to yield. The maroon children's ring games and songs such as "Walk Together, Children," as well as community members' reliance on the healing capacities of the John de Conqueror root, are among the cultural practices that are derived from the African gods (Mikkelsen, *Virginia Hamilton* 135). The novel presents them as fruits of preserved cultural memory. Initially introduced by Pretty Pearl, her adult alter ego Mother Pearl, and their trickster companion Dwahro, these and other practices quickly take root in the Black community's lives. Pretty, Mother Pearl, and Dwahro represent the spirit of African creativity, productivity, and genius that is expressed through African American persons and communities. These characters lack the psychological weight of realist characters, but they personify founding principles that continue to inform aspects of Black diasporic cultures in the United States.

Pretty Pearl's evolution into the role of storyteller and preserver of cultural knowledge resonates most with Lester's emphasis in *Time's Memory*. Focusing on Pretty Pearl's life within a maroon community of African Americans who support themselves through farming and trade with members of a Cherokee community, *The Magical Adventures of Pretty Pearl* is Hamilton's attempt to present a mythology that connects Africa and African Americans, and to explain the links between legendary figures like John Henry and John de Conqueror, on the one hand, and ordinary African Americans, on the other. The novel's protagonist Pretty Pearl, who is Hamilton's creation, is the sister of these two personages, who both support her acculturation into the society of maroon people whom she discovers in a southeastern forest. Pretty Pearl is a reminder that not only male figures had leading roles in African American cultural history: Pretty Pearl, a god child through much of the novel, has left the haven of Mount Kenya to help enslaved Black people (Hamilton, "The Spirit Spins" 121). She loses her divine status after being irresponsible with her powers, but by the end of the narrative, she emerges as a productive, resourceful member of the Black Midwestern community that the maroons found after having to leave their sanctuary. As a human, Pearl becomes a farmer who tends to one of the community's key crops, which signifies her commitment to the group's ecologically responsible farming practices and symbiosis with Cherokee trading partners. Just as importantly, she becomes a storyteller who shares stories that form part of the basis for the Black American vernacular. Although Pretty Pearl forgets her divine identity, the gods allow her to retain her memory of her brothers' feats and struggles, which as Nina Mikkelsen has noted, represent "contrasting avenues to power for the oppressed (open action as opposed to subterfuge)" ("But Is It" 135). John Henry and John the Conqueror, as representative of Black physical power, endurance, and competitiveness and of Black ingenuity, respectively, are figures in Black folk expression that suggest a range of survival strategies. The novel presents Pretty Pearl's storytelling as an indispensable means of conveying core cultural values; her stories are necessary vehicles for keeping and expressing cultural memory.

Another way of putting *Time's Memory* into aesthetic perspective is to consider its relation to other works by Lester. As one of many historical narratives he has written about slavery, *Time's Memory* explores the external and internal experiences of enslaved African Americans and their descendants, the observable and the hidden. This dual focus on Black interiority and material reality has been central to Lester's writing about slavery since he created his first book for children, *To Be a Slave* (1968), which presents testimony about enslaved persons' private and public selves. Drawing on former enslaved persons' written and oral narratives, the book documents ways in which Black persons' self-conception was shaped by slavery and challenged its destructive powers. Through *To Be a Slave*, Lester sought to offer stories about slavery that expressed enslaved persons' perspectives and challenged the standard reduction of slaves to the status of objects of white control and brutalization. The book can be understood as a foundation for much of Lester's historical writing, including *Time's Memory*. *To Be a Slave*'s collection of enslaved persons' voices, combined with Lester's historical reflections, manages the difficult balancing act of acknowledging the horrific experience of slavery and showing how many Black persons struggled to retain agency within its oppressions. The book accordingly registers Lester's emphasis on both the importance of individual African American voices and a carefully constructed historical frame that facilitates understanding Black persons' tangible and intangible realities.

Lester would go on to create other children's books that expand on his vision of what it meant to be enslaved, creating realist narratives about enslaved persons' physical, social, and affective experience, and books that highlight Black vernacular culture, especially folktales (Bishop, *Free Within Ourselves* 255–56). It is as if no one genre is enough to encompass his vision of Black historical experience. Lester's realist texts include the short narratives in *The Long Journey Home: Stories from Black History* (1972) and *This Strange*

New Feeling: Three Love Stories from Black History (1981), whose subtitles underscore their reliance on historical sources and re-creation of lived experience. Also in this category is *Day of Tears* (2007), a novel that relies on historical documents and fictional constructions to re-create an 1859 slave auction that was purported to be the "largest" in US history ("The Largest Slave Auction"). As Rudine Sims Bishop has pointed out, these books are Lester's attempt to make history present to young readers and awaken their responsiveness to and understanding of the past; the books acknowledge the horror and trauma of slavery, even as they imagine ways in which many African Americans survived them (*Free Within Ourselves* 256).

Complementing such historical narratives are Lester's renderings of African American folklore, including *Black Folktales*, four *Uncle Remus* collections, and single-story picture books such as *The Old African*. The folktales convey the priorities, values, and beliefs of the Black cultures in which they were developed and shared, and thus offer insights into the belief systems of enslaved African Americans and the succeeding generations who inherited and adapted the tales.[6] These texts constitute a major contribution to children's literature by acknowledging and portraying how Black persons creatively expressed their values and beliefs through oral arts. When considered together, Lester's historical texts offer a holistic picture of African American slavery that challenges facile assumptions about African American epistemological and cultural deficiency.

Time's Memory (2006) brings together many of the generic, formal, modal, and thematic features of these historical and folkloric texts. Through realism and fantasy, Lester is able to explore obscured and more familiar aspects of African American historical experience (Atkinson 66; *Writing for Children* 104). The novel combines these narrative modes to portray the physical and emotional experience of enslavement and forced migration, and the reach of spiritual belief and power. Its protagonist, Ekundayo, is an emissary of the god Amma, and appears first as a disembodied spirit. *Time's Memory* tracks his impact on enslaved African Americans' lives; initially, he enters and possesses their bodies, and later, after he attains human status, he adapts Dogon customs of remembrance for African American culture. The novel shows how African Americans' practices of remembering affirm individuals' ongoing connection to their ancestors and other loved ones and negate the destructive power of slavery. These cultural practices challenge some of slavery's most disturbing legacies, including lingering socioeconomic inequities and assumptions about African American inferiority and pathology. The novel also insists that the transfer and evolution of Dogon beliefs and practices contributed to a distinctly African American culture that nourished and empowered many Black persons, enabling survival and growth within a divided US society.

LESTER'S ADAPTATION OF DOGON BELIEFS

Hamilton's novel locates Pretty Pearl and her godly associates' African home on Mount Kenya in East Africa, perhaps inspired by Black Arts Movement writers' claiming of East African cultures as a basis for Pan-Africanism, their dedication to the idea of a common African culture. Several children's books reflect this assumption about East Africa, including Tom and Muriel Feelings's book *Jambo Means Hello*, and show an optimism about the potential of the East African liberation movements in the late twentieth century. *Time's Memory*, by contrast, focuses on the influence and adaptation of the complex Dogon culture of Mali, a part of West Africa where a majority of persons taken into the transatlantic slave trade came from. Lester relies on the Dogon belief in the ongoing, intricate relationship between the living and dead to portray the devastating losses and disruptions enacted by slavery. Set in mid-nineteenth-century America, Lester's novel centers on Ekundayo's efforts to alleviate the suffering of enslaved Africans. Ekundayo initially focuses on those who have already died and whose spirits have survived them, adapting the Dogon concept of the *nyama* to refer to the inner force that defines selfhood. In the Dogon belief system, each person has a nyama and a soul, both of which are immortal, though they have different functions and trajectories during and after life (Masolo 80). Lester does not concern himself with this difference, in effect, conflating the two spirits. Yet he does present the nyama in accordance with scholar Dismas Masolo's description of traditional Dogon belief in the nyama as "a principle spread in the blood of man . . . a vital force transmitted from father to son and from generation to generation. It makes beings have life" (81). When a person dies, his or her nyama survives and must be honored and cared for. In traditional practice, the dead person's survivors prepare a figurine that houses the nyama and that is kept at the family's home. The novel's narrator and protagonist Ekundayo explains, "The nyama remained part of the household and blessed it with prosperity and health" (*Time's Memory* 21). The survivors' caretaking entails maintaining an altar, providing sacrifices, and remembering what qualities made the relative distinct. As Lester points out, the dead have an ongoing role in the lives of survivors, continuing to receive their survivors' love and care, but also perpetuating the vital force that enables living and future family members to flourish (Masolo 76).

This system of belief emphasizes reciprocity, remembrance, respect, and balance among different realms of being, and in the novel it functions to emphasize the importance of an inclusive understanding of community. For Lester's contemporary readership, as for the African and African American characters in *Time's Memory*, understanding Dogon beliefs requires a creative response that prioritizes human connection over individualism. "To care for nyama," Ekundayo ponders, "one had to love the dead as much as one loved life" (Lester, *Time's Memory* 70). Living human beings maintain a relationship to their dead family members, and thereby participate in a world that intricately connects the tangible with the intangible. When love and care for the dead are missing, the nyama of the dead wander, disrupting the lives of individuals and the order of society (21). The Dogon deity Amma expresses concern that the transatlantic slave trade and racial slavery in the United States are interrupting this process of affection, reciprocity, and remembrance, and he tells Ekundayo that the United States "is a land in which death is more important than life. The Soul Stealers fill the air with nyama and do not know that so many nyama without a place to be, without people to care for them, can cause the heavens to fall into the chaos that existed before I ordered sun to number the days" (47). Not tending to the nyamas' need for recognition and care amounts to forgetting one's responsibility to participate fully in the cycles of life, but social conditions for African Americans and African transplants make this participation difficult: Many who have survived are too traumatized by the slave trade to carry out tradition (45). To remedy this grave situation, Ekundayo tries to find the most viable ways of supporting the dead and their survivors in a social context that disrupts ties to family, suppresses ethnic heritage, and assaults traditional African modes of consciousness that emphasize family. Like Hamilton, Lester uses superhuman characters to bring order, insisting that allegiance to the past, as well as adaptation, were necessary for African American individuals and communities to overcome the deprivations of slavery.

As *Time's Memory* opens, Ekundayo waits in the body of the sixteen-year-old Amina, whose husband and father have been killed in a raid on their Dogon village, and who is being transferred to the United States on a ship. After helping Amina acclimate herself to her life in the US South, Ekundayo moves to the body of Nat, an enslaved carpenter on the Chelsea plantation in Virginia. Nat is a weak-willed young man whose grandmother has forbidden him from growing close to his father Gabriel, a violent, visionary preacher. Although Nat and his enslaver's daughter Ellen Chelsea love each other, he has tried to keep their relationship secret. As Ekundayo takes possession of Nat's body, the young man's own spirit dies, but not before transferring his forbidden love for Ellen to the Dogon spirit. One way in which Ekundayo manifests his difference from the passive Nat is by supporting Gabriel's plan to rebel against the slaveholding class. Yet, when Gabriel, leading a small number of enslaved men, begins to kill white persons and orders Ekundayo to kill Ellen, Ekundayo turns on Gabriel and kills him. Afterward, the god Amma, despairing that the dead can ever know comfort in such a horrible place, tries to relieve Ekundayo of his duty and return him to Africa. Yet Ekundayo opts to become human and find a way to restore order to the nyama and enslaved survivors on the Chelsea plantation. The novel ends with a description of Ekundayo's descendants, who have carried on his healing efforts into the twenty-first century.

SPIRIT POSSESSION AND CULTURAL CONTINUITY

Although *Time's Memory* examines aspects of enslaved persons' experience in ways that are compatible with many realist fictional and autobiographical accounts of slavery, the recurrence of spirits entering human bodies, changing form, and affecting human characters' thoughts and behavior introduces a fantastic dimension that challenges the Euro-American epistemological framework that informs many enslaved Black persons' autobiographies. Such texts usually privilege and legitimate realism, rationalism, and empiricism: Antebellum narratives emphasize the verifiable nature of their accounts of slavery, relying on the texts' credibility as a galvanizing force to support abolition. Yet as A. Timothy Spaulding has acknowledged, African American postmodern writers often diverge from these conventions, with many embracing fantasy as a way of challenging the limits of realism for presenting Black historical experience (6–7). Writers like Virginia Hamilton and Zetta Elliott draw on the fantastic to highlight the interplay between the past and present and challenge the concepts of empiricism and authenticity upheld in traditional historiography (Spaulding 7). Although *Time's Memory* does present many of the outer realities common in literature about slavery, it also, as historical fantasy, foregrounds intangible experiences and the relationship between the intangible—the felt, remembered, and spiritual—and the tangible or observable. Realism is insufficient for presenting this worldview and the nuances of Black psychological and social experience that are informed by it. Lester's historical fantasy allows him to foreground spirit work, with spirit possession in particular serving as a principal means by which African cultural influences persist within persons who have been displaced from their homelands, as well as American descendants of persons taken from Africa.

For the novel's Black characters, spirit possession signifies the continuity both of African modes of thought and feeling and of affective relationships.

Lester uses spirit possession as a trope that not only facilitates Amina's continuing adherence to and preservation of her Dogon culture, but also allows her to survive the trauma of displacement and slavery. Bound in the hold of a slave ship during the Middle Passage, Amina is traumatized by the memory of her father's and husband's deaths and confused by feeling the presence within her of another life, even though she is a newlywed virgin. It turns out that Amina is carrying not a child, but her father's nyama, implanted through a kiss he gives her just before his death. And his nyama is a collective spirit: As a *hogon* or spiritual leader, Amina's father represents Dogon tradition; he has carried the nyama of Amma's divine son, Lebe, as his own and he passes this nyama on to his daughter; the kiss serves to underscore her status as a person enmeshed in Dogon culture (Lester, *Time's Memory* 49). That Amina contains transhistorical spiritual power, the power of Lebe and subsequent hogons, including her father, suggests that she will have the resources to withstand the abuses of the system of slavery, even if she is understandably consumed by pain, grief, and confusion during the Middle Passage and afterward, when the ship captain Josiah rescues her from slavery. Amina, longing to die and end her pain, chooses to drown herself in a river, but the god Lebe appears in the form of a giant serpent that envelopes her, leading not to death, but rebirth. Wrapped in Lebe's embrace, Amina feels love and support, and she becomes aware of the figure of Ekundayo, who also holds Amina as they are held by Lebe. Ekundayo's presence manifests the accessibility of Dogon spirituality. Moreover, identifying Ekundayo as the grown embodiment of the "seed" she has felt growing within her, Amina is ready to confront her new reality as a displaced African in America. Although still confused, she is mindful that Lebe, Amma, and their spiritual assistants will continue to have a place in her life.

Amina commits herself to life in America only after she realizes that she will continue to think and believe as a Dogon woman and that she can continue to practice Dogon spirituality. Her possession by spirits is allied with the belief, which the novel ascribes to the Dogon, that "Each person is the sum of the generations that went before.... Those generations live within everyone, pulsating with each heartbeat and each breath" (Lester, *Time's Memory* 22). Spirit possession saves Amina, for it is part of a complex process of identity formation that depends on persons' and generations' interconnectedness. For Amina, this means that her personhood will continue to be rooted in her Dogon heritage, even as she encounters new challenges and realities in an island off the southern coast of the United States.

The novel insists that Amina's personhood is expressed through her staying true to her native culture, and her adjusting to the different circumstances in America in ways that align with the practices, beliefs, and emotions that she has known. Moreover, Amina will exercise influence of her own, sharing her Dogon cultural knowledge with the white American man, Josiah, who becomes her friend and husband.

In addition to allowing for the survival of her Dogon culture, spirit possession will also allow her and Josiah to acculturate to their roles within a racially and ethnically mixed marriage, a process that Lester portrays as involving Amina and Josiah's adaptation, mutual respect and interdependence. Amina, for instance, will expand her perspective to include his first wife Hannah's nyama and to acknowledge Josiah's connections with his dead family members. Lester hereby imagines a complicated process of integration that is not equated with Amina's succumbing to the white dominant culture, and that acknowledges the appeal for some white Americans of alternatives to a toxic, racist, and patriarchal social order. In effect, the process involves white and African characters' adaptation and integrity. Although Amina is shocked when she is asked to become a living "resting place" for Hannah's nyama, she agrees to do so once Ekundayo explains that harboring the nyama of Hannah, Josiah's dead wife, will not hurt her. He indicates that the enormity of slavery and the displacement of Indigenous people necessitates adopting new ways of surviving: Taking in and caring for Hannah's nyama will help Amina adjust to her loss of family and community; it will also facilitate her integration within southern US culture on her own terms. Ekundayo explains that Hannah "will share with [your nyama] all she knows—how to cook and make clothes as she did, the songs and stories she knows, her memories, everything you need to know to live here" (40–41). This cultural knowledge, which includes proficiency in English, supplements rather than replaces her enculturation as a Dogon woman. In the novel's formulation, at least with Amina, integration does not erase aspects of selfhood and past enculturation, but rather allows for the coordination of past and present influences that can enrich the self. For young readers, the text offers assurances that captive Africans were not simply objects of exploitation and pity, but strong and resourceful persons whose lives were more than their diminished social status as enslaved. Lester's portrayal of character encourages readers to see identity as a complex issue that includes contradictory elements such as personal integrity, subjugation to spirits, the force of circumstantial and environmental influence, and resistance against negating powers. These portrayals complicate popular American ideas about personal autonomy.

Through Ekundayo's ministering to Amina, Lester suggests that her finding her footing entails embracing her own past and complementary influences in her new home. Lester thus acknowledges—and indeed, accelerates—the transformation of an African identity into an African American one. As her sojourn with Josiah suggests, Amina's decision to accept aspects of US society, including a white American husband and the accoutrements of US southern middle-class life, is in many respects an isolated case. Amina lives with Josiah on a remote island where they presumably create an alternative to the repressive, racist society on the mainland. And Lester does not depict much of Amina's acculturation, for the novel leaves her after its first few chapters, and when she reappears near the end, she is happily married to Josiah, with whom she has two young children. Amina's experience nevertheless demonstrates her reliance on the spiritual resources of Dogon culture, which she will share with Josiah as they both continue to heal.

It is notable that Lester represents Amina's possession in a way that is different from many popular iterations, in which a person is overtaken by a spirit they cannot control that makes them lose their bearings; this experience is parasitic, draining, and in opposition to the idea of personal integrity. In *Time's Memory*, being possessed, by contrast, is collaborative and constructive, providing benefits to the possessing spirit or the god it serves, as well as the person who is possessed. Although the words *possession* and *possessed* convey the intrusive nature of the process and the foreign spirit's manipulation of selfhood, they also signal, in *Time's Memory*, the status of the affected person as possessor, owner, or agent who contributes to and benefits from aspects of the process. Taking refuge within Amina permits Ekundayo's transfer to America, but it also facilitates Amina's recovery from the trauma of captivity and her adjustment to life in America. Lester, through his portrayal of Amina's early experience in America, assures young readers that the Black historical legacy was not a simple one of Black submission and self-erasure, but a complicated process in which Africans negotiated to maintain their ties to their past, even as they reinvented their lives in America.

Ekundayo's possession of the African American Nat also emphasizes the continuing influence of Dogon culture. While Amina's possession is informed by her femininity and family inheritance, Nat's possession by Ekundayo is gendered in ways that are traditionally masculine, involving competition, conflict, and an impulse toward aggression and violence, rather than the harmony achieved between Amina and her past and present influences. Yet the relationship between Nat and Ekundayo is arguably productive, too, and grounded both by the continuity of Dogon influences and an adaptation that is responsive to Nat and Ekundayo's needs and to pressures and opportunities in US society. Through this process, Lester encourages his readers to see Black people's complicated negotiation of the oppression they have faced in America, which entailed adherence to tradition, as well as compromise and change. For late twentieth-century readers of Lester's novel, this emphasis affirmed African American ties to a rich African cultural past, and emphasized Black agency, even when confronted with destructive forces.

Time's Memory portrays Ekundayo's acculturation on the Chelsea plantation as a form of possession in which he inhabits and controls the enslaved Nat's body, which in turn affects the Dogon spirit. At one point, while contemplating changes in his way of thinking, Ekundayo realizes he is becoming a different being: Nathaniel—an uneasy sum of Nat's predispositions and his own Dogon consciousness:

> As long as my nyama had merely occupied Nat's body, my purpose had been clear. Find the way to bring peace to the nyama of the dead. But my nyama was not the same anymore. Instead of me using Nat's body and nyama, Nat had used mine to bring Nathaniel into existence. And Nathaniel cared passionately about life and love, and he had listened eagerly to Gabriel's words of rebellion and freedom. Nathaniel knew nothing of *nyama* and their needs. He wanted happiness for himself. I did not understand such selfishness because my desire could not be separate from Amma's desire. (Lester, *Time's Memory* 122)

Identifying Nat's US identity as egocentric, Lester sets the stage not for the continuing conflict between Ekundayo's warring identities, but rather for their integration. Ekundayo's self-division ultimately serves Lester's message about the importance of balancing personal desire with communal obligations, which encompass one's duties to the living and the dead.

In portraying Ekundayo's possession of Nat, Lester encourages readers to see the empowering continuities between African and African American cultures, showing how serving others can be wedded to personal desire. At a time when success in the US mainstream was often measured by individual achievement and status, this message encouraged readers to see the generative power of community and ancestral ties. Lester does this first through Ekundayo's critique of Nat's love for Ellen, which is associated with a myopia Ekundayo sees as a common quality of enslaved persons on the Chelsea plantation. This short-sightedness is associated not only with romantic love, but also with a focus on personal emotions at the expense of communal obligations and welfare. A concern with individual feeling that is not attached to ancestors or the community is also manifest in Nathaniel's curiosity about Gabriel's planned fight for freedom, which ostensibly could serve the enslaved community's interest. Gabriel and his partner Ezekiel, however, are arguably more motivated by anger about white aggression than by concern for their fellow Black community members. Gabriel and Ezekiel seek to avenge the humiliation and deaths of loved ones by destroying slavery and all who support it. Similarly, Ekundayo, bound to Nat's body and the more militant Nathaniel's will, becomes consumed by anger and the need for retribution, at least temporarily accepting Gabriel's argument that "Death in the cause of freedom gives life to a man, while life as the white man's slave is the worst kind of death" (Lester, *Time's Memory* 130). This assessment suggests the extent to which individual rights and desires are important to the nascent Nathaniel's sense of self.

Yet Lester underscores the importance of acting in ways that integrate personal and communal welfare, a message that is meant to apply not only to the novel's action, but also to readers' lives. During the rebellion, Ekundayo rejects Gabriel and Ezekiel's vision, because it opposes his own respect for the dead and for the cycles of life, which emphasize social connection rather than alienation. Gabriel's actions are derived from a "madness born from the inability to withstand pain" (*Time's Memory* 148), an incapacity that keeps Gabriel from empathizing with others who are pained, unless they have the same outrage that he does. Although Gabriel's grievances are understandable, Lester suggests that he is a flawed hero, because he resists rather than connects to the heterogeneity of African American experience. Nathaniel Ekundayo, the character who synthesizes Nat's and Ekundayo's identities, on the contrary, makes community knowledge and preservation priorities, providing a model of inclusive leadership that the novel suggests remains relevant.

During the time that Ekundayo is persuaded by Gabriel's call to fight for personal dignity, he does not understand that the elder is discrediting the less overt ways that enslaved persons resisted the system and expressed their need for dignity and personal authority. Lester acknowledges this tendency through characters like Nat's enslaved grandmother Harriet, a Christian.[7] Gabriel sees Harriet's Christianity, which emphasizes love, kindness, and forgiveness, as weakness, and Harriet herself as a "'white folks' n-----,'" a pliable tool of the enslaver (Lester, *Time's Memory* 158). Yet she explains to Ekundayo that acting on Christian principles of love, kindness, and forgiveness draws on reserves of personal power, "What Gabriel couldn't understand was how much strength it takes to be a slave and to care about the one who's keeping you a slave" (158). Harriet's perspective reflects the pacifist approach to confronting social exploitation that the Reverend Martin Luther King Jr.

embodied, as opposed to Black Power figures who rejected conciliation and promoted a violent response. Rather than echoing Gabriel's rejection of Harriet's approach, however, the novel presents it as one legitimate way of navigating injustice. It might be argued that Harriet's approach facilitates the continuity of enslavement and encourages complacency rather than resistance. Yet her self-discipline and her love and support for others help maintain a sense of community that challenges the alienating and brutalizing aspects of slavery. Harriet's care extends to her grandson, Nat, other enslaved persons, and the motherless Ellen, establishing a basis for an inclusive, caring community.

Similarly, Nathaniel Ekundayo, though he is first paralyzed by the conflict between individualism and his social and historical conscience, ultimately brings together these competing values in a productive way. If anything, his love for Ellen and desire for individual dignity become part of his social vision, which is informed by his loyalty to his Dogon heritage. This vision is manifest in Nathaniel Ekundayo's later work to record the stories of nyama. Thus, Lester suggests both a way an African consciousness is altered by immersion in a new social context, and highlights preexisting Dogon structures of feeling and understanding that shape the change. According to Lester, a person does not lose contact with a culture completely, for it continues to orient that person in a new place. Moreover, he suggests that one foundational aspect of African American identity, as exemplified by Nathaniel Ekundayo, combines self- and community interest, and that this dual concern is born of African Americans' ongoing negotiation of their inheritance as African and American.[8] His memory work encourages Black and non-Black readers to share their feelings of loss and loneliness and to build on this communication to re-create a society founded on respect for the living and the dead. Indeed, he finds ways of emphasizing the ongoing presence of the dead through different forms of embodiment, and Lester suggests that Nathaniel Ekundayo's methods are necessary for contemporary readers—not only as a means of preserving the past, but also as a way of tapping into and sharing creative energies that affirm and enrich Black lives.

VISUAL CULTURE AND MEMORY

Lester presents African-derived visual culture as an especially effective way of reinforcing this cultural orientation. In addition to bodily possession, Lester foregrounds the Dogon tradition of memorializing the dead through wooden altar sculpture, one of several means by which the Dogon affirm the connections between the past and present. For *Time's Memory*, Lester adopts perhaps the most familiar form of this memorial sculpture—vertical, elongated figures either in kneeling or standing positions. Although the novel is not illustrated, it includes descriptions that reference this traditional style. Lester presents the first such sculpture in detailing Ekundayo's efforts to help Amina and Josiah: "It was the figure of a man. His head was shaped like a thin oval, the body long, with a protruding belly and slender legs. The figure rested on a flat pedestal, which would allow it to stand" (Lester, *Time's Memory* 52–53). When Ekundayo gives this statue to the traumatized, suicidal Amina, she instantly recognizes it as the container she will use for her dead husband Menyu's nyama. "She took it with trembling hands and clasped it to her bosom" as if she were reuniting with a friend (53). Seeing the statue, she understands that the ways she cherishes her husband can remain a part of her life; they will serve as an anchor that will allow her to orient herself in her new circumstances. Indeed, Lester seems to be drawing on contemporary discussions of trauma and recovery that emphasize the importance of establishing a ritual that lends order to a life disrupted by events beyond one's control. The statue becomes part of the process that Susan J. Brison describes in which the victim of trauma recovers "not only by transforming traumatic memory into a coherent narrative that can be integrated into the survivor's sense of self and view of the world, but also by reintegrating the survivor into a community, reestablishing connections essential to selfhood" (39–40). Amina's connection to the statue facilitates her surviving the trauma of displacement, enslavement, and loss by affirming her past cultural orientation and abiding aspects of selfhood. The sculpture makes tangible the ongoing presence of her dead husband in her life and thus their ongoing relationship; it makes the presence of the past tangible in a new setting.

Furthermore, even as she takes in the values and language of Anglo-American culture, she, in turn, imparts aspects of her own to Josiah, including her care for her loved ones' nyama. The sculpture functions to make public a private relationship or experience so that it can be shared. Josiah joins her, for instance, in the ceremony marking the move of her first husband's nyama into the sculpture. And later she joins him in honoring his and the deceased Hannah's dead son, whose nyama will inhabit another sculpture. The ceremonies encompass lamentation, as well as the hope that Amma will "set [the dead] on the correct path" and that the dead will be inspired to support and protect their survivors (Lester, *Time's Memory* 54). Through the sculptures, Ekundayo has helped Amina and Josiah to share with the nyama of the dead a culture that acknowledges their particular needs. The sculptures are instruments in a shared ritual that pays respect to both an individual's distinct life force and their connection to living and dead family members. Moreover, rather than simply focusing on the past, these functional works of art help to create meaning in the present, providing a basis for Josiah's and Amini's recognizing each other's losses and common humanity. The ritual of maintaining the sculptures and memorializing the dead helps maintain the belief in "personal and collective immortality" and "the harmony of the spiritual and material worlds," to borrow from Barbara Wilcot's discussion of some of the distinctions of Black folkways (10). It evinces a connection to intangible, but real, powers that reinforce the couple's commitment to a shared life integrating the past, present, and future. As Lester suggests, through Josiah's acceptance of Amini's spiritual framework, these generative powers can serve as a basis for a cross-racial, cross-national culture in the United States.

If Amina and Josiah's example is an important, but isolated, case of maintaining African tradition, the novel also presents Ekundayo's broader influence at the Chelsea plantation, where he takes action to influence the practices of an evolving African American culture. This refocusing involves a shift from Ekundayo's concern with the nyama of the dead to the psychological and spiritual health of the living, after the revolt in which several community members die. The new focus resonates with a late twentieth- and early twenty-first-century readership, who may have encountered concepts of holistic health and mindfulness in schools. It also connects to Black communities' reckoning with the relatively high rate of African American youth mortality. According to data collected by the US Department of Health and Human Services, the Centers for Disease Control, and the National Center for Health, between 1980 and 2016, Black children and adolescents ages five to nineteen died at higher rates than white children ("Infant, Child, and Teen Mortality").[9] The shift in *Time's Memory* to a concern with survivors' pain thus imagines a background for contemporary Black people's concern with African American mortality, as well as disproportionately high rates of illness and incarceration among Black persons. In this section dedicated to Nathaniel Ekundayo's socialization as an enslaved young man, Lester shows the process by which enslaved persons endured suffering, including the commonality of death and other losses. The novel's refocusing calls attention to Nathaniel Ekundayo's own new status as a human being who must negotiate the continuing hold of Dogon tradition and the need to address features of African American life that are discordant with it but representative of the Black experience within America. Lester shows Ekundayo's efforts to recognize and assuage the devastating, inescapable pain of slavery among survivors of the revolt, and to bring them back from the grip of an enervating grief. Central to Ekundayo's work in this part of the novel is the importance of recognizing trauma and finding creative, generative means of coping with it.

After the revolt fails, the survivors must watch the white enslavers who live near the plantation torture and kill the surviving rebels and callously dispose of their bodies. The enslaved persons on the Chelsea estate are overcome with sadness and unable to cry from or speak of their pain. As one woman explains, "Wouldn't do no good. Us slaves got so much to cry over, I be afraid that once I started crying I might not be able to stop" (Lester, *Time's Memory* 192). Lester depicts their trauma through the image of a fog that emerges from and oppresses the Black community: "Each day the fog was getting more and more dense around everyone from whom it poured. Some of them were in danger of being suffocated by their grief" (195). The fog signifies the grievers' isolation and confusion; Ekundayo comes to understand this as "grief that did not know itself," and he believes they must confront and share it (193). Although many are affected by this fog, their incapacity, or unwillingness, to turn to one another for comfort and understanding suggests the negative ramifications of American individualism and of slavery's systemic alienating processes. To counter these, Ekundayo puts in place a ritual that helps strengthen communal ties and facilitate personal healing.

Nathaniel Ekundayo uses a set of crude figurines he has found hidden in the plantation carpentry shop, particularizing them by adding to each the name of one of the dead men and a sign of his individuality. Nathaniel Ekundayo carves a Bible on the statue for Gabriel, a dancer on a statue for a man who has loved to dance, and a flame on that for another known for his passionate spontaneity. These statues are like tombstones, but they do not represent sites where the bodies lay. Also, they do not contain the nyama of the dead. According to him, engaging with the memorial sculptures promotes community members' self-expression and critical engagement with memory—-distilling key defining qualities through which survivors remember the dead men's lived experience and personalities: "What mattered was [not the presence of the bodies but] that those who remained had a place to come to and let the tears flow, a place where they could talk aloud to the dead one, and speak of their love and the lacerating pain of cruel loss" (Lester, *Time's Memory* 200). This self-expression also honors the fullness of the dead men's being, ways of living that evoke the survivors' sadness, as well as their joy. One woman recalls that Horace, the dance-lover, had danced inside his mother when she was pregnant, and remarks, "Sometimes I wished I could be inside his head to hear what he was hearing that got him to moving his feet the way he did" (201). She thus expresses her sense of Horace through what she and associates remember about him, and these memories come together into a story that transcends the official valuation of Horace as an object that could be destroyed when it can no longer be manipulated or exploited. Ekundayo helps free the Black community to place value on their thoughts and experiences. He provides groundwork for an African American culture that thrives on expressing a productive, life-affirming connection to the past and to community members' emotional responses to history. This is a necessary privileging of Blackness, Black selfhood, and community at a time when both Black history and Black people's emotions were all too often casualties of white hegemony.

Recognizing that Black persons' feelings and lives matter disrupts the assumption that whiteness is supreme, "a ruling episteme that privileges that which [black persons] can never be" and that actively punishes many African Americans for their failure to be white (Cheng 7). Lester suggests the painful ramifications of anti-Black racism through his portrayal of the enslaved laborers at the Chelsea plantation, but he also points to means by which African Americans coped with racial trauma. In this way, his portrait relates to a tendency Éva Tettenborn has observed in much African American literature, which, she says, "locate[s] loss as something from which a group or community can paradoxically derive its bonds and its strength" (250). According to Tettenborn, "the melancholic's grief in African American literature often signifies resistance to a historiography that has systematically neglected the African American experience in antebellum southern history" (249).[10] Lester's foregrounding of grief, mourning, and remembrance not only challenges conceptions of African Americans as emotionally superficial, but also guides young Black readers to counter alienation and nihilism and to find more life-affirming ways of handling personal and cultural loss.[11] Lester's portrayal of Ekundayo's efforts to establish generative mourning rituals suggests that past African American trauma holds lessons for a current generation of readers. In portraying the Black Chelsea community's acceptance of Ekundayo's sculptures, Lester acknowledges that such rituals grew out of African ones and developed into something different. In this sequence within the novel, the process of remembering is detached from the elaborate system of belief and practices that the god Amma seeks to uphold; most obviously, at least in this instance, it becomes detached from the nyama. Ekundayo asks himself, "Was this fog the nyama of the twelve [rebels]? No, I decided, because the fog was coming from inside people" (Lester, *Time's Memory* 190). The dead retain importance, but survivors' welfare and individual voices and visions have become significant concerns. Survivors' practice of remembering, Lester suggests, provides an orientation and purpose that strengthen the self. Remembering lends balance to a world that is off kilter, just as it does in the traditional Dogon practice. Bearing memory validates the person who has been lost and the person who remains; it counters the forces of slavery that negate the Black self, privileging Black feeling and encouraging communal connections, communication, and an imaginative engagement with the world.

BAD MEMORY

Time's Memory acknowledges a range of Black affective experience, opposing Ekundayo's memory keeping and Gabriel's and Ezekiel's violent reckoning with memories of loss. The rebellion, and the emotions fueling it, resonate with militant forms of Black activism throughout African American history. Gabriel and Ezekiel remember past injustices perpetrated by white persons that have contributed to personal and familial ruin. The two men rely on these memories to fuel and justify their own actions and incite others to attack the white power structure. Yet Lester suggests that while Ekundayo provides a pathway out of destructive pain, Gabriel and Ezekiel are energized by replaying their memories both in their own thoughts and in speech to others, an approach that Lester suggests leads not to creative transformation of their circumstances, but to a kind of spiritual entrapment. Part of Gabriel's motivation comes from the memory of a white woman who falsely accused his brother of looking at her, which leads to the brother's death and to their parents' debilitating trauma. "That white man's daughter had killed three people with her life," he explains to himself, comparing her to Ellen Chelsea, who he sees as a dangerous, ruinous presence that must be removed from his son Nat's life (Lester, *Time's Memory* 118). Ezekiel's anger also stems from a concern with familial well-being, for he has seen his daughter courted and cosseted by the plantation owner Mr. Chelsea, and then sold, only for her to kill herself and their baby. Around white persons, Ezekiel appears to have reconciled himself to the loss of his daughter, but he speaks openly of his hatred for Chelsea when he is with other resistant enslaved persons. It is Ezekiel who kills Ellen during the rebellion when Ekundayo refuses to, addressing the absent enslaver, "We even now. . . . You took my daughter from me. I just took your daughter from you. We equal now. You and me. For the rest of your life, you gon' feel what I been feeling every day" (149). Ezekiel's statement succinctly demonstrates his difference from Ekundayo: Where the latter encourages mourners to grapple with the complexity of a dead loved one's life and character, Ezekiel thinks less of his daughter as a whole person and fixates on her exploitation and his own emotional response to it. Certainly, his pain is a poignant testimony to the lingering power of slavery to undermine selfhood, for Ezekiel never heals. He manifests his power not by acting to heal from horror and loss, but instead by imposing them on another to perpetuate the cycle of pain and destruction. Of course, African American militancy is not necessarily defined by such destructive, parochial urges, but Lester makes Ezekiel's and Gabriel's activism the antithesis of creativity: It stops short of reckoning with how to live in a world after revolt. They refuse to envision and plan for alternatives to the white supremacist regime they attack.

In a novel that emphasizes the creative power of memory, Gabriel and Ezekiel stand out as limited characters because of the recursive nature of their thoughts and feelings. Gabriel, whose typological imagination conflates his experience with that of the biblical angel, Old Testament prophets, and Christ, believes that he acts in accordance with God's will and serves "the God of the downtrodden" (Lester, *Time's Memory* 111). He has grown up, like the historical Nat Turner, with a rare ability to read that he believes was granted spontaneously by God. Also like Turner, Gabriel sees himself as a special, true servant of God, who has empowered him to lead a revolution against evil. Yet Lester's use of the biblical name "Gabriel" functions ironically to underscore the character's shortcomings. The biblical Gabriel interprets one of the prophet Daniel's dreams and reveals the coming of John the Baptist and Christ to their mothers. As dream interpreter and messenger, Gabriel tells of the rise and inevitable fall of human rulers and suggests God's everlasting power; his annunciations associate the Judeo-Christian God with renewal and positive transformations. Similarly, Ezekiel summons, through his biblical name and professional identity as a blacksmith, associations that ironically highlight his limitation. The prophet Ezekiel, who lived during a time of great international turmoil, also bears messages about human evil and society's discontinuities in light of God's omnipotent power, which includes merciful divine intervention in human affairs. Lester also contrasts Ezekiel with the West African role of artisan and African American traditions of agency among skilled laborers. Ezekiel's revenge, for instance, signals his distance from the traditional Dogon position of blacksmith. According to art historian Kate Ezra, "As in other West African ethnic groups, the blacksmiths' mastery of earth, air, and fire, and their ability to make the iron tools on which Dogon farmers depend, accords them a privileged place in Dogon society.... [Blacksmiths] serve as intermediaries and peacemakers, not only between other Dogon, but also between the living and the ancestors and between mankind and Amma, especially in order to bring rain" (25). This vision of professionalism transcends the manual tasks of manipulating metals and suggests the artisan's integral role in a complex social and natural matrix. Such a communal, integrative vision was apparently important to the skilled artisans who proved indispensable to actual slave revolts, including those led by the blacksmith Gabriel Prosser and carpenter and church founder Denmark Vesey (Vlach 110). Ezekiel's status as a skilled enslaved laborer, which brings him a rare mobility, might position him to be a bridge-builder, but even within the Black community, he foments division. Before the revolt, he derides Nathaniel for being "nothing but a house n-----" and rejects him as a potential collaborator, calling him "Judas" (Lester, *Time's Memory* 127). He is poised to kill the young man for any misstep. And in killing Ellen, who disapproves of slavery and has been close to Nat and other African Americans, he shows insensitivity. Moreover, he never demonstrates much concern for the welfare of other enslaved persons. Though Lester's Ezekiel and Gabriel experience social horror, their response is a self-righteous resistance that applies Judeo-Christian ideas about meting out justice and defying social custom in destructive ways. Both characters, it might be argued, function as cautionary examples of their kind of militancy, encouraging readers to question hate-fueled activism and to think critically about ways to redress racist grievances.

TELLING AND WRITING TALES OF SELFHOOD

Lester contrasts these two elders with Nathaniel Ekundayo, emphasizing his ability to see events and persons in their complexity; his efforts at memorializing the dead and comforting the living relay a very different sense of reality. Writing, the ultimate way in which Ekundayo meets his dual obligation to the living and the dead, offers a way of recording the complexity of African American lives. It is the last form of embodiment that Lester presents to memorialize the dead, and Ekundayo's discovery of its possibilities resonates with Lester's own approach as a crafter of historical narratives. This aesthetic emphasizes an intimate bond between a writer and an historical human subject that bridges temporal distance and very different circumstances and experiences. Written and oral tales of selfhood allow for, indeed, seem to facilitate, transcendent apprehension of other persons' experiences, according to Lester; they can enable a present-day person's imaginative relocation to another time and way of being. This transcendence is evident in the account Lester offers in his 2004 memoir of being possessed by the spirit of an enslaved man:

> I was standing at the edge of a field in Laurel, Mississippi. I don't recall how I happened to be standing there. I only remember that I was. Suddenly, it was not 1964 but 1854 or 1844 and I was a slave who paused from working the cotton to lean on my hoe. Gazing northward I wonder: What was on the other side of the horizon line far in the distance? If I could walk to that line and step across it, would I be free? What would that feel like? To be free? I stare for a while longer. Then, not wanting to think about it anymore and before the overseer notices me looking off into space and lays his whip across my sweaty back, I go back to hoeing. (*On Writing* 90)

Here, Lester connects the experience of possession by another consciousness to his conviction that he must acknowledge the person out of whose eyes he has seen and try to reconstruct and tell the stories of this man and of other enslaved persons theretofore obscured by history. "Though I did not know his name, I knew I had to tell his story and as many stories as I could of those who had been slaves. I had uncovered my subject" (*On Writing* 90). In *Time's Memory*, writing becomes the means of narrating and fixing this experience of possession, of honoring access and sensitivity to another person's perspective and life.[12] Writing a life, and telling stories about lived experience more generally, for Lester, lead the author and their readers to a fuller engagement with history and to a better understanding of an individual's purpose within the cosmic order.

In the novel's final chapters, Lester emphasizes the legitimacy of imaginative and biographical writing by stressing the authenticity of Ekundayo's written texts about loved ones' and strangers' lives. Indeed, after tending to the Chelsea community members' grief, Ekundayo sits down over several hours and writes about Ellen, having inherited Nat's love for her (and his ability to read and write). Ellen's nyama has appeared to him previously and expressed concern that she will not be remembered once he dies. Unbeknownst to him, Ellen's nyama looks over his shoulder as he records his impressions of her in a notebook and, once he is done, thanks him for what he has written. Her nyama then enters the book, accepting its status as lieu de mémoire, both a receptacle and a representation of memory (Dixon 22). Ellen's evaluation of Ekundayo's text as true to her sense of herself validates the biographical mode, and serves as a meta-narrative parallel to Lester's ideas about his authorial practice. Yet it is important to remember that this evaluation occurs in "the context of historical fantasy" (Lesley), a narrative mode that Lester uses to affirm his faith in stories' power to carry the essence of a life. Lester suggests that what is real and important is tied not just to the objects of empirical proof but also to imagination, affective experience, and other intangibles. The belief in a narrative's truth ignores influential theories about language's arbitrariness and life-writing's conventionality and artifice.[13] For Lester, such writing is a "gift" that opens a "deeply personal" connection to another (*On Writing* 123, 77).

Lester is not naïve—he knows that language can be misleading, indirect, and ambiguous, which he demonstrates in some of the stories in *The Tales of Uncle Remus: The Adventures of Brer Rabbit* (1987), his retelling of Joel Chandler Harris's Uncle Remus tales.[14] In *Time's Memory*, however, Lester's faith in language shows the influence of Romanticism, his upbringing in the Baptist faith, and his embrace, as an adult, of Judaism. Each orientation upholds the truthfulness of inspired language and storytelling, which confers a serious, even mystical cast to the practices of reading, hearing and writing personal testimony and narrative. As Rudine Sims Bishop has pointed out, this faith in language as a means of revealing reality is also central to the mission of children's book authors (*Free Within Ourselves* 1). Lester sees such "writing [as] a sacred trust" between himself as author and both his subject matter and his readers, a trust that allows for a profound and productive trinity (*On Writing* 155, 157).[15] *Time's Memory* suggests that this trinity has substantial political weight, validating the idea that speakers and writers intent on revealing themselves can use words honestly and precisely. And in turn, receptive readers can take in their words and hear their voices.[16] In Lester's view, writing is a people's art, reflecting and expressing the people's experience—a philosophy that reflects an emphasis of the Black Arts Movement. Moreover, though writing in Black expressive traditions acknowledges individuals' experiences, it also often envisions the individual in relationship to others, both living and dead. The configuration recalls poet, novelist, and critic Melvin Dixon's observation that "orality and memory transmitted orally require communal expression" (22). Lester's conception of writing down oral testimony is informed by this sense of orality's community foundations, and opposes Euro-American tendencies to separate orality and literacy. Furthermore, Lester's vision of the interdependence between self and community challenges myths of American individualism and exceptionalism. *Time's Memory* conceives of writing as a political force and of writers as truth-tellers who are at the service of a complicated, inclusive reality.

Lester displays a part of this trinity when Nathaniel Ekundayo turns to recording the life stories of dead African Americans, a "sacred trust" that his descendants will continue (*On Writing* 155). After Ellen's nyama disappears into the book Nathaniel Ekundayo has been writing in, the nyama of a man, Mose, appears and signals for Nathaniel Ekundayo to listen to and record his story next (214). In this instance, although the autobiographical subject, Mose, who was formerly enslaved, depends on the writer's materiality and literacy skills, Mose's voice is authoritative; Nathaniel Ekundayo remains in a supporting role. Similarly, the personal qualities of his descendants are temporarily subordinated to the nyamas' storytelling, as Nathaniel, Nathaniel Ekundayo's grandson, indicates in an explanation that appears in the novel's epilogue. First of all, he says, "the nyama would choose one child of each generation to record their stories. No one knew why" (*Time's Memory* 218). As an only child, he begins to fill this role as an adolescent:

> one day during my junior year of high school, I was sitting in math class, not my favorite one by any means, and was looking out the window not thinking about much of anything. Suddenly, an old black woman appeared. She wasn't outside, nor was she in the classroom. The only way I can explain it is to say she was in the window glass itself, except her voice, sounding as ancient as wind, was speaking inside me. For a moment I thought I was going crazy, then I remembered my mother's words about the spirits and how they had chosen our family to record their stories. Quickly, I opened my notebook and began writing what she was saying. (219)

Here, Lester underscores the spiritual nature of a kind of writing, in which authorship is associated with an elemental force that moves and empowers an agent to act in accordance with the speaker-author's will. The author, an "old black woman [who] appeared," is a spirit and only discernible in a threshold that gives the young Nathaniel some access to a world of the dead and unknown. The window suggests the speaker-author's transparency and authenticity, and these attributes extend to the oral and written versions of her story, which are true to her life.[17]

This process of life writing privileges African American voices and preserves some of the spiritual quality of Dogon memorial practice. Indeed, Lester suggests that the tradition Nathaniel Ekundayo establishes defies some influential scholarly conceptions of Black literary tradition: It inverts, for instance, the influential concept of the talking book, the text whose codes were discernible to a white readership but not the displaced, enslaved African (Gates, *Signifying* 155–56). According to scholar Henry Louis Gates Jr., who identified this experience of exclusion as a motif in many early African American texts, the exclusion of the Black person from white print culture engendered desire and associated the ability to read (to hear what the book has to say) with freedom and power within Anglo-American culture. Gaining the ability to read and write, to engage with the talking book, was associated with competency within the dominant culture, self-mastery, and freedom (Gates, *Signifying* 135–37). As Gates has also acknowledged, this process involved shedding or suppressing African ancestry and aligning with European influences (139, 157–58). Yet, rather than emphasizing the dispossession and assimilation that the talking book often marks, Lester has African Americans define the material entity of the book as an apt means through which their voices can be heard. Nathaniel Ekundayo's books are extensions and representations of self, even sanctioned holders of self.

Even more than the novel's possessed bodies and memorial sculptures, an as-told-to book is a product of a nyama's distinct powers: It foregrounds the subject's voice and shaping of their experience. This distinction is not insignificant, for voice has been an enduring trope in African American culture because of the dominant culture's long tradition of silencing and marginalizing Black Americans.[18] As bell hooks has said about women's development and expression of agency, "Speaking becomes both a way to engage in active self-transformation and a rite of passage where one moves from being object to being subject. Only as subjects can we speak. As objects we remain voiceless—our beings defined and interpreted by others" (53). In hook's conception of voice, there is an equation of identity and voice; voice is a means of expressing that identity. Lester does not accept the idea that, in general, African Americans lacked a voice and were only defined by others in nineteenth-century US society. Although the character Nat has not been able to establish his voice (and commit himself to his love for Ellen), other Black characters manage to express themselves. Yet like hooks, Lester does accept the equation of being and voice. For him and for Ekundayo, the nyama's oral stories are unquestionably true ones, and their printed, literary forms are legitimated by the nyama's endorsing presence within the material reality of the books: Just as Ellen endorses the story Ekundayo tells about her by entering the book he has written, the nyama disappear into and thus authorize the books he and his descendants write about them. The stories are answers to the call of a current generation of artists and readers to reclaim the voices of the past.[19]

This interpretation of African American expression rejects the influential argument that print culture has long excluded authentic self-expression by African Americans. The scholar John Sekora has asserted that the slave narrative, one of the most studied of African American genres, displays limited "literary authority" by Black writers, because they crafted their stories to fit into a "white envelope," the set of textual formulas that define the genre (484). Writing about the genre's requisite truthfulness, he notes: "The facticity sought was not that of individualized Afro-American life, but rather the concrete details of lives spent under slavery" (482, 497). According to Sekora, the choice and presentation of experience yielded a generalized view of Black life and character, and "the suppression of the personal slave voice" (510). This suppression is evident, according to Gates, in much of African American literature, because it caters, in great part, to a white readership that is out of sync with Black experiences, attitudes, and languages ("Lifting" 154–57). Many scholars reject this argument. Robert S. Levine, for instance, in writing about slave narratives, sees, for example, "black voices, or messages, that emerge from their not entirely white 'envelopes' and that can be productively examined in relation to a tradition of American autobiography" (101–2). Acknowledging the influence of white literary conventions, white editors, and white readers' literary tastes, Levine and many other critics note African American authors' ingenuity in manipulating standard language and literary forms. In many ways, Lester sidesteps this debate about the integrity of African American literary voices by affirming the truthfulness of his nyama narrators and presenting their participation in a different culture of the book, one that features understanding, supportive editors, and amanuenses whose personalities and politics do not interfere with the narrators' visions or voices. As Lester admits in *On Writing for Children and Other People*, his own participation in the world of publishing has not always been as smooth: For instance, the editor of two of his Uncle Remus books found fault with his manipulation of voice in retelling the tales (121). In *Time's Memory*, however, he envisions a realm that lacks obstacles to effective communication.

The novel's alternative culture of the book would seem ideal, for in addition to foregrounding the oppressed and the silenced, it includes women and men, both as narrators and authors. It brings together the living and the dead, as well as orality and writing. With Lester's representation of the Ekundayo family's culture, he rejects dichotomies that often inform our understanding of non-Black and Black Americans. The long-standing comparison of African Americans' and white Americans' cognitive abilities is one such dichotomy. Throughout the nineteenth century, African Americans' illiteracy and vernacular speech were used against them as signs of intellectual deficiency. Gaps remain that separate many African American children's achievement on tests from that of white and Asian American children. In spite of much evidence to the contrary, the stereotype that "Black People Don't Read" lingers.[20] Perhaps, *Time's Memory* functions, at least in part, to affirm that African American literacy has deep roots and is not opposed to vernacular forms, such as African-derived sculpture and oral storytelling. Lester points to a book culture founded on integration—on the mutual interdependence of different states of being and different ways of keeping memories. Writing has not been foreign to African

Americans, Lester avers, but rather it has been a form they have adopted to serve their interests. It has been an especially versatile tool because it can represent, or at least evoke, other forms of memory-keeping: the sculpted figures are prompts for memories of and storytelling about the dead, and oral testimony is the basis for the books the Ekundayo family maintains. *Time's Memory* itself epitomizes the potential of the print medium through which Lester hopes to reach readers and encourage them to carry on the work of keeping memories of the dead.

By the end of *Time's Memory*, Lester does admit, however, that his culture of the book is limited. The Ekundayo family's spirit books have proliferated in their home library, but they do not seem to circulate. Even family members seem to be ignoring the books, and other aspects of the tradition have been lost. The Dogon word nyama, for instance, has been dropped, and replaced with "spirit." Perhaps more tellingly, the family does not grasp its own history. The epilogue's narrator, Ekundayo's great-grandson, says that "By the time I was born, all memories of Nathaniel Ekundayo had vanished from my family" (*Time's Memory* 218). It turns out that Ekundayo has not yet narrated his story, because he will come back to life and take possession of the epilogue's narrator, who will marry the reincarnated Ellen (or at least, their nyamas will possess the bodies of the descendants). Lester treats the lovers' reunion as a closure that necessitates the end of the Ekundayo family line, and he uses this narrative outcome as grounds for inviting readers to take active roles in preserving the past: The epilogue's narrator asks, "who will listen to the dead, record their stories, and give them the peace that comes when they have told their stories and had them written down" (224). He continues, "I have done all that I could. If there is to be hope for the living, someone else must care for the spirits of the dead" (225). For Lester, the practice of listening and recording the nyama's stories is not just one man, woman, or family's job. The world is full of nyama ready to be discovered and integrated into our lives, and we must embrace and listen to the nyama and, in turn, tell stories that will possess a new generation, who will position themselves to maintain and pass on the practice of remembering.

In the next chapter, I turn to more commercial narratives that explore issues of communication, focusing on Black girls' empowering combination of the Black vernacular with literacy. As with Ekundayo, the protagonists in these narratives rely on the resources of Black support systems as they learn to read and write. Rather than simply endorsing the primacy of an Anglo-American tradition of literacy, these freedom narratives show young African American protagonists make reading and writing extensions of their Black culture.

Chapter 4

STEALING LETTERS

Freedom Narratives, Literacy, and Black Vernacular Traditions

Many historical texts designed for children present literacy as a principal means through which enslaved persons secure freedom and are thus aligned with nineteenth-century slave narratives' portrayal of the liberating power of literacy. Yet as Paula Connolly has observed, neo-slave narratives do not simply conform to the conventions of antebellum slave narratives; they transform them (200). This is demonstrated by the freedom narratives I discuss in this chapter: Charles Burnett's *Nightjohn* (1996), Patricia McKissack's *A Picture of Freedom: The Diary of Clotee, a Slave Girl* (1997), and Joyce Hansen's *I Thought My Soul Would Rise and Fly: The Diary of Patsy, a Freed Girl* (1997). These narratives present literacy in league with other means of reaching freedom derived from Black folk culture, including songs, tales, and character types, like the trickster. These features of the Black vernacular were long important within Black communities for cultural definition, orientation, and education, as well as entertainment. Literacy, by contrast, functioned as one of the "master's tools," the expressive and political powers controlled and employed by white patriarchy; before the Civil War, African Americans had limited access to literacy (Lorde 112). In Burnett's, Hansen's, and McKissack's narratives, as well as in other freedom narratives, Black children bring literacy *and* aspects of Black vernacular, especially oral, culture together to empower themselves, whether they are enslaved or newly free. With the help of print and oral traditions, all three narratives' Black girl protagonists rise above dire conditions and begin to fashion better lives for themselves: They speak and act for themselves both within and outside the Black community; they manipulate words to secure social advantages for themselves and others; and they help to shape and preserve a body of Black communal knowledge. In manifesting the girls' creativity and agency, these actions reflect the liberatory values of the Black Arts Movement, particularly the importance of freeing Black self-expression. Surprisingly, these characters and narratives are products of large media companies, Disney and Scholastic, and thus these particular narratives suggest the viability in the late 1990s of popularizing radical Black thought, although their messaging was by no means commonplace.[1]

My selection of primary sources for this chapter allows me to show how commercial, mass-marketed texts convey the Black aesthetic in revising the myth of literacy's predominance as a path to freedom. The revisionary trope conjoining literacy and folk culture is central to Burnett's *Nightjohn*, a film adaptation of the award-winning novel by Gary Paulsen, and McKissack's *A Picture of Freedom: The Diary of Clotee, a Slave Girl* (1997) and Hansen's *I Thought My Soul Would Rise and Fly: The Diary of Patsy, a Freed Girl* (1997), two novels in the Dear America series. These freedom narratives' transformation of the literacy myth suggests the possibility of Black agency within the contexts of slavery and the postslavery South, where exploitation of African Americans continued. The trope also claims literacy as a mode of expression that Black people have been able to adapt and use to express themselves, a power they have made their own, rather than primarily an accoutrement of the dominant culture or a register of assimilation to white society. Not all freedom narratives foreground the confluence of literacy and orality to the extent that Lester's *Time's Memory* and the focal texts in this chapter do, but many portray characters developing leadership skills and using various modes of communication to advocate for themselves and others.[2] Generally, freedom narratives suggest that fluency in various communicative modes provided African Americans with means of asserting selfhood fruitfully and ingeniously in a variety of social frameworks.[3] I have chosen to concentrate on Burnett's film and the Hansen and McKissack novels because they make the power of Black cultural expression thematically central and highlight the conjoining of literacy and the Black vernacular.

This revised trope takes aim at many African American children's purported bias against literacy and formal education in general. In presenting a history of literacy aligned with both individual and communal Black achievement, such texts address children who associate reading and writing with a white mainstream from which they may feel estranged. The books' and movie's affirmation of print and oral traditions stresses that reading and writing are rewarding parts of the African American heritage, that literacy is aligned with the oral riches of Black culture, and indeed, that Black folk and print cultures are not at odds. As in Julius Lester's portrayal of the synergy between orality and print culture in *Time's Memory*, these emphases reflect the central role of Black orality and written expression in the Black Arts Movement, as well as its commitment to fostering children's cultural awareness (Smethurst 92–93; Batho 26). The lessons target the many children whom sociologists describe as "oppositional"—those who resist formal schooling because they see it as a denial of Blackness and as culturally inauthentic (Finn 42).[4] The freedom narratives I explore here confront this issue by delivering the message that African American girls, and African American children in general, are inheritors of a rich tradition of intellectual and creative expression.

In fusing folklore with literacy, the narratives render historical situations that demand cultural sensitivity and, indeed, foster this sensitivity to an impressive degree. The folkways the freedom narratives portray include indirection, lying, stealing, and duplicity, which the texts seek to contextualize, showing that during both the eras of slavery and Reconstruction, Black persons had few other means of establishing their authority in a world dominated by white persons hostile to manifestations of Black agency. African Americans' situational ethics are not only presented as signs of African American ingenuity and resilience, but are also attached to, even conflated with, the acquisition and spread of literacy in Black communities at times when the dominant culture limited African Americans' access to formal education. Stealing letters was a cultural triumph, with book learning and folkways working in tandem to include and validate African American practices of self-affirmation at a time when the dominant culture required that Black Americans remain silent and subordinate.

Of course, this focus on indirection and theft can lead to historical misunderstanding and reaffirm stereotypes that might undercut the texts' cultural work. Subversion, deception, cunning, and trickery are not uncommon in children's literature, but freedom narratives take pains to show how actions that might be classified as negative forms of behavior are understandable, given the proscriptions against African American expressions of power. In focusing on the protagonists' necessary stealth and subversion, the narratives at times come close to reinforcing the stereotype of girls as covert manipulators of others. And, to varying extents, they concentrate so much on their girl protagonists' capabilities that their representations of power may seem contrived, even fantastical; at the very least, the girls seem poised to develop into the stereotypical indomitable Black woman (T. Harris 19). Thus, even as the texts aim to challenge some racial stereotypes, they may be reinscribing others. Yet to suggest that Black persons had to rely on clever indirection and covert one-upmanship rather than overt activism in order to achieve goals reflects historical necessities. Stealth and secrecy were central to many acts of African American defiance and to African American survival more generally, and these behaviors suffuse Black folktales. Yet these maneuvers were likely more complicated and less theatrical than the novels and film suggest, informed by a delicate, shifting balance of self-interest, stealth, boldness, feigned and actual submission, and self-denial.

This dramatic approach to presenting Black children's resistance may result from the texts' status as popular entertainment and demands attention, but the work that the narratives primarily do is to offer versions of history that show African Americans in a variety of roles as shapers of their experience, even when their powers are severely circumscribed. *Nightjohn*, *I Thought My Soul Would Rise and Fly*, and *A Picture of Freedom* challenge stereotypes of Black passivity, laziness, violence, and stupidity that outlasted the era of slavery and persist today. If the narratives perpetuate other stereotypes, the effects of these shortcomings might be diminished by readers' fuller engagement with history, and by complementing the novels' and film's portrayals with other, more balanced perspectives on slavery and Reconstruction (Schwebel 129). The three texts can serve as springboards for discussion about protocols for representing Black history through fiction for late twentieth-century child audiences. Furthermore, the books and film, primarily aimed at young girls, promote the idea that young women are central to the work of adapting, maintaining, and passing on a rich cultural legacy. If *Time's Memory* is pronounced in calling on readers to be active in seeking and preserving Black history, the film *Nightjohn* and the novels *I Thought My Soul Would Rise and Fly* and *A Picture of Freedom* encourage their audiences to respect the psychological and social experience of young Black girls intent on developing their voices in social contexts that demand their self-denial.

Much of my description of the Burnett adaptation and the Hansen and McKissack novels applies to Paulsen's *Nightjohn* (1993), which I will also examine. Yet I do not classify it as a freedom narrative because it ultimately does not reflect the positive evaluation of Black culture central to the 1960s Black aesthetic that defines the genre. Paulsen's novel limits access to Black characters' interiority and only indirectly and ambiguously suggests that Black culture strengthened and sustained the protagonist Sarny before and during her embrace of literary. The novel certainly offers a searing portrayal of a community of enslaved persons that is victimized by enslavers and by a social system that supports slavery. Paulsen's *Nightjohn* portrays important dimensions of slavery that are necessary for young audiences to understand, but the freedom narratives complement this more familiar narrative of subjection in essential ways. While Paulsen's novel promotes literacy as both an extension and critique of folkways, the film adaptation of *Nightjohn* offers an appreciative account of the interworkings of folkways and literacy in its astute protagonist's resistance to enslavement. The Dear America novels translate this focus on a girl's power through folkways and literacy into the diary form, with each centering on a Black girl's voice and perspective: *A Picture of Freedom* uses the trickster character common in Black folklore to portray the protagonist Clotee's witty manipulations, and *I Thought My Soul Would Rise* references a range of Black vernacular culture to show Patsy's agency. These focal texts' status as mass-marketed suggests both the viability of presenting girls' power in historical circumstances and the possibility of presenting radical history in meeting the demand for multicultural children's literature in the 1990s.

THE SLAVE NARRATIVE AS MODEL

Hansen's and McKissack's novels and the Burnett film complicate traditional ways of conceptualizing African American cultural expression. Long-canonized Black literature by Frederick Douglass, Richard Wright, and others, as well as much of today's hip hop, has presented Black culture as largely oral. For a long time, literacy in African American communities has been associated with only a privileged few (Mullen 670). As Elizabeth McHenry has asserted: "Historically much has been written about the absence of literacy skills among African Americans. While their verbal performance arts, from folktales and proverbs to testifying and rapping, have received wide recognition, the singular identification of African-American culture as 'oral in nature' has obscured facts surrounding other language uses—especially those related to reading and writing" (477). McHenry, Deborah Brandt, and children's literature scholars such as Anna Mae Duane and Katharine Capshaw have begun to uncover a rich history of reading and writing practices in Black America.[5] For many years, however, critics' attention to intersections between literacy and African American culture fixed on slave narratives' portrayals of efforts to attain literacy (McHenry 477). Henry Louis Gates and Robert Stepto have described this narrative trajectory as central to African American literature: "the correlation of freedom with literacy not only became the central trope of the slave narratives, but it also formed a mythical matrix out of which subsequent black narrative forms developed" (Gates, *Figures* 108). Yet the stories that such eighteenth-, nineteenth-, and early twentieth-century narratives often tell help perpetuate a troubling opposition between Black literacy and folk culture, between an elite group of reading and writing African Americans and the unlettered majority.[6]

The popularity of *Narrative of the Life of Frederick Douglass, an American Slave* (1845) and scholars' many examinations of the text have been especially influential in conceptualizing this opposition in a way that abets popular misinterpretations of literacy and Black orality. The heroic Douglass, though periodically adapting the role of trickster to get his way (and to learn to read), nevertheless discounts folk experience, including medicinal practices and community rituals. Even in his much-heralded discussion of enslaved persons' singing, Douglass offers an ambiguous portrait of Black creativity that approaches the stereotype of African American anti-intellectualism, even as it touts the depth and double-voiced nature of Black expression: Although slaves' songs were characterized by "unmeaning jargon," they "were full of meaning" to the singers themselves. Douglass, however, "did not, when a slave, understand the deep meaning of those rude and apparently incoherent songs" (14). Rather than attributing his lack of understanding to his youth, he paradoxically explains that membership in the group—"I was myself within the circle"—obscures the meaning of the songs. Only education and freedom allow access to their significance. As the critic David Van Leer has remarked, "the dual focus of Douglass's understanding of the slave songs, in fact, characterizes his whole conceptualization of slavery as the prohibition of knowledge" (129). According to Douglass's way of thinking in the 1845 narrative, vernacular expression and folkways, bound as they were by slavery, constituted limited means of self-expression; they were rich in meaning but limited in reach and social capital.

Later in the narrative, in comparing himself to enslaved persons who could not read, the literate Douglass, believing he is stuck in slavery, bemoans his learning and admires his peers for their supposed ignorance:

> I would at times feel that learning to read had been a curse rather than a blessing. It had given me a view of my wretched condition, without the remedy. . . . In moments of agony, I envied my fellow-slaves for their stupidity. I have often wished myself a beast. I preferred the condition of the meanest reptile to my own. Any thing, no matter what, to get rid of thinking! (40)

Douglass suggests here that thinking critically depends on learning and knowing how to read, thus denying the powers of perception and understanding people may develop without training in letters. Literacy here trumps folk forms; it is a path to freedom, but one that isolates the literate person from a community of uneducated others. Although Douglass's *Narrative* and many other formerly enslaved persons' autobiographies offer models of heroism, they often do so at the expense of a fuller portrait of Black culture. Most, after all, have as their chief purpose detailing the horrors of slavery and showing the need for its immediate end. Offering a portrait of the richness of Black culture would be superfluous and possibly counterproductive (F. Foster, *Witnessing* xxx). Yet one consequence of many antebellum slave narratives' focus on the brutality of slavery, and on the fortunate escape of the brave, often literate narrator, is that the connections between literacy and folk culture that sustained many enslaved persons are obscured (Graff 155–56).

Gary Paulsen's *Nightjohn* conforms to this pattern, adapting conventions common in nineteenth-century male slave narratives to chart a preteen girl's developing consciousness. Along with the academic prominence of Douglass's 1845 account of his education, *Nightjohn* has proven to be influential in demonstrating the viability of narratives about enslaved children's struggle to become literate and free. Named a "Best Book for Young Adults" and a "Notable Children's Book" by the American Library Association, *Nightjohn* features graphic treatment of its young narrator Sarny's constrained, potentially dehumanizing experience. The novel's language marks her as a confident, perceptive beginning writer who is set on exposing the horrible abuses of slavery. Primarily promoting the power and possibility of literacy (and the power won by defying slave laws), the novel presents a folk consciousness through Sarny's often sarcastic, assured critical voice, but it also encodes the deficiency of folkways alone as a path to self-possession and freedom.

The novel opens with Sarny noting her emotional distance from her enslaver and his family, a distance she shares with other enslaved members of the community. Yet the Black community is defined more by silence, passivity, and anonymity than by any observable resistance, suggesting the extent of its subjection: Along with Sarny's often critical commentary about life as an enslaved person, one of the few manifestations of resistance is Sarny's caretaker Delie's prayers to God in secret in defiance of the enslaver, Clel Waller. Yet Delie's subjection is suggested by how often other characters refer to her not by her name, but rather by her role as caretaker or "mammy." John, having been purchased by Waller, enters this environment willing to trade letters for tobacco and promptly stirs things up, inspiring Sarny to direct her rebellious energy into learning to read and write. Juxtaposed with scenes of her education are her graphic descriptions of the atrocities slavery permits, including severe punishment for those who try to escape or resist in other ways. John continues to teach Sarny even after Waller discovers his subversion and punishes him for it. After escaping the plantation, John comes back briefly to take Sarny to a secret "pit school," where she begins to teach others.

In emphasizing the bleakness of enslavement, the novel mirrors the focus of most slave narratives, whose purpose was not to analyze Black communal resources, but rather to demonstrate the moral, physical, and social costs of slavery. Paulsen's *Nightjohn* shows little of how enslaved persons may at times have partly circumvented these costs and attained some measure of autonomy (Wohler; D. White 124, 126). This is an important omission, given the prominence of historiography that gives attention to both the horrors of slavery and evidence of African American subversion (beyond that of the slave narrator's escape). One might argue that this omission is a byproduct of Sarny's narration—her suggestions, but not full renderings of the Black community's solidarity and resistance may result from her being so familiar with these states that she does not think to show them. Yet the omission works to limit the portrayal of African Americans' humanity and to suggest that Sarny and John, the manipulators of letters, are the rare enslaved persons who have evaded slavery's harshest self-stunting effects.

Like the narrator in nineteenth-century slave narratives, Sarny often presents scenes of Black victimization that exclude representations of a strong community, but many of her perceptions are informed by a Black folk spirit, and by an understanding of her world that she shares with other enslaved members of her community. Indicating her estrangement from Waller and the system of enslavement, she records that

> He wants that we should call him "master," and they's some do when he can hear but we call him dog droppings and pig slop and worse things yet when he ain't listening nor close. He ain't no master of nobody except that he's got dogs and a whip and a gun and so can cause hurt to be on some, bad hurt, but he ain't no master for all of that. We just call him that when we have to. Keeps him from whipping on us. (14)

Sarny's canny assessment of Waller and her perception of the irony he embodies expresses an interpretation she apparently shares with her people. Through her words about Waller, she reveals some of the autonomy she has within the system of slavery and her solidarity with other enslaved people who define themselves in part against an enslaver. Her confident tone and use of the second-person plural in this passage suggest that Sarny and her associates have not been dulled by enslavement in the ways Douglass describes. Yet the novel does not fully illuminate the communal solidarity and strength that the passage above suggests. Instead, it renders African Americans as a largely indistinguishable, ineffectual mass. Occasionally, individuals emerge from this mass to signify either the terrible abuses of enslavement (for example, the beating and defeat of Alice, a girl who "was addled in the head, off dreaming sometimes" [42]) or the possibility of a singular enslaved person's resistance. The novel does not offer scenes of folkloric exchanges, such as storytelling or oratory, through which unlettered group members worked out and communicated their values and established ethical standards that could both challenge enslavement and support survival.

One of the rare gatherings in the novel of the Black community signals the group's weakness, precariousness, and virtual invisibility in clear opposition to the spirit of initiative and possibility associated with literacy. After finding Sarny making letters in the dirt, Waller chooses to punish her surrogate mother Delie to manipulate her and other enslaved persons into identifying Sarny's teacher. Waller hangs Delie from a wall while the others, mostly field workers, are away. Returning from the fields, "They had to walk past the spring house and they saw mammy but there wasn't nothing they could do" (68). For most of the scene, rather than charting the slaves' actions and responses or mentioning their words or even their silence, Sarny focuses on Waller's cruelty and Delie's victimization, with Waller hitting the woman with his fist, tearing off her clothes, dragging her to his buggy, and ordering her to put on the harness so that she can pull the buggy. Although Sarny offers an insider's view of slavery's brutality, this view does not give readers access to the inner experience of other enslaved community members. Instead, she indicates their inadequacy, as opposed to her bravery as seer and testifier. When Delie begins to pull the buggy, Sarny recalls, "I couldn't keep my eyes down. But the men did, they didn't look at her. Looked at the ground" (71). Sarny can only register her enslaved neighbors' actions and underscore their subjection, rather than their subjectivity. Although the men's downcast looks can signify their defiance of Waller, who wants the men to see his power over them, Sarny's description primarily signals the men's subjugation and their inability to act to help Delie.

John stands out from the group as the only Black character present, other than Delie, who speaks. His words save her from further torment; once he speaks them, she drops out of the spotlight until the end of the chapter when John has been wounded. Both of these characters express their power in part through their adeptness as tricksters, particularly as able manipulators of words. Delie, for instance, when faced with Waller's threats, responds with a spirited self-defense that combines lying with her assertion of not knowing anything, both of which tie her to folkloric representations of the trickster. "I don't know nothing about reading or writing," she says; though she does know that John is teaching Sarny to read and write, she refuses to help Waller get this information. In spite of her illiteracy, she has an epistemological advantage over Waller and is intent on maintaining it. John, whose subversive teaching has remained veiled from Waller and from some enslaved community members for most of the novel, emerges in the scene as one who is willing to affirm his actions and thus step beyond the veil of trickery and deception. John assures those gathered that Delie "don't know nothing. It was me that taught the girl the letters" (72). According to him, "It was all me" (72).

Although John does not oppose the folk spirit of defiance, he represents an ostensibly superior means of resistance, one that can encompass and supercede folkways. When the other enslaved men are stunted by their silence in the confrontation between Waller and Delie, John can speak and, because of his teaching, Sarny can write about what she has witnessed. In justifying his efforts to teach Sarny, John explains to Delie: "They have to be able to write.... They have to read and write. We all have to read and write so we can write about this—what they doing to us. It has to be written" (58). What John is proposing is a form of resistance that involves communicating outside the community of enslaved persons on the Waller farm. He is not advocating for the double-voicings of the enslaved group's songs with their different messages for different groups. Instead, he is calling for a straightforward documentary treatment of slavery from the perspectives of those who are enslaved. Also, he is suggesting that literacy completes a person by allowing them to reflect themselves through words, to present the self in a way that retains its integrity. According to Sarny, John brings her people "the way to know" (Paulsen 92). Literacy here becomes the tangible means of resistance that builds and improves on the more inchoate, random acts that enslaved persons have formerly used.

For John, writing can be a social remedy, and his concern with written records of life experience, which recalls that of Ekundayo in *Time's Memory*, translates into a plan to prepare community members, including Sarny, to write their narratives. Yet the writing practice that he promotes has limits. Sarny's storytelling, as effective and moving as it is in revealing slavery's hardships and in characterizing her and Delie's resilience, reflects the emphasis of many slave narratives: Sarny can show the psychosis of an enslaver and the physical suffering, incapacity, and even, as in Delie's case, dignity of his victims. She does not, however, evoke the feelings behind most other enslaved persons' masks or the voices beneath their silence. This refusal to reckon with their complexity shows the obvious influence of an abolitionist program that has little space for humanizing the many African Americans who represent "the soul-killing effects of slavery" (Douglass 14). John and Sarny's sense of documentation conforms to the didactic purpose of prodding a largely white readership to antislavery action, which depends on scenes of brutality and deprivation and identification with a clever narrator.[7] Some slave narratives, such as Douglass's *My Bondage and My Freedom* (1855) and Harriet Jacobs's *Incidents in the Life of a Slave Girl* (1861), offer visions of Black family and communal life that go beyond this program, but they arguably have not been as central to the tradition as it was long defined by literary scholars. Indeed, Paulsen's foregrounding of a smart, but naïve, insider, apparently unattuned to the range of Black emotional responses, mirrors Douglass's account of his response to slaves' songs, the sounds of suffering, while "within the circle" (14). As discerning as she is, Sarny misses a lot. In making her choices as a writer, she shows how persons become casualties of slavery, but she does not show how African American communities fostered at least some security against complete subjection. This community has fostered Sarny's ability to critique Waller sharply, but Sarny sees her security against slavery coming from the world outside the Black community: the world of letters, which sheds light on the darkness of slavery and shows its victims the way to freedom.

This idealist view of literacy coexists with another in the novel: *Nightjohn* also presents literacy as access to a world of material plenty and white middle-class values. At the novel's climax, John, Sarny, and enslaved persons from various farms meet at the pit school where John uses a store catalog as a primer. He explains to his students, "It is full of things you can send for and own if you have money. They use it all the time. It has pictures and writing to talk about the pictures" (88). All the students look, but in typical fashion, Sarny focuses on her own response to the catalogue:

> I can't believe it. Here in the school, pit school covered over so the light won't show out of the ditch from the torches, we look at the catalog. All the things we don't have. Dresses and shoes with buttons and little gloves and pretty hats and overalls and I started crying. Thinking of all the things, all the pretty things, and then I see it. Picture of a horse. Got a thing around his head for feeding him, around his head and hanging over his nose. *BAG.* (88–89)

Caught in the darkness of slavery, the small group gains enlightenment through a marketing tool. Sarny's recognition of the word "bag," a container not just for the horse's feed, but potentially for all the products she would like to accumulate, caps a passage in which literacy facilitates consumption and materialism, where education aids a burgeoning consumer economy, and where learning delimits one's desire for things. This scene brings to mind Henry Giroux's characterization of neoliberalism's affordance that "the market, rather than politics, gives people what they want" (*On Critical Pedagogy* 89). Freedom is associated in Paulsen's vision with epistemological advantage and social mobility, as in much Black folklore, but it also seems devoid of spiritual nourishment. At the end of Paulsen's novel, freedom is a process that prepares an African American for a new role as a desiring subject in a mercantile society, with individual power directed at shopping for and acquiring property of her own.

THE GIRL POWER PARADIGM

In award-winning filmmaker Charles Burnett's adaptation of *Nightjohn*, Sarny moves beyond Paulsen's protagonist in terms of her ambition and achievement. The film locates its action and characters in realistic settings, such as the historic Rip Raps Plantation in Sumter, South Carolina, but it endows Sarny with almost fantastical powers. During the months that she takes instruction from John, for instance, she goes from illiteracy to an advanced form of print literacy that includes reading the newspaper and the Bible and writing passes for her friends. Moreover, although she is never equated with the folkloric character of the conjure woman—a member of the enslaved community with extraordinary, even magical, powers—Sarny bears some of her capacity to affect others' experience. The film makes clear, however, that Sarny's interventions, which often occur in secret, are not magic, but rather the product of her astute observations, her virtual invisibility to white persons, and her ability to capitalize on this social obscurity to manipulate others. This kind of characterization not only shows the influence of its folkloric roots in the trickster tradition, but also resonates with many literary visions of childhood. According to Lissa Paul, "child protagonists create options that are simply unthinkable to grown-ups whose conditioned responses have already closed in on them" (189). The film's characterization of Sarny is modeled on both African American folk traditions that emphasize a code of situational ethics and Romantic ideals of childhood innocence free of the diminishing force of socialization. By maintaining this balance, even as she is gaining skill with alphabetic literacy, Sarny suggests that learning to read and write does not necessarily entail sacrificing one's instinct and imagination; it does not entail becoming subject to the suspect values and assumptions that may be embedded in language. Grounding literacy in the ethos of the Black rural vernacular keeps the literate Sarny poised for actions that defy white hegemony.

The film adaptation of *Nightjohn*, like the Dear America novels *A Picture of Freedom* and *I Thought My Soul Would Rise and Fly*, presents a narrative paradigm that is not guided as much as Paulsen's novel by the polemical imperatives of the nineteenth-century slave narrative. These freedom narratives present their Black girl protagonists as active, versatile participants in a culture that often dignifies Black individuals and communities even as they are restricted and hurt by racism, economic exploitation, and violence. Literacy becomes an important means by which the protagonists express their ingenuity, one key tool among others that they can use to challenge the ruling class's authority. The particular forms of literacy promoted in the books and the film express the folk spirit and advance a conception of individuality that serves this spirit. Literacy is also associated with a familiar Romantic vision of the individual as an artist, a namer and shaper of experience, and someone endowed with power in the world because of her gifts of insight and imagination.

Burnett and screenplay writer Bill Cain's adaptation reshapes a novel championing literacy into a new narrative that endorses both literacy and the Black vernacular as expressions of a girl's social power.[8] In this way, the film conforms to the neo-slave narrative genre as described by Connolly, showing "necessary respect for those who had been enslaved" (196). Building on the book's characterization of Sarny's defiant spirit, the film makes her into a habitual trickster, a regular subverter of the social order. Though her relationship to John remains central, the film interweaves numerous melodramatic threads involving Sarny, the Wallers, and Delie. In addition to learning her letters and numbers from John, Sarny helps Mrs. Waller by carrying messages and books between her and her lover, a visiting doctor. She also wins Mrs. Waller's favor by taking over the youngest Waller son's potty training, which allows time for Sarny to learn to read and for Mrs. Waller to meet with her lover. As a go-between and nurse, Sarny finds ways to help herself and other enslaved persons. By the end of the film, when she reveals how much she knows about the Wallers' marital and financial problems, she is sold off the farm. Yet her spirit is not broken, for she continues to show her defiance by teaching the band of enslaved persons she will travel with. Sarny has become like John, an itinerant teacher whose trickery in combining literacy and folk values challenges the system of enslavement. In opening up the book's action and tempering its violence, the film offers Sarny more opportunities than the novel does to demonstrate her power and resourcefulness, particularly her effectiveness at anticipating and impacting others' actions.

In the film, Sarny's subversive actions recall female protagonists in a tradition of girls' books, which often cast their heroines as "defenseless" and have them rely on deception to overcome their troubles (Paul 192). Sarny's subversion not only benefits her, but also reinforces and protects the Black community, and thus demonstrates the ties between self and group. A scene from the middle of the film illustrates her ethos and underscores the competing perspectives on literacy and folkways that she manages to fuse. The scene opens with a group of enslaved adults entering a light-filled building and discovering a cake on the table. As they express their surprise about the cake, Sarny speaks to make her presence known and the camera simultaneously reveals her position in the rafters at the top of the frame. Sitting on a beam over their heads, she announces that she did not steal the cake but received it as a gift from Mrs. Waller for taking over her youngest son's toilet training. Then, Sarny confesses that she has stolen something and produces alphabet blocks as she proudly calls out several letters. The light tone of the scene ends as Old Man, an elderly enslaved laborer on the farm, declares, "Anybody in this cabin teachin' letters I go right to Waller and give him a name." He goes on to explain, "They will kill you they find you reading! Worse than kill you, and for what? Words? Words ain't nothing." John counters by asserting, "Words are freedom. . . . Cause that's all slavery's made of. Words. Laws. Deeds. Passes. All they are is words. White folks got all the words and they mean to keep 'em. You get some words for yourself and you be free." At a climactic point, Old Man reveals that he knows the alphabet and that this knowledge got one of his fingers cut off as punishment. Thus, he disputes John's claim and explains his own perspective: "Slavery is when the man with the whip got the gun, so you let him whip you. You let him take everything away from you and you got nothin.' "

The scene features a number of important points. First of all, in spite of their clear opposition, Old Man and John are both presented respectfully. Both characters have a chance to assert their opinions, with the camera capturing each man in low-angled one-shots, a visual composition that lends authority to what is pictured. The two are the most educated men in the cabin, and they both embrace a code of situational ethics, as evidenced by their early enthusiasm for what they believe to be a stolen cake. The film suggests that Old Man's threats to expose anyone who defies the dominant culture's law against Black literacy are understandable consequences of enslavement. Old Man, a character created for the movie, recalls Paulsen's characterizations—he has learned the lesson that the enslaving class demands: to limit learning and thus his access to freedom. Yet he is primarily motivated by fear that Sarny and other ambitious members of his community will be hurt in the same way he has been. Old Man, like Delie in Paulsen's novel, is concerned about Black individuals marking themselves with a potentially disabling cultural difference, one that makes them more vulnerable to white resentment and punishment. Old Man is also motivated by the need to protect the community's few "stolen" advantages. The film, however, does not suggest that this preserver of communal integrity is antithetical to the progressive spirit that informs John's teaching of letters. Sarny, who watches both men intently in the scene, does not choose John's ethos above Old Man's: She embraces both. For her, freedom lies in using various means of establishing an epistemological advantage over those who would control her.

Moreover, the film promotes the idea that trickery and literacy are not mere signs of cleverness or intellectual sophistication, respectively; instead, they are endowed with spiritual and religious power because Sarny uses them to re-create her community, and help transform it into a group of more advantaged, whole, and knowing persons. Sarny facilitates her friends' fuller understanding of their place and power in the world. One scene underscores the spiritual cast of her reading. After she has expended much effort to learn how to understand words (and numbers), as opposed to simply identify lexical (and numeric) marks, Sarny has an awakening as she sits with the Waller family in church. As the congregation sings, she realizes that she has been reading the Bible she holds. When the white minister sees her joyous response and asks if she has been saved, Sarny looks up at him and answers affirmatively, mindful of their different uses of the word "saved." For Sarny, this personal salvation through mastering letters is inextricable from the larger Black community's welfare and access to freedom. In later scenes, for instance, her reading about Nat Turner before her friends fosters their sense of possibility and enhances their sense of agency. This trajectory recalls W. E. B. Du Bois's descriptions of the long-standing ideals of many African Americans as "strife for another and a juster world, the vague dream of righteousness, the mystery of knowing" (142).

Ultimately, the film *Nightjohn* indicates that a girl's power can destabilize an unjust society. It presents Sarny as a kind of artist, a manipulator of words, persons, and plots, who acts for personal and communal freedom. Like the novel's climax, the film's is concerned with literacy and material wealth, but it exposes the limits of the enslaving class's material values in comparison to African Americans' more humanistic commitment to freedom, individual self-expression, and communal strength. Earlier in the film John pronounces that "all you got is what you remember," after speaking of the loss of his wife and son. The statement recalls the ongoing connection that Amina of *Time's Memory*, Kofi of *The Captive*, and Amari of *Copper Sun* feel to their dead loved ones. Whereas the Wallers' conspicuous display of fine material goods both represents their high social status and conceals their financial precariousness, John, Sarny, and other members of the community (even Waller's oldest son) promote the idea of human connections as wealth. In a confrontation with a gun-wielding Waller at the church, Sarny reveals the extent of Waller's debt and tells her people that he depends on them for his own success. She thus publicly exposes the extent of her power—her literacy, her cunning, her knowledge of white people's business and romantic affairs, and her ability to use this knowledge to save her life and empower other Black persons. The confrontation occurs when Waller returns from an unsuccessful search for two fugitives from his farm whom Sarny and her friends have helped escape. He enters the church bearing a gun and threatens to shoot whoever is responsible for the note he has found that authorizes the fugitives' travel. Although Sarny has written the note, other members of the community have supported her efforts. Thus, Sarny protects herself and her friends by challenging Waller's threat. She tells her enslaved community members that he will not shoot, because they are his only "wealth." When he turns the gun on her, Sarny calmly asks Mrs. Waller to "speak for her" so that Sarny will not have to speak further to Waller and expose his wife's adulterous relationship. In promising to trade words for Waller's threatened gunfire, she shows her ability to read much more than letters and numbers.

Sarny's achievement in this scene reiterates the spiritual importance of her work and reflects the common blurring of secular and spiritual experience in African American culture. The film dramatizes the idea that a girl's singular power is inflected by a communal soulfulness combining daring, discretion, and testimony, which is impacted by the demands and dangers of the marketplace but is not diminished by them. Thus, as the Wallers leave the sanctuary, with Mrs. Waller ordering her husband to sell Sarny, she stands nobly awaiting her community's response, for this is what counts to her. And the Black community rewards Sarny with an outpouring of the song of Moses and Miriam from Exodus 15 that recounts the Hebrews' escape from slavery and the Egyptian army's defeat. From the balcony, Sarny's friends, including Delie, a religious skeptic, and Old Man, sing: "I sing unto the Lord / For he hath triumphed gloriously / Horse and rider she hath thrown into the sea." The group's performance changes the pronoun referring to the patriarchal God to one that refers to Sarny, conflating her and the deity. Such typological referencing and revision is common in African American culture, according to scholars of folklore such as Harold Courlander and John Roberts; nineteenth-century African Americans often adapted Biblical materials with epic dimensions in crafting songs and stories about their own conditions and aspirations (Roberts 109; McKissack and McKissack vi). In fitting this particular song to Sarny's battle (and invoking the model of Harriet Tubman, the Moses of Her People), the group endorses her play with letters and defiance of enslavers, using their own play with words. The scene thus reconstructs and valorizes the African American practice of oral testimony and registers the individual and communal benefits of witness, literacy, and folkways.

In embracing vernacular culture, Sarny shows how effectively an oral-based communal culture intersects with her individual interests. In championing literacy, she defies the notion that in learning to read, one simply adapts oneself to the dominant culture. For her, literacy signifies self-affirmation, bending a given language by using it to represent a Black self and express a Black cultural disposition, just as Amari of *Copper Sun* and Kofi of *The Captive* do. In advocating making meaning with a variety of tools from white and Black American cultures, the film's Sarny joins protagonists from other recent texts to point to the revolutionary potential of African Americans' spoken, sung, and written words. The film *Nightjohn*, like the Dear America novels, portrays for a contemporary readership how girls' personal resistance might be translated into social power.

LITERACY AND ORALITY IN DEAR AMERICA BOOKS

The congruence between folk expression and literacy is also prominent in McKissack's *A Picture of Freedom* and Hansen's *I Thought My Soul Would Rise and Fly*, which appeared in the Dear America series published by Scholastic Books beginning in the 1990s. Indeed, these two books use the diary form common in the series to document individual girls' acquisition of literacy and folk life skills. The Dear America series paralleled the popular American Girl line of books and toys, albeit for a slightly older group, featuring historical novels by award-winning writers as well as videos, a CD-ROM, and an interactive website. Aimed primarily at girls aged eight to twelve (and their parents and teachers), the novels relate their protagonists' individual and family experiences to major social phenomena, from colonial discord to slavery and emancipation to the changing mores of the 1960s. Encouraging an intimacy between late twentieth-century readers and nineteenth-century Black girls, *A Picture of Freedom* and *I Thought My Soul Would Rise and Fly* emphasize how enslaved or only nominally free girls have the power to shape aspects of their experience and navigate social influences and obstacles. In both novels, print and folk practices are the base of the girls' power, serving as instruments that the protagonists can use to challenge laws and conventions that would otherwise constrain them. The diary form aids in these endeavors, for it becomes a freeing space, a locus of resistance that equates the protagonists' writing with artistic and epistemological control. Patsy's and Clotee's diaries belong to the category of antislavery literature, but they oppose the traditional slave narrative's adherence to a strict abolitionist agenda, foregrounding instead often hidden dimensions of girls' personal and communal lives.[9] These fictive diaries, though aimed at young readers, recall the liberating narratives that Angelyn Mitchell has described—historical novels for adult readers that privilege a private discourse to reveal a fuller range of emotional and cognitive experience than most traditional slave narratives allow (4).

Hansen's *I Thought My Soul Would Rise and Fly* is set just after the Civil War and tracks the progress of enslaved persons who have been freed but remain in limbo due to the persistence of class and racial stratification in the South. Although inspired by the promise of Reconstruction, particularly the opportunity to become educated landowners, the newly emancipated African Americans in Mars Bluff, South Carolina, learn that they will have to depend on themselves to ensure their communal and individual welfare. The Freedman's Bureau inadequately addresses their concerns, and the structure of southern society continues to disadvantage them. The novel foregrounds the consciousness of the twelve-year-old Patsy, whose uneven leg length and stuttering obscure, at least for white community members, her intelligence and curiosity. Equating Patsy's physical condition and speech disorder with stupidity, the plantation's white children cast her as dunce whenever they play school, and, consequently, she learns to read and write without their knowledge. Having attained literacy, the shy Patsy grows in confidence to the point where she becomes competent in her work as a household maid and, more importantly, realizes her aspirations to speak clearly and teach others. The novel ends with the once nearly invisible Patsy asserting her identity as a teacher and renaming herself Phillis Frederick, after her heroes, the poet Phillis Wheatley and the writer and civil rights leader Frederick Douglass. (Conveniently, Patsy's longtime romantic interest, who the epilogue tells us she eventually marries, is named Douglass.)

In associating her with these two widely known Black writers and representing her frequent diary writing, *I Thought My Soul Would Rise and Fly* emphasizes Patsy's place in a culture of print and reading. She reads fiction privately, and her social leadership in the Black community begins with her agreeing to read the newspaper to a group of plantation workers. Thus, Patsy recalls the models of literacy associated with Douglass and Wheatley, who are known for their knowledge and public appropriation of Euro-American literary forms.[10] These models are subversive because of Douglass and Wheatley's embrace and mastery of discourse that the dominant society had defined as beyond them. Clearly, Patsy shares in this kind of subversion. Yet Hansen also emphasizes Patsy's difference from Wheatley's and Douglass's public personae, for Patsy relies on the Black vernacular in her writing in ways that her precursors never do. Patsy's storytelling embodies a synthesis of print and oral cultures. She uses the ostensibly private form of the diary to reflect on and record the value of Black culture.[11] She relies on the diary to safeguard her view of the world and the ethos she is developing in response to its pressures. In a society in which Black discourse is systematically devalued, suppressed, or stereotyped, the private space of Patsy's diary yields a respectful reckoning of the virtues of Black culture. Among the many examples of this process is one involving Patsy's exposure to the call and response at a Black worship service and another involving her recording of a West African story she hears.

First, Patsy's introduction to African American worship, particularly its ritual of call and response, allows her to feel part of a community, and this sense of community inspires a greater sense of personal confidence in the clever, but skittish, girl. Previously, Patsy has either avoided church and stolen away with one of her enslaver's books, or been forced to attend a white Protestant church that required all Black congregants to speak a demeaning catechism. For instance, the long series of questions and answers designed to indoctrinate the Black people to their subordinate social station includes the following:

> *Question*: Who gave you a master and a mistress?
> *Answer*: God gave them to me.
> *Question*: Who says that you must obey them?
> *Answer*: God says I must.
> *Question*: What book tells you these things?
> *Answer*: The Bible.
> *Question*: Does God have to work?
> *Answer*: Yes, God is always at work.
> *Question*: What does God say about your work?
> *Answer*: He that does not work, does not eat. (27–28)

According to Patsy, "these words were only for us up in the gallery. The white people didn't have to say them," an inequity that make church attendance a reinforcement and justification of the dominant culture's objectification of enslaved persons (28). Her visit to the grove where African American workers worship, by contrast, allows for a stirring, affirming harmony of self- and communal expression. It inspires writing that also fuels Patsy's resistance to abuse and subjection. Indeed, Patsy's record contrasts with the less ennobling representation of Black religious fervor that appears in nineteenth-century South Carolina writer Mary Boykin Miller Chesnut's popular diary, which foregrounds her elite, white perspective on the South during the Civil War and describes a Black religious ceremony as all sensibility and no sense.[12]

As Patsy arrives at the service, she hears the spiritual leader commenting on the group's good fortune now that their marriages can be legalized: "by the grace of God we is now married like all free peoples in this here country" (56). He then goes on to say, "We are free at last" (56), which prompts married and single members of the group to offer some version of this last phrase through speech or song. The spirit of freedom, which informs group members' conception of the marital relationship and of the other possibilities in postbellum society, inspires a young man to sing "Thought my soul would rise and fly." Echoing this assertion in her diary, Patsy notes: "The bush arbor, the quarters, the prayers and songs made this seem like a place apart. Friend, I thought my soul would rise and fly, too" (57). Here, Hansen conveys the transcendent power of call and response, an exchange of words and phrases whose tautologies affirm and reinforce the community's creativity and collaborative spirit. As Patsy comments, "How different from St. Philip's Church! There, no one talks but Father Holmes and people only sing the hymns written down in the books. Nobody makes up a song from their hearts together, like 'Free at Last'" (58). Hansen thus affirms through folk expression the power of personal agency, creativity, and freedom in the realm of community. She also affirms Patsy's power as a crafter and preserver of experience, for through her diary, she captures ways of being that generally do not appear in print because they do not conform to the conventions of proslavery or antislavery writing. Patsy records a rich ethnographic experience that enables her to feel stronger and assert herself even when she is away from the grove. Diary writing, like call and response, is an alternative to subjugation, one that allows Patsy to experiment with finding words to communicate her vision of the world.

The power of spoken and written words is also central to Patsy's retelling in the diary of a West African folktale she hears from her friend Mister Joe, whose family has passed the story down. In it, Africans have gained the ability to fly with the help of magic men. But when the Africans are "captured and stuffed into slave ships," their wings, already invisible to the white captors, atrophy. The captives struggle for years in South Carolina until an elderly man among them speaks words he remembers from the magic men and the wings come to life. The captives then fly back to their homes in Africa. Patsy comments that she loves this story and records it "so that I will always remember it" (65). Having placed her faith in written and spoken words, Patsy recognizes that freedom can depend on knowing the right words and on remembering words that have worked in the past. In this instance, she uses her diary to preserve an oral tale that reinforces her sense of the power of language and the practice of storytelling itself.[13]

Exploring the transformative power of a girl's language is also central to McKissack's *A Picture of Freedom*, which recounts the twelve-year-old Clotee's self-conscious attempts to transform her observations of her world into appropriate words. Set in 1859 and 1860, the diary follows the orphaned Clotee's efforts to learn to read and exercise some personal agency on the Henleys' Virginia plantation. In waiting on the plantation owner's son, Clotee stealthily takes in whatever the tutor Mr. Harms is trying to teach him. Eventually, she realizes that Harms is a conductor on the Underground Railroad, and she aspires either to escape the South or to work on the Railroad herself. Her aspirations are fueled by the loss of several of her closest connections, including her mother, her surrogate father, her preacher, and a longtime friend. After Harms becomes an object of suspicion within the white community, Clotee's trickery helps to protect him from enslavers. She takes Harms's place as conductor and becomes a trusted teacher of enslaved children and adults. Repeatedly in the diary, Clotee tries unsuccessfully to envision a "picture of freedom," and finally on its last page, she determines that she is such a picture (169).

Like Hansen's novel and the film *Nightjohn*, *A Picture of Freedom* defines the Black community through its creative resistance to racism and classism and through its reliance on an oral culture that encourages activism. The folkloric cast of the novel results mostly from Clotee's performance as a trickster who, like Sarny in the film *Nightjohn*, manipulates the powerful for the benefit of her enslaved friends. Yet *A Picture of Freedom* also depicts the cultural resources of a community of enslaved persons, especially oral communicative practices that served to challenge the hegemony of slavery. Oral storytelling has an important role in *A Picture of Freedom* as a means of preserving and conveying commentary about African Americans' experiences and sustaining a sense of community. Clotee relies on stories to draw closer to her apparently aloof friend Spicy; shared stories make both girls understand how the condition of slavery limits them. Moreover, the older Black community members' stories about Clotee's mother help her determine her own place in the world.

One of the first lessons that Clotee learns in the novel is the need to go beyond the literal meaning of Bible stories to arrive at more usable knowledge. Early in *A Picture of Freedom*, Clotee is not getting much from the stories she hears about Adam and Eve, Noah, Jonah, and David. She quickly develops, however, from a relatively passive receiver of stories into an interpreter who understands a story as commentary on her and her people's experience. Thus, she becomes associated with a model of interpretation that is compatible with folkloric practice, in which listeners weigh and take potentially usable meaning from a folk text. According to Clotee, for instance,

> I got on to [the Black minister] Rufus's Bible stories today. All the weeks he been leadin' us in service, he been tellin' us two stories in one. His stories are 'bout Bible times, but they is 'bout our times, too. Jonah in the belly of a big fish, Daniel and the lions, and David and the giant is like us bein' in slavery, facin' the mas'ers. But God delivered Daniel, David, and Jonah, and he'll deliver us one day. Rufus can't say all that right out or Mas' Henley will make us stop havin' service. But Rufus tells us in other ways. (54–55)

Although Clotee has already achieved a proficient level of reading, in this diary entry, she acknowledges her membership in an interpretive community that encourages her to exercise her imagination and to see points of connection between a text and her world. In completing the diary entry, she admits: "I didn't understand the stories at first, but now I do. For the first time, I said 'Amen' and knew why I was sayin' it" (55). Like Patsy, Clotee provides a model of activism that blends community and individual efforts, public knowledge and private, cognitive work, and print and orality. In particular, Clotee underscores how girls' power entails active play with words and ideas and putting this intellectual play to use in a world of contingent values. Girls' power also involves recording this process of play, work, and potential social transformation in order to affirm selfhood and sustain community.

BEYOND THE PAGE

Works such as McKissack's, Hansen's, and Burnett's belong to a large and growing group of children's texts that includes glimpses of Black folkways to authenticate historical accounts of slavery or Reconstruction. Hansen's *Which Way Freedom?* (1986) and *Out From This Place* (1988), Walter Dean Myer's

The Glory Field (1994), and Jabari Asim's *The Road to Freedom* (2000), like the Dear America novels and the Burnett film, conscientiously reconstruct the texture of Black lives and depict the tensions between Black individuals and communities, the destructive effects of economic and political oppression, and the many creative ways African Americans adapted. *Out From This Place*, for instance, focuses on Easter, a teenage girl, and her efforts to reunite with loved ones she became separated from because of the chaos of the Civil War. The novel highlights Easter's crafting of baskets and blinds, learning and teaching of letters, and taking part in various ways in a productive, nurturing Black community. More representative of the majority of Black historical narratives than Hansen's *I Thought My Soul Would Rise and Fly* and Burnett's and McKissack's texts, *Out From This Place* acknowledges the complementarity of folkways and literacy tacitly. The more emphatic, even didactic, message of the Dear America novels and the Burnett film may be a function of their mass-market status, but it also suggests an urgency about the need to reinforce the connections between folk and print for late twentieth- and early twenty-first-century readers.

This urgency grows out of Hansen's, Burnett's, and McKissack's particular commitment to presenting folklore and literacy as viable tools for coping in a society in which economic and social inequalities have long limited many Black persons' achievement. McKissack and Burnett are especially well known for their conception of Black folklore as a means of coping with the tribulations of life and challenging damaging stereotypes. They adapt components of the Black vernacular that forge connections between individuals and tear away at barriers to community. In writing about the crisis of drugs, violence, and familial instability in today's cities, for instance, Burnett asserts that filmmaking can be a means of remedying social problems when it defies Hollywood conventions and presents useful models for living. For Burnett,

> A major concern of story-telling should be restoring values, reversing the erosion of all those things that made a better life. . . . The issue is that we are a moral people, and the issue need not be resolved by a pushing and shoving match or taken in blind faith, but should be continuously presented in some aspect of a story, as for example in the negro folklore which was an important cultural necessity that not only provided humour but was a source of symbolic knowledge that allowed one to comprehend life. ("Inner City Blues" 224)

Burnett has expressed this commitment to the Black vernacular in his ventures in independent filmmaking, and in the 1990s, in his efforts to reach a broader audience through popular theatrical film and television. For McKissack, the folkloric materials that she uses in *Mirandy and Brother Wind* (1988), aimed at preschool and primary school students, the anthology *The Dark-Thirty* (2001), designed for preteens, and much of her other work allow her to characterize the resilience and resourcefulness of her protagonists. For her, folklore remains a vibrant, viable, and entertaining way of dramatizing moral options.

McKissack, Burnett, and Hansen are no less positive about the ramifications of literacy. The lessons their characters learn and the teaching they offer reflect an optimism shared by commentators and theorists who analyze the effects of literacy. As James Paul Gee admits in writing about children's acquisition of mainline literacy,

> We should not fool ourselves into thinking that access to essay-text literacy automatically ensures equality and social success or erases racism or minority disenfranchisement. . . . [Yet] Short of radical social change, there is no access to power in the society without control over the discourse practices in thought, speech, and writing of essay-text literacy and its attendant world view. (Gee 60)

Clotee, Patsy, and Sarny demonstrate that the process of gaining control over such communicative practices is not selling out. In a much-anthologized essay about how she learned to write academic prose, Barbara Mellix describes how the process can be empowering and liberating. Acknowledging her fear of betraying her race, "of turning away from blackness," and of the resulting destabilizing of self, Mellix explains that "To recover balance, I had to take on the language of the academy, the language of 'others.' And to do that, I had to learn to imagine myself a part of the culture of that language, and therefore someone free to manage that language, to take liberties with it" (119–20). Mellix's learning to write academic prose is analogous to the protagonists' mastering the language of those most powerful in their societies: The girls do not submit to their oppressors' linguistic standards, but rather exercise their ingenuity in making the dominant culture's language satisfy their need for freedom.

Clotee, Patsy, and Sarny illustrate for contemporary young readers the power of literacy and the opportunities it offers for freedom, creativity, and personal and communal well-being. The Dear America novels and the two versions of *Nightjohn* present literacy informed by a spirit of rebellion and resistance congruent with Black communities' frequently oppositional stance toward the dominant culture. The texts also affirm for their audience in the late 1990s and beyond a tradition of literacy in Black communities that is aligned with critical thinking, social justice, and intellectual wholeness, thereby embodying the Black Arts Movement's embrace of orality and writing. Clotee and the other girls' actions as learners and teachers challenge stereotypes of Black passivity, submission, and ignorance.[14] Part of the texts' cultural work has been to show late twentieth-century Black readers that they inherited a rich academic tradition that develops intellect and character and that reinforces the ties of community. The Dear America novels and Burnett's film in particular indicate that this tradition has encompassed reading, writing, stories, and values from the Black oral tradition.

Stories about Black children's educational successes parallel the work scholar Jacqueline Jones Royster undertook with Black women at Spelman College starting in the 1980s. Royster found that motivating young women to develop and pursue intellectual interests involved showing them that intellectual work was not out of sync with their heritage. In effect, through a variety of pedagogical and social encounters, Royster and her colleagues sought to help their students "understand their 'intellectual ancestry'":

> We did not need to convince them they were competent and capable women. Instead, a critical task became helping them to broaden their definitions of their strengths—in ways that, at the time, women in general and women of African descent in particular did not habitually do.... Our task initially was to help them situate themselves within a community of women (especially women like themselves, that is, of African descent) and to help them see a historical continuum within which they were participating, consciously or not. (266)

The students could then build on this knowledge to understand their particular relationship to power structures within society (265).

In reading the Dear America novels or watching the Burnett film, young girl readers might similarly have broadened their understanding of the stakes of their intellectual development, to see it within a larger picture of economic and social deprivations, legalized oppression, and individual and communal resistance. This cultural work continues to be relevant, of course, because of continuing racism and socioeconomic inequities in US society that result in many African American children's disadvantage and failure in school. The values that the film and books affirm—individual drive, skepticism, persistent effort, cleverness, and community support—are more necessary than ever. Although contemporary society features educational and social opportunities aplenty, their availability to African American children from a spectrum of social classes is debatable. The middle-class children to whom *Nightjohn* and the Dear America books are directed are probably not those most in danger of social precarity or failure. But the texts are offering them a lesson about nineteenth-century life that is still applicable: Education is not something everyone can expect—it is a process that many have to fight to gain access to; it is a process that must be shaped in accordance with individual and communal needs and cultural frames of reference (Sola and Bennett 108). The texts affirm that girls (and boys) overcome barriers to education and identify ways to manipulate their schooling to suit their intellectual needs—to steal their letters from an ungenerous, restrictive system, as it were—rather than forsake them.

In my next chapter, I build on this chapter's discussion of the subversive power of Black literacy and folklore, concentrating on freedom narratives' representation of African American children's play, yet another means by which they exert power and express both personal agency and Black cultural inheritances. As with Patsy and Sarny, protagonists in the focal texts of chapter 5 rely on culturally specific forms of trickery. In addition to tricks to gain social advantages, however, the next chapter explores ways that historical narratives can envision Black children using their ingenuity to entertain themselves and others. The chapter will show how, as in the case of much trickery, African American play entailed both fun and serious business, involving the high stakes of personal and often communal freedoms.

Chapter 5

LET'S PLAY

Black Children's Agency and the Pursuit of Fun

> Even in the wickedest times, you got to find some enjoyment.
> Or you not gon' survive.
> —P. DJÈLÍ CLARK, *RING SHOUT* (2020)

In balancing portrayals of social hardship and injustice with demonstrations of Black autonomy and cultural integrity, some freedom narratives combine scenes of labor, exploitation, and racist discrimination with displays of African American leisure and entertainment. These juxtapositions depict Black children's agency within oppressive social systems and suggest that African Americans' lives were not completely determined by white enslavers' or employers' demands or the trauma of victimization. Youth at play animate Mildred Pitts Walter's neo-slave narrative *Second Daughter*, plus Marilyn Nelson's *My Seneca Village* and Joyce Hansen's *Home Is With Our Family*, which are both about a community of free African Americans in antebellum New York City. I analyze the depiction of play in three other texts in this chapter: Christopher Paul Curtis's novel *Elijah of Buxton* (2007), Zeinabu irene Davis's film *Mother of the River* (1995), and Jewell Parker Rhodes's novel *Sugar* (2013). These three texts, a novel set in the free North, a film about an enslaved South Carolina girl, and a Reconstruction novel set in Louisiana, demonstrate that play is crucial in spite of characters' social conditions and locations. This message resonates with Karen Sánchez-Eppler's finding in a study of nineteenth-century working-class children that "the need to play figures as a powerful site of identity, the demand for at least a little fun is ardently claimed as characteristic of self that survives these children's quite drastic geographic and class relocations" (54). Play affords opportunities to express private energies and wishes, test ideas and identities, and develop strategies for navigating problems. Play is liberating in *Sugar* and *Mother of the River*, allowing their protagonists to express their creativity, command their time, and shore up their community in ways that challenge the hegemony of the dominant culture. *Elijah of Buxton*, by contrast, offers a more cautionary message about the freedoms of play. Examining these texts' messages about Black children's play helps illuminate freedom narratives' contributions to debates about the nature and extent of children's powers. While Curtis's novel emphasizes its African American child protagonist's limitations in confronting slavery, Rhodes's novel and Davis's film, though acknowledging the importance of adult mentoring and care, envision Black children as resourceful in resisting social oppression, during and after the era of slavery.

Freedom narratives, then, do not tell a single story about the importance of African American children's play, and the forms of play they foreground are various, including word games, storytelling, clowning, playing tricks, acting up, play-acting, manipulating toys (or converting other objects into toys), moving the body, and exploring the world. Many texts present play as expressions of Black folkways that affirm Black psychical health and culture, often through intergenerational exchanges. Indeed, play has an important role in child protagonists' socialization within Black communities; it is part of the community's culture and informs its members' perspectives and actions.[1] Play is also portrayed as a feature of interracial friendship that fosters experimentation that challenges standards of white domination and Black subordination. *Mother of the River* and *Sugar* both represent the liberatory possibilities of play and its role in resisting and circumventing racist exclusion and exploitation. These texts illustrate the pattern Katharine Capshaw Smith describes in which "play . . . betokens an imaginative restructuring of social exchanges, experimentation with identity roles, and the transformation, if only temporarily, of the nature of reality" (124). In Curtis's novel, play has a more conservative function, often serving as a counter-example of Black communal success and supporting the message that pragmatism is ultimately more beneficial than fun and games, which detract from the necessary work of community building and preservation. In each case, however, play has serious functions: It is a means through which African American children test and demonstrate their agency. Play orients their participation in a racially divided society and signals the imaginative ways in which children control their time and space and interpret and express their cultural inheritance. It can either aid or limit individual efforts to act for the good of a community that has common experiences and perspectives.

The juxtaposition of fun, games, and laughter with slavery, in particular, continues to be hazardous terrain in youth literature. The result too often, according to critics, oversimplifies the experience of slavery and the effects of racism. Critiques of Emily Griffin and Sophie Blackall's picture book *A Fine Dessert* (2015) are instructive.[2] It presents four children from different eras involved in making a blackberry fool. Controversy has arisen from the representation of an enslaved African American girl who smiles both while picking berries with her mother and later while finishing a taxing kitchen chore. Critics of the book see these images as diluting the horror of slavery, and argue that their juxtaposition with similar images of free, non-Black children is misleading (Campbell). This attempted parallelism obscures significant differences between the conditions of enslaved and free children, and may foster a sense of sameness or parity that is not historically accurate. Moreover, the smiling Black child recalls stereotypes of "the happy darky," the Sambo character for whom slavery fits like a glove that delights rather than constricts and hurts.[3]

The Sambo stereotype counterbalances assumptions that African American children are disruptive, threatening, and even criminal, negative associations that inform many Americans' perceptions of Black children at play. The example of Tamir Rice, who was killed in 2014 by a police officer who mistook the toy gun Rice was holding for a real one, can be seen as representative of a larger phenomenon of seeing Black children as predatory and their play as dangerous. A study of white college students that was conducted by University of Iowa psychologists found that even images of very young Black boys prompted study participants to think of guns rather than toys ("Faces").[4] The Kirwan Institute reports that African American children, compared with white children, are seen as disproportionately disruptive (Rudd). Such studies are relevant to a consideration of play because they reveal a tendency within the dominant culture to define African American children as threats to social order and to justify methods of control, whether through segregation in school settings or the criminal justice system or, in extreme cases, such as Rice's, through extermination. Although many forms of play teach and reinforce the order of society by imitating adult roles or neutralizing passions and energy, play can also unsettle or disrupt the status quo, and it seems that African American children are often associated with forms of play that are taken to be excessive, disruptive, and destructive and that prompt restraint and containment.

Black children's literature often counters this assumption by normalizing Black children's play, and it does this in various ways. In the historical narratives under investigation here, this normalizing process involves relating African American play to its cultural roots in an African past or to an alchemy of empowering inheritances from Black and other cultures.[5] In presenting enslaved and free children's play, such texts underscore the routine nature of Black children's culturally oriented play. It shows a range of personal and group benefits that counter the destructive consequences of slavery, and the racism and economic exploitation that hampered legally free African Americans before and after the end of slavery. Play is a means of personal and group survival, because it enables children's agency in ways that other behaviors and tasks may not. Play becomes an expression of selfhood and culture that resists, at least to some degree, the imperative to work and serve another. In *Mother of the River* and *Sugar*, in particular, play becomes a guide to life and thus a revolutionary statement, confronting and redefining the association of Blacks with "out of control" behavior.

Scholars have offered various definitions of play that are pertinent to the three narratives. In her study of enslaved African American children, historian Wilma King describes play as "a stark contrast to work, [which is] the keystone of slavery" (108). It is recreational activity whose principal aim is to provide pleasure and that usually lies outside the realm of social responsibilities, whether forced or chosen labor. Work is ordered or imposed by forces outside the self, while play is "intrinsically motivated" (R. White 6). In her overview of research on Western play, Rachel White states that it operates by its own rules and has its own goals (6). This system that runs by its own logic is appealing because it allows children to establish what Tadese Jaleta Jirata, in her study of contemporary Ethiopian children's riddling, describes as a "discrete" "sphere for children's autonomous entertainment and knowledge acquisition" (273). Within this realm, children can, according to Nicolas Argenti, affirm their personal power through role-playing, namely practicing, experimenting with, and performing roles that imitate adult social identities (Jirata 226).[6] They use the realm of play to revise and challenge the routines and conventions of everyday life. In addition, play can involve interactions and collaboration between children and adults, which usually has an educational purpose.

Elijah, *Mother of the River*, and *Sugar* are representative of freedom narratives because they tap into these definitions of play, while amplifying its cultural significance as a measure of African American survival and freedom. In *Mother of the River* and *Sugar*, with their focus on southern racism and labor exploitation, play is a concerted or impromptu departure from exploitative work, but not from the freeing possibilities of education and experiment. Moreover, the narratives portray African American characters defying social demands for self-denial, drawing on the lessons of Black oral culture to serve the interests of Black individuals and groups. *Mother of the River* and *Sugar* demonstrate how Black cultural teachings are expressed through individual African American girls' play; both narratives emphasize the conflict between the creative, group-centered ethic of minoritized cultures and the exploitation and instrumentalism of the dominant American culture. By contrast, *Elijah of Buxton*, which is set largely in a free Canadian town, offers a different assessment: Play, though an accepted part of childhood experience, can be at odds with the vision of mature experience needed to empower Black individuals and communities. Given this important distinction, the texts encourage child readers to see the forms and functions of play as important but variable factors in understanding African Americans' survival of racism and economic exploitation. To a great extent, these variables reflect the texts' different ideas about the substance and integrity of Black communities. *Mother of the River* carries forth the disruptive energies of the L.A. Rebellion, the group of fiercely inventive, politically engaged Black independent filmmakers who sought to remake cinema by telling authentic Black stories. The film presents its protagonist Dofimae's Black world as a resourceful and empowering one that coexists with and resists the dominant culture that would control her. Although *Sugar* and *Elijah of Buxton* are from roughly the same period, they suggest to varying extents the discursive and interpretive constraints informing twenty-first-century neoliberal-informed multiculturalism. *Sugar* more emphatically reflects the Black Arts Movement's revolutionary spirit in envisioning an alternative to a white-dominated society and not providing easy narrative closure. By contrast, *Elijah of Buxton* presents a Black world that's parallel in many respects to middle-class white American culture: a model of social order and harmony that depends on moral conservatism—hard work, frugality, and self-discipline. This parallelism reflects neoliberal multiculturalism's tendency to promote characters' economic viability and to discount and punish social differences that obstruct it.

PLAY'S JUST FOR CHILDREN

Although *Elijah of Buxton* associates play with creativity and imagination, the novel also suggests that it can be an illusory, limited, and misleading experience. In the realm of childhood, it is acceptable, Curtis suggests, but it is insufficient for effectively confronting many social challenges and must give way to reason as characters grow up and seek to wield positive influence in the world. Moreover, at worst, the novel suggests, play, including that by adults, can be destructive. These cautionary messages undergird the novel's plot, much of which explores the eleven-year-old protagonist Elijah

Freeman's often humorous interactions with adults and reflections on his experiences and observations. The jokey tone and meandering plot of the first part of the novel shift in the second part to more sobering, unpredictable, and fateful happenings that occasion the sharpening of Elijah's awareness (Connolly 184).

Elijah of Buxton focuses on a relatively prosperous Canadian community of Black Americans who have fled slavery in the United States. Having established a communitarian society, they are able to choose their labor and view work as a means of maintaining self, family, and community in the present and for the future. Yet childhood, in Curtis's novel, is largely free of labor, and what chores the young protagonist Elijah has are not onerous but rather an expression of agency; and as in many boy's books, play is a realm of experimentation and freedom (Tribunella 35).[7] The first child born in Buxton and the first town resident born in freedom, Elijah, like other residents, helps to maintain its status as a haven for fugitive slaves, joining with other children to ring the church bell when fugitives are in sight and, with the fuller community, to welcome them. Other routine aspects of his life resemble that of a typical middle-class American boy of his time and suggest the middle-class comforts of Buxton, including Elijah's school attendance, fishing, chores, and play with his friend Cooter. Yet the novel also reveals that Elijah's understanding of history, which he conveys in his pretend play in the game of "abolitionists and slavers," is self-deluding, a revelation that emerges during his travel to Michigan to help his friend Mr. Leroy purchase his family's freedom.

Elijah's journey, as Paula Connolly notes, makes him confront the business of slavery and liberation in a new light (184)—it is not the easy heroic endeavor that he has believed it would be. After Mr. Leroy learns that his emissary the Preacher has gambled with the money earmarked for buying his wife's and children's freedom, Elijah accompanies Mr. Leroy to Michigan to retrieve what is left of the money. When Mr. Leroy falls ill, he gets Elijah to pledge to find the Preacher and the money. The "adventure" into reality that starts with Elijah leaving Buxton without his parents' permission continues with Mr. Leroy's death and Elijah's subsequent encounter with the hanged body of the Preacher and with a group of captured, chained Black fugitives (Curtis 273). The novel ends with Elijah headed back to Buxton with one of the fugitives, an infant, after his plans to free them all prove to be untenable. As a resident of a town populated by people who have emerged from slavery, Elijah has conceived of it as an escapable condition, an experience that is capped by a happy ending. Yet, as Danielle Price has astutely noted, "While Elijah is not culturally naïve, he is removed from the full weight of history because of his birthplace" (206). Mr. Leroy's death and Elijah's subsequent encounter with the hanged Preacher and the captured fugitives cause Elijah to recognize that his assumptions about slavery and means of escaping it are wrong (307).

The antislavery stories he has learned at school and the game of "abolitionists and slavers," which he and friends modeled on them, have fostered his innocence. Although pretend play often allows children to practice roles and envision goals associated with adults, the novel suggests that Elijah and his friends' game has resulted in misunderstanding about the real hardship of enslavement and the danger of attempts to fight the social system that allows it. The game emphasizes the conflict between the savior abolitionist and the defenders of slavery, de-emphasizing enslaved persons themselves: he and his friends "had to pull straws to see who would get to be the abolitionists 'cause didn't no one want to pretend to be somebody bad as a slaveowner" (307). And it exaggerated the ease with which slavery could be destroyed: "I remembered how we'd act like we were sneaking up on a plantation to kill a lot of slave masters and make a run for Canada with some happy, smiling, free slaves" (308). This view, referencing the stereotype of the simple, happy enslaved person, is one that the reality of the captives deflates and ultimately transforms, but not before Elijah shows the extent to which heroic stories and games prevent him from seeing the firm hold of slavery and the beleaguered humanity of enslaved people.

Elijah's innocence is so great that when he first encounters real enslaved persons, he does not recognize them as human beings. He also does not see the hanged Preacher as dead. In searching for him, Elijah enters a barn and sees the man's body some distance away, but Elijah does not understand that he hangs dead from the rafters, most likely having been lynched for overstepping racial boundaries by trying to play cards with white men and cheat them out of their money. Elijah moves toward the hanged body, surprised that the Preacher does not acknowledge him, and is scared by the darkness and "a humming sound so near my left-hand side that my blanged legs and breathing frozed up" (293). After identifying the source of the humming as a bundle near the barn's wall, he gradually discerns two sets of arms and assumes the entity before him is a "haint," which scares him enough to cause him to lose his balance and make enough noise to arouse other "bundles," which together make "a powerful horrible sound" (295). His next conclusion about the figures is that they are "demons" (296). It is only after one of the figures asks him if he is real that Elijah perceives her as a scared, vulnerable woman who has been shackled to the wall and deprived of clothing. He goes on to learn her name, Chloe, along with those of two other captives, and to hear some of their story. Though Elijah becomes more attuned to their humanity, his vision of their abjection and impotence disturbs and repels him. Yet his understanding of the captured fugitives' circumstances and his own current situation remains skewed, informed by an innocence that leads him to believe he can free them. His "can-do" thinking is shaped by the optimism of his pretend play back home, and signifies the difficulty of evaluating and acting against the often intractable forces of slavery. The episode teaches him that fighting slavery and helping enslaved persons are not a game.

Ultimately, Elijah acknowledges that helping to free enslaved persons "was a whole lot harder when things were real and you had to worry 'bout shotguns and chains and coughing little babies and crying folks without no clothes" (308). Finding it impossible to free Chloe and the other adult captives, Elijah must admit that "our playing didn't have nothing to do with the truth" (308). In proceeding, he must find a way to hold on to a hopeful commitment to concerted action that helps others, but the novel suggests that this orientation must be tempered by a more mature appraisal of real pressures, obstacles, contingencies, and possibilities. The novel suggests that he must abandon much of his playful orientation in order to achieve the objective of helping Chloe's unchained child attain freedom, rather than single-handedly, or with help from nearby African American adults, freeing all six captives. Although *Elijah of Buxton* does not reject imaginative resolutions to problems, it does cast doubt on the viability of play as a means of fighting slavery, and instead upholds the importance of confronting facts and probabilities, or as Elijah's father, Mr. Freeman, pronounces, "You caint let your wantings blind you to what's the truth. You always got to look at things the way they is, not the way you wish 'em to be" (252).[8] Mr. Freeman's advice establishes a standard of pragmatism that the novel associates with the Buxton ethos of responsibility and maturity. In this respect, the novel conforms to Perry Nodelman's conception of children's literature as validating the standards and values associated with adulthood and underscoring the deficiency of children's perspectives (77–78).

The fitness of Mr. Freeman's advice is underscored by the Preacher's fate. A trickster who becomes deceived by his ability to play tricks on others, the Preacher relies on wordplay and lies to establish his superiority over others and enrich himself. Among the few things that Mr. Freeman and other Buxton residents know about the Preacher is that he is not employed, does not live in Buxton, and is a young man, all of which help associate him with the freedom from convention and conscience of the youthful and unsocialized. His behavior fits within a spectrum of African American play, including trickery and verbal competition, but it is antithetical to liberatory forms of play that affirm Black social bonds and promote integration into the Black community (Lesley). Belying the honorifics of "Preacher" and "Deacon," he effectively manipulates Elijah into giving up four of ten fish, saying that they amount to a 10 percent tithe. The Preacher poses a complicated, fantastical mathematic problem that factors in the weight and age of the various fish, out-talking the mathematically proficient Elijah, who has been trained to respect his elders.

This trick deprives Elijah of fish he planned to give to family members and neighbors and foreshadows the Preacher's more egregious theft of Mr. Leroy's savings. The Preacher exploits Mr. Leroy's eagerness to recover his family members quickly, and, against Mr. Freeman's more cautious judgment, takes control of the plan to negotiate with the slaveholders, invalidating alternatives that do not give him a central role. The Preacher's tricks certainly show his creativity, but his egotism ultimately prevents him from caring about their destructive consequences on others. This narrative strain reflects the cautionary note in many African American animal tales, which according to scholar John Roberts, critique trickery against a peer or a potential mentor. According to Roberts, trickery was appropriate when it was designed to neutralize a more powerful figure's unfair advantage; deviating from this pattern often leads to the trickster's comeuppance (45). The Preacher's trickery hurts not only his neighbors, but also himself, for he apparently discounts his vulnerability as a Black man in the white-dominated society of rural Michigan. Although his efforts to gamble with white men test the racial status quo, this challenge simply underscores his self-absorption; it has no relevance to a larger struggle against social oppression and indicates the danger of egotism.

Elijah's "adventure" into the reality of enslavement and resistance does, however, oppose the Preacher's destructive, selfish play, for the novel presents Elijah's experience as part of his movement toward responsible adulthood. Further underscoring the difference between maturity and immaturity, Curtis's novel presents adult play in a negative light in another telling way. When Elijah is looking for help in his quest to free Chloe and the other captives, he runs to the group of African American gamblers who have told him how to find the Preacher. The gamblers are Black men who embrace gaming because the village offers little to do outside of work (279). Yet the novel suggests their games of chance ultimately manifest their limited social power, serving as consolatory entertainment that redirects energies they might use to fight against oppression. When Elijah interrupts their game to ask for their help, one player laughs at him and another tells him to be realistic, noting that the law supports the captors, not the captives. This man, who has previously provided help to Elijah and Mr. Leroy, explains that the gamblers' freedom to help is limited and they would be punished severely if they started freeing enslaved persons. When Elijah tries to appeal to his compassion, another man verbally and then physically attacks him, emphasizing that self-preservation takes precedence over empathizing with and helping others. Although these men are willing to gamble with their small amounts of cash, they are not inclined to risk their limited freedom to challenge the power structure. They see Elijah as a distraction from the practical business of living, which allows for the excitement of certain kinds of play, but excludes the idealism of "freeborn Buxton fools" (325) and the real struggle for fuller liberation. The men's embrace of gaming takes the place of significant, transformative action. Joined with the demonstration that Elijah's play at "abolitionists and slavers" results in a distorted view of the world, the men's limited action suggests that play can promote a self-absorption and escapism that oppose the hard work of tackling messy social problems. In spite of the very different features and effects of the men's gambling and Elijah's pretend play, both do little to change an unjust status quo. Yet Elijah's play, for all its limitations, does show an optimism about changing and improving society, optimism he is able to adjust and transfer to his efforts to taking Chloe's baby, Hope, back to Buxton.

In Curtis's novel, Buxton residents channel their creativity into their daily lives, which on the surface, seem shaped by rules of family and church and the demands of economic endeavors and civic participation. Although the Michigan gamblers call them idealists, the novel's portrait emphasizes their practical approaches to sustaining community. The town requires a certain amount of standardization (68, 72); for example, all the houses' exteriors must look the same. Yet these constraints do not prevent families from designing their homes' interiors according to their inclination (68). Moreover, the upstanding Freeman parents are not above playing a trick on their son to teach him the lesson that "what's sauce for the goose is sauce for the gander," or that Elijah will need to take what he dishes out. After Elijah hides a toad in his mother's knitting basket, she gets back at him by putting a snake in a jar of cookies she has offered him. Watching his shocked reaction, Mr. and Mrs. Freeman laugh so much that Elijah as narrator remarks, "If people could die from laughing too hard, I'd be a orphan" (21). His parents' practical joke is purposive, designed to help Elijah think before he acts and be careful about making someone else look and feel foolish. In choosing a practical joke, rather than a lecture, for instructing him, they show their delight in using their wit and sharing a laugh. Yet if the parents' play suggests their imaginative resources, it also shows how play serves their African American community's mission, maintaining social harmony among neighbors and encouraging self-regulation. Curtis's novel encourages readers to see the benefits and constraints of a free Black community that embraces enslaved African Americans who flee slavery. In the process, *Elijah of Buxton* offers a powerful critique of the individualism central in many antebellum slave narratives and in many myths of American progress and success. At the same time, it promotes social conformity and suggests that Black children must learn to tailor their creative energies to serve their community. This conservative message resonates with neoliberal ideas about conforming to a socioeconomic system that benefits those who fit in.

GETTING WISE WITH WORDS

The protagonist Dofimae's wordplay in *Mother of the River* also promotes her family and community's welfare, and serves as a principal means by which she expresses her agency. In telling a story about a Black family's effort to survive the abuses and losses of slavery, *Mother of the River* focuses on the creative and liberating resources of Black oral vernacular traditions and critical thinking practices, often presenting them through intergenerational and interracial play that challenges the status quo. *Mother of the River*, which has aired on BET and PBS, was directed by Davis and written by her husband and frequent collaborator, Marc Arthur Chery.[9] Davis is an African American feminist artist, whose films generally focus on Black women; she made *Mother of the River* specifically for young female viewers, highlighting the experience of an enslaved girl "who provides a role model of independence, spirituality, determination, loyalty, and community-mindedness" (G. Foster 19). As film scholar Gwendolyn Audrey Foster has noted, Davis is intent on remaking "constructions of blackness and femaleness" in ways that oppose the distortions of "the colonial white gaze" (10). Her challenges to Hollywood's and the larger culture's often narrow conceptions of Black girlhood and womanhood are manifest in *Mother of the River*.[10] Davis and Chery point to traditions of resistance, imagination, and play that the protagonist Dofimae embodies and that serve as manifestations of the resourcefulness and creativity of Black communal culture.

Set on a South Carolina plantation in the 1850s, *Mother of the River* focuses on the preadolescent Dofimae, who is mentored by her father, Cudjoe, a skilled laborer who uses riddles to encourage her to think critically about the world. He insists in his quiet way on an education that promotes self-reliance and communal responsibility. He is also trying to fill the void left by his wife's forced departure: she has been sold away because of her independent spirit, and his daughter laments her absence. Yet Dofimae does engage in play with her close friend Emma, the daughter of the plantation owners: The girls share games, jokes, and laughter. Perhaps because of the freedom she feels with Emma, Dofimae is disobedient with the mistress Anne and is punished with a whipping and the threat that she will be separated from her father. Dofimae befriends the mysterious Mother of the River, who is injured and in hiding, after having helped lead Black fugitives to freedom. Mother of the River intervenes later when Dofimae is about to be beaten again, and Dofimae reciprocates, using the magical eggs the elder has given her to save her from capture. The film ends with Mother of the River's promise that Dofimae and Cudjoe will remain together and a vision of the pair reuniting with Dofimae's mother in an idyllic setting.

These components signal *Mother of the River*'s rejection of realism as the principal means of telling a story about an enslaved girl and her associates, departing from the realist renderings of slavery commonplace in many adult and children's neo-slave narratives. Along with the magical Mother of the River and transformative interracial friendship, the film anachronistically portrays the power of other women to shape public experience. The revisionary portrayals of Emma's mother, Mistress Anne, and her alter ego, the overseer Miss Anna, depart from conventional images of the demure southern lady and emphasis on white male southern honor, suggesting that white women, rather than being passive onlookers, contributed to and perpetuated slavery in various ways. Davis complicates this exaggeration of history by presenting it through a documentary style: *Mother of the River* uses a sharply focused camera to present these white women serving patriarchy in ways that grant them power to inflict harm on others.[11] Countering the film's realist rendering of this white supremacist power is Mother of the River highly stylized appearance, which underscores her otherworldly status.[12] The actress Joy Vandervort-Cobb's slow, deliberate gestures and speech lend grandeur to the portrayal that is enhanced by low camera angles. These features signal Mother of the River's distinction from others in Dofimae's world. With her promise to help Dofimae and her father escape, her ability to predict and influence the future, and her talk of meeting "ghost people," Mother of the River opposes the ordinary and routine. She represents the promise of social change and the possibility of realizing ideals of freedom. And she underscores for young viewers the importance of elders who foster intellectual and moral growth and model the pursuit of social justice. With her roots in folklore, the figure also promotes imagination and magic and thus challenges the logic of white mastery and the expectation of Black subjection. The elder also reminds viewers that Black lives include dimensions that realism, with its focus on the predictable, habitual, and observable, does not admit (G. Foster 20). The film's play with narrative form and common expectations of slave narratives provide a fitting context for demonstrating the power of the word and for showing Dofimae's empowerment through her facility with language.

Dofimae's affective and cognitive experience are central to her characterization, and the film's representation of her language games with her father, Emma, and Mother of the River are especially relevant to her personal growth. In beginning the film with a scene in which Dofimae and her father share riddles and puzzles, Davis suggests that her purpose is to show not only the horrors of slavery, but also the "world that the slaves made," to borrow a phrase from historian Eugene Genovese.[13] Through their play with words, Dofimae and Cudjoe have created a private space that is both a temporary retreat from white-dominated slavery and a training ground to prepare her to navigate society's challenges and injustices. When Cudjoe gives her the riddle, "something that runs all day, runs all night, and never stops running," he is referring to something that is defined by its strength and persistence. Dofimae correctly answers "the river," which summons a comparison that is central to the film's vision of African American resilience: It equates the river's power and flow with Black persons' determination. Davis's conception of the river recalls Langston Hughes's "The Negro Speaks of Rivers," with its refrain, "My soul has grown deep like the rivers," and the affirmation of its speaker's relationship to African civilizations across time and space. Dofimae's answer, "the river," then, suggests an orientation for her that defies the stasis and constraint of slavery. The river represents continuity and flow, freedom, renewal, movement, and life. As the answer to Cudjoe's riddle, "river" establishes an array of meanings that signal the seriousness and defiance of linguistic play.

Davis is relying on an understanding of riddles that is common throughout the African diaspora, whereby the person who answers riddles is "display[ing] both cultural wisdom and linguistic skill" (Okpewho 89). Indeed, the riddles foregrounded in the film show Dofimae's grounding in the Black community's values and defiance of the white ruling class. Her play represents not only her identity as a child, but also her participation in a distinctly Black culture. As Isidore Okpewho has explained, riddles are "word games" grounded in "observation of life and nature," often emerging from "a skillful contraction of existing proverbs" (241).[14] The riddles that Dofimae and her father share are "within the circle" of Black community, as Frederick Douglass calls it, a sphere largely hidden from the enslavers' class. This realm is both safe and dangerous, however, because Dofimae is learning to think independently and be imaginative rather than simply to follow orders. Word games are not only mental exercise in *Mother of the River*, but also keys to Afrocentric metaphysical thought. Associated with the realm of children and play, African riddles can be thematically dense and metaphorical and demand attention and intellectual rigor (Jordan 29). In some African societies, riddling is an activity that children share among themselves, one through which they refine their critical thinking and linguistic skills and express agency by exercising some control over their lives (Jirata 273). Often in the film, riddles serve as shorthand for important cultural beliefs that have to be guarded from the dominant class.

Such in-group knowledge is also highlighted in other questions, as when Cudjoe asks "What has eyes and cannot see?" Dofimae correctly answers "potato," which seems simply to signal the importance of observing ordinary aspects of life carefully and freshly (Okpewho 241). Yet sight and blindness are important tropes in the film—for instance, Dofimae and Emma like to aim stones at targets; at one point, Dofimae's slinging of magic eggs seems to blind the overseer and her assistant. Potatoes can have sightless eyes, but the film suggests that girls like Dofimae need to be discerning to maintain whatever autonomy they can manage and to push for more. Of course, the lesson that discernment is self-protecting and self-empowering is familiar in children's literature, but it has special relevance in treatments of slavery and other hierarchical socioeconomic structures, in which disadvantaged individuals and groups depend on their powers of observation to find opportunities that they can use to their advantage.[15] As Okpewho has commented, riddles and proverbs were a means of "social education" that "sharpen[ed] the intellect" (246) and offered an orientation for action. The film's epigraph, "Riddles are the horses of discourse," indicates that language games are a means of conveyance, a means of getting from one point in discourse to another. Yet in practice, riddles are also substantive, conveying ideas and values that may be indispensable for meeting life's challenges.

Dofimae not only responds correctly to her father's riddle about unseeing eyes but also internalizes the wisdom that informs it. Dofimae resolutely rejects passivity and imperception, repeatedly demonstrating her attentiveness and curiosity. In the next scene, for instance, she walks among laborers in the field and focuses her eyes on a white overseer abusing an enslaved Black person. She takes on the active role of witness, even as she embodies the public role of a yoke-bearing slave. If the yoke signals Dofimae's subjection, her watchfulness suggests she has not been reduced to a tool. After she discovers Mother of the River's hiding place, she takes pains to keep it secret. It seems as if Mother of the River, a conjure woman who often pauses to read

Dofimae's expressions and bearing, is able to trust the girl because she has learned the necessity of being responsible with information. Emphasizing the importance of keeping secrets is another of Cudjoe's sayings, "Eyes see. Mouth silent." And more indirectly, "sifter," the answer to the film's second riddle ("What's round as a saucer, deep as a cup, and the river couldn't fill it up?"), indicates the need for being active and discriminating when taking in information, that is, choosing what is most relevant out of an excess of detail. Cudjoe is teaching Dofimae, and she is learning how to be an active, critical thinker: She is not "the horse [that] only knows where his stable is," to refer to another riddle from the film, spoken by the enslaved domestic worker Joseph, who claims allegiance to their enslaver. Dofimae is not willing simply to go through the motions of life as dictated by enslavers, and riddles are a means of exercising her discernment and fostering her autonomy.

The riddles that highlight Dofimae's creativity and humor convey her independent spirit and resistance to the white ruling class and its values. These include riddles about the tallest and shortest men that allow her to move beyond the literal and empirical and express her imagination, particularly her skill at exaggeration. In identifying "the tallest man I ever saw," Dofimae describes a man who bridges an extraordinary distance in "getting a haircut in heaven and a shoeshine in hell." At one level, this figure is the stuff of a tall tale, but at another, her answer points to a duality of selfhood that is quite human. Her tall man is associated with good and evil, salvation and damnation. He displays a gift for fitting into contrasting environments and for being well served in each. Dofimae's answer shows her capacity to use comic exaggeration to comment on extremes within human nature. Similarly, the riddle about "the shortest man I ever saw" derives its humor from picturing a man who is less successful at negotiating challenges: For him, mounting a bit of sand is a challenge. Although several interpretations of the riddle are possible, it may refer to a morally deficient, "small" person whose ambitions prove both over-taxing and petty. Fitting this description is the film's Joseph, a well-dressed enslaved man who works in the plantation mansion and who tries to win favor with enslavers, particularly Mistress Anne and Master Charles, by betraying Dofimae and Mother of the River. Yet he ends up being humiliated in front of other enslaved persons, with the overseer calling him "n-----" and repeatedly prodding him to whip a girl. His pride and supposed prestige as a house servant are deflated, and though the film does not indicate that Dofimae has Joseph or any particular person in mind when she gives the riddle, the film certainly exposes Joseph as an overachiever who is stunted rather than ennobled by his ambitions. Although A. C. Jordan, an important early theorist of African literature, describes riddles "as hardly more than entertainment" (29), the film's matching of riddle, character, and situation underscores the practical nature of Dofimae's language games: They are a way of commenting on human capabilities and flaws, on social limitations and possibilities. This commentary, along with the powers of observation and discrimination that guide it, are part of a cultural process enabling the critical thinking and act of witnessing that marginalized persons can exercise in an unjust society.

The dynamics of Dofimae and Emma's friendship more emphatically reveal the subversive social function of riddles and of play more generally. Supplementing Dofimae and her father's apprentice-master relation, the girls' riddling leads to collaboration that also destabilizes the status quo. In an extended scene that alternates between the girls' play and images of Emma's mother, their status as affectionate, collaborative, and yet competitive peers is evident in their positioning within the film frame: In the first part of the scene, the girls are seated at the river's edge, partly facing each other, though Emma is centered and Dofimae is to the left, slightly elevated. Each girl, as it were, has a visual advantage. The scene continues with a cut to the girls trading riddles as they toss stones at paper boats in the river. After Dofimae's apparently innocuous riddle about the night sky ("In the daytime, there's nothing in the garden but at night it's full of potatoes"), Emma poses a distinctly shocking one—"White man licking a Black man's backside"—to which Dofimae answers, "Fire under a pot." In this instance, the question seems more crucial than the quotidian answer. Emma's riddle is ambiguous—"licking" can refer to either beating or kissing—and conveys forbidden knowledge, a homoerotic reference to a man touching another man. Such a touch overturns US slavery's power relation of white male dominance and Black male subordination, suggesting her engagement in a world of play allows for social experimentation and flights of imagination. In response to Emma's riddle, Dofimae offers another that neutralizes the abiding social order: "Stick that beats the black dog also beats the white dog." This straightforward statement of equality in punishment elicits the girls' simultaneous response: "What goes around comes around." In the world they have created in play, Dofimae and Emma are aware of social standards and divisions, but their play enables and expresses girlish intimacy, friendly competition, equivalence, and wit that challenge the status quo. The first part of the scene ends with them running from the frame, holding hands, and with the camera shifting focus to the paper boats the girls have been using for target practice: The boats are made out of the wanted ads for Mother of the River. Emma and Dofimae have appropriated papers essential to the business of upholding slavery and converted them into toys that become part of their fun and part of the river. The girls' subversion is also on display when Emma is picnicking with her mother, and Dofimae hides in the bushes behind Mistress Anne and makes faces at a pleased Emma. When Mistress Anne notices and confronts Dofimae about this disobedience, Emma provides her with a pastry, foreshadowing her willingness to act on her alliance with Dofimae and defy her mother.

The film does not gloss over the girls' social difference. The intercut shots of Mistress Anne on her porch and walking over her big lawn underscore the family's wealth and social capital, just as Emma's ruffled bloomers and ringlet curls do. Yet Dofimae seems to have the advantage over Emma in riddling, for the last riddle that Dofimae gives is one that Emma cannot solve:

> DOFIMAE: Twelve pair hangin' high and twelve pair hangin' low. Twelve king come riding by. Each he took a pair. How many pair left hangin' there?
> EMMA: None left. They all gone.

The exchange continues with Dofimae telling her "That ain't it. Give up." Although Emma has been standing at some distance from Dofimae, who is seated with a bowl doing a chore, she moves closer and sits across from her friend, admitting "That one is hard." After Emma tells her "I give up," Dofimae reveals the riddle's logic and linguistic trick: "Twelve pair high, twelve low, equals 24. A man called *Each* takes one, leaves 23." Emma has assumed that the riddle's language is simple: her answer assumes that "Each" serves as an adjective referring to the missing noun, "king," rather than as a proper noun. She ignores the possibility that a word might mean more than one thing, and that the receiver of words must be mindful of this variety. Although Dofimae and Emma's riddle is part of their play, it has some serious implications. Dofimae's relative mastery of language is the kind of edge over a social better that is common in African American trickster tales, and supports the idea that she has strengths that she can rely on in facing those with social advantages that she lacks. Yet the scene ultimately emphasizes Dofimae and Emma's strong friendship. When Emma cannot answer the riddle, she moves closer to Dofimae, seeks insight, and is delighted by the riddle's cleverness, rather than becoming defensive and resentful and refusing instruction from a subordinate. The film assures viewers that the girls are able to overcome barriers resulting from their racial and class differences.

Emma is an important part of Davis's didactic revisioning of history: Although she is a white lady-in-training, she is so affected by the friendship, puzzles, and games she shares with Dofimae that she ultimately will stand by their alliance in defiance of her parents. Emma, according to Mother of the River, will choose Dofimae's welfare over her parents' desire to punish and control the girl. Emma, like Dofimae, is aligned with the world of nature and imagination, with the processes of vision and intellect opposed to the wealthy but insensitive Mistress Anne and Master Charles, and to other less affluent white persons like the overseer Miss Anna, who strive to make money by catching Black fugitives and take pleasure in scaring children. Emma represents the possibility that a person with a large stake in the dominant class can understand and accept enslaved African Americans' worldview and accept their rights as a given. Emma's belief is manifest in one of the riddles she and Dofimae share, in which the latter states her question as an assertion, "It belongs to those that till it," and Emma responds, "The land." The riddle's answer—that the workers own the land they farm—suggests an understanding of labor and property ownership that departs from Emma's mother's assumption of authority.[16] And though the film does not show her acting as Mother of the River promises, it does nothing to suggest that she will not. Indeed, the film suggests that Emma has been radically transformed by her play with Dofimae and by the epistemology that informs that play.[17] The substance of their linguistic play shows how the pair are able to mock and ultimately transcend the barriers of class. The promise of Emma's intervention in her parents' business affairs and the preservation of Dofimae's home indicates that the girls' play marks their ability to transform the rules of social engagement and social organization. Emma has the power to do what is right by Dofimae and her father and to reject her parents' attempts to control and limit Dofimae. Although Emma's intervention in her parents' business affairs is incredible, it fits within a narrative economy including a woman overseer, magical eggs, and communion with ghost people. Through the fantastic, the film suggests the possibilities of interracial friendship, imagination, and play, in both the antebellum era and our own.

TRANSFORMATIVE, FREEING PLAY

Rhodes's Reconstruction novel *Sugar* also expresses optimism about the potential of cross-racial and -cultural friendship, suggesting that it can promote greater understanding across rigid social boundaries and destabilize the status quo. The novel's protagonist Sugar establishes a friendship with the son of her employer, a plantation owner who has previously enslaved Sugar and her Black associates. While *Mother of the River* emphasizes a Black girl's empowerment through her African-derived, play-infused education, *Sugar* portrays a greater range of play and a more catholic sense of the cultural influences surrounding it. The novel also makes manifest the film's suggestion that play can be transformative: Where Dofimae realizes transcendence from slavery through fantasy, the novel, in focusing on Sugar's life in postbellum rural Louisiana, provides a realist exploration of the psychology, dynamics, and consequences of child's play. And this play is serious business, a means of Black self-assertion within an exploitative system of subjugation that both draws and expands on antebellum slave narratives' familiar tropes of resistance and escape.

Modeling her protagonist partly on the Black vernacular figure of the trickster, Rhodes has the clever and energetic Sugar engage with Chinese, American, and African cultural traditions. In addition to Sugar's embrace of the trickster tales that she has learned from her neighbor and surrogate parent Mister Beale, Sugar's cultural framework is influenced by her engagement with southern American landscapes and river-scapes and her friendships with her white employer's son and African American and Chinese neighbors. These associations function in ways similar to Dofimae's, for Sugar also sees her world's injustices, and is eager to act on self-sustaining principles. Like Dofimae, Sugar resists the restrictive, stereotypical racial and gender categories often associated with Black and working-class persons. These stereotypes converge in notions of dull-mindedness, lack of self-motivation, laziness, and intemperance. Sugar, by contrast, uses her intelligence to resist a work ethic that is designed to exploit workers' energy and provide little compensation, and she tries to circumvent it. Like *Mother of the River*, the novel *Sugar* represents child's play as a means of resisting domination and diminishment. Sugar learns how to use her playfulness to help to remake lives and reorder her world, thereby nodding toward but radically revising the social reform work of Harriet Beecher Stowe's Little Eva, the passive embodiment of white girlhood innocence and redemptive grace (Bernstein, ch. 1).

Sugar's play is informed by four interconnected features: her reliance on trickery; her love of and engagement with nature; her transgression of racial boundaries; and her integration of play and work. With each of these aspects of the novel, Sugar demonstrates that for her, play is not only a tangible action, but also a predisposition and perspective that guide her behavior. Sugar has embraced the advice her mother gave on her deathbed: "Do. See. Feel" (41). In a world in which she is a child who is expected to earn her keep, this advice serves as a motto affirming Sugar's delight in play and pursuit of personal freedom. As a ten year old, she feels an intense desire to break free of the finger- and back-numbing labor of growing and harvesting sugar, work that has killed her mother and that she finds so distasteful that she has come to hate sugar's flavor. She often gets depressed and frustrated by the amount of work she must do, as if her real self is suppressed and unnourished. Her play, accordingly, often has an edge, for it defies the economic system that drains workers' energies, saps their imaginative powers, and limits their will. This edge surfaces when she uses tricks to control her time and direct her energies as she likes. And over the course of the novel, her priorities as the crafty manipulator of time and other people will expand from a focus on self-satisfaction to include the welfare of her multiethnic community. Like Elijah, she has to adjust her ideas about play, but unlike him, she does not have to abandon it.

Sugar is the only African American child on the Wills plantation during a time when many formerly enslaved persons have left rural Louisiana for places with a greater range of jobs and promise of less racist exploitation and intimidation. At the beginning of the novel, Sugar finds that even her longtime best friend Lizzie is leaving. In describing the maturing Lizzie, Sugar identifies some of her own priorities as a child still interested in play, "When we aren't working, we've always had fun together. We're the only kids left. But Lizzie doesn't climb trees anymore (she sighs instead), she doesn't run (she swishes), and she doesn't like pranks ('Childish,' she says)" (11). Although Sugar takes comfort from her older neighbor Mister Beale's folktales, she must confront Missus Beale's dismissal of "made-up tales" as "a waste of time" (10). She also searches for fun and adventure in the fields and on the river, getting in trouble with her guardian Missus Beale and other adults in the tight community of African American laborers. While on one of her larks, she befriends Billy Wills. And though each child has been cautioned against playing with persons of different races, Sugar and Billy take to each other, settling into a routine of playing together, as Dofimae and Emma do in *Mother of the River*, in remote areas of the plantation and its environs. Billy shares his father's secret with Sugar about having hired Chinese laborers to work the fields, and when the migrant workers appear, they pose a threat to the aging Black laborers who have remained at the plantation, but Sugar gets the Chinese immigrant and African American residents to work together. Their collaboration leads to several changes on the plantation, including the fair-minded Billy, who works beside the other laborers, replacing the exploitive overseer, the Black and Chinese workers trusting one another, and Mr. and Mrs. Wills mostly accepting Billy's friendship with Sugar. After the displaced overseer burns the harvested sugar, the Wills sell the plantation, and the community of workers, including Billy, disperse, with Sugar accompanying the Beales north to reconnect with their family.

Early on, the novel establishes that Sugar's play is a central means of expressing her desire for freedom. Sugar's unsupervised play is transformative for her, allowing her to express her sense of agency in ways that her role as a field worker cannot. The novel also underscores the way that her play encompasses several modes, with her running around shifting quickly into role-playing and then into collaborative play with Billy. This variety indicates both her great hunger for the pleasure that play provides, her fluency in different forms of self-expression, and her openness to experimentation. The pleasures of freedom are evident in a scene that occurs the morning after harvest is completed, when Sugar wakes up earlier than everyone else and sneaks out of the quarters, escaping chores so that she will have her time to herself. Occurring in a chapter entitled "Freedom," Sugar's escape emphasizes the imaginative and physical nature of her play. Her flight counters the stillness of the workers' quarters that she leaves behind where "Everyone else is still asleep. Sleeping on the floor of our old slave shacks. Even Rooster Ugly hasn't stirred" (15). Sleep can be an empowering experience, of course, but here Rhodes's diction connects the Black laborers' sleep and impoverished domestic spaces with stasis, shackles, and the slavery of the past. Sugar moves away from this confinement:

> I'm off, running. Free. Sprinting to the river, my soles flapping against my bare feet. I run, swallowing big gulps of air. I run past cane fields, then up the grassy knoll where the big house sits to keep dry when the river overflows. I smell the Mississippi before I see it. Muddy and tangy from algae, marsh grasses, and sedge. Nothing like sugar! I whoop down the riverbank, kicking up dust, tiny rocks. I startle a raccoon. I pass trees. (16)

This passage foregrounds Sugar's energy and delight in moving through a rich, uncultivated landscape that is free of obvious signs that it exists for human use. Sugar delights in the freedom to control her own body: "running," "sprinting," "flapping." Sugar achieves an idyll through play that emphasizes the intensity of her relationship with nature; she actively consumes its bounty, "swallowing big gulps of air." Her appetite here contrasts with her disgust with the taste of sugar, which makes her vomit. And her keen senses are responsive to nature's variety: "I smell. . . . I see. . . . I whoop." She is wild, having abandoned the self-restraint of her adult neighbors and even her closest peer Lizzie.

Sugar's flight aligns her with notions of the idealized Romantic child, who, as Marah Gubar has explained, is "a solitary figure who roams the natural world, blissfully uninfluenced by adult ideas, practices, and discourse" ("Innocence" 131). This concept usually applies to white children and informs such characters as Stowe's Little Eva and Mark Twain's Huckleberry Finn. Although Little Eva is associated with domesticity and Huck with the outdoors, both characterizations, as is standard in Romantic iconography, emphasize the child's deflection of the corrupting influences of society. According to Robin Bernstein, the concept of white childhood innocence, and such ancillary traits as physical beauty, emotional delicacy, moral rectitude, empathy, and imagination, operate and are perpetuated in great part through opposition to stereotypes highlighting African American children's difference (ch. 1). Where the white Romantic child is sensitive, the Black child is supposedly insensitive, coarse, and immoral, like Stowe's Topsy before her conversion. Although Sugar is undisciplined and borders on the intractable, her misbehavior and commitment to play grow out of a love for freedom that parallels Huck's resistance to the domesticating forces of convention. The outdoors is a realm of freedom for her, in which she can reinvent social roles and take joy in movement that is not bound to imposed rules and labor. If anything, Sugar's flight and subsequent play resemble some of Huck's romps and refashion his celebration of childhood freedom to suit a young Black girl.

Like Huck, the tomboyish Sugar has an affinity for play-acting through which she displays a different challenge to the current social order: casting herself in the role of a lady who controls the transfer of the sugar crop, and thus redefining her relationship to labor. Watching the sugar being hauled onto barges, she mimes orders to sailors to take it away. Then, she acts the part of a gentlewoman when a sailor acknowledges her, "I twirl, pinch my shift, and curtsy" (16). And she runs along the river, imagining that she is "a ship chugging to St. Louis. Then I turn around and run south. *Chug-chug-chugging* down to New Orleans" (17; Rhodes's emphasis). Sugar's mobility and role-playing attest to her need to express herself as a child and to suspend the adult responsibilities she has assumed since her mother's death. She expresses her joy in pretending to act out a superior role and exercise control over the commodity that she dislikes and associates with exploitation.

In this extended scene, Sugar's play is not the kind of escape from slavery that is central to antebellum slave narratives; instead, it allows her to imagine her freedom from sugar and its painful associations. Although the role of lady would seem to be entrenched within a world that depends on the marketplace, labor and exploitation, and a racial and economic hierarchy that disadvantages African Americans, Sugar's appropriation of the role is ambiguous. Her mimicry seems different from the play among enslaved children in Octavia Butler's *Kindred*, in which the children restage a slave auction, competing for the role of trader and dreading that of enslaved person (The Fall). In Butler's novel, children's imaginative play underscores their limited social options and their acceptance of society's stratification, but in this scene of play, Sugar avoids referring to the exploitative relations of the slavery and the postslavery labor system. And unlike Elijah in Curtis's novel, she does not get lost in the role's illusions. Her role is a momentary performance in a liminal space at some distance from the actual business of the sugar trade. There she can claim the qualities of gracious hostess without taking on the limitations of the role or becoming fixed within it.[18] Moreover, she quickly abandons the role of lady to become a riverboat that cuts through the river, alluding to Douglass's apostrophe to the cargo ships on Chesapeake Bay.[19] Like Douglass, Sugar can suspend the onerous characteristics of trade and emphasize those compatible with her need for freedom, mobility, and adventure.

Similarly, her play with Billy, which begins later in this episode, often allows her to suspend her awareness of their very different status. The children belong to two different categories according to society: "Mainly, I work. Billy's tutor makes him read books. Sometimes, he practices a violin" (24); her house is a "gray shack" and Billy's the "yellow plantation home" (24). And although Billy occasionally betrays some of his father's bias, for much of the time, Sugar and Billy have a friendship that accommodates differences and builds on their parallel experiences. Just as Sugar defies her deceased mother's proscription against socializing with white persons, Billy ignores his parents' rule against playing with Black persons. Both have recently lost close family members, are about the same age, and are willing to risk getting in trouble.[20] They take turns leading or they lead together. Returning from the river, "Me and Billy walk side by side" (24). He gives her a Chinese finger trap, and she eventually tells him a story about Brer Rabbit. Through their partnership in play, Sugar and Billy can, at least temporarily, establish a tentative social equality in the liminal physical spaces away from the plantation's social centers and defy social norms.

Sugar and Billy's first encounter leads to successive days of "adventuring" in which they leave their home routines to experiment in nature, and these adventures have social implications. After revealing a makeshift raft he and his brother have built, Billy is willing to give up his ambition of being principal captain and serves as pirate co-captain with Sugar. This is a characteristic moment that shows Sugar's ability to assert her interests and Billy's ability to overcome his egotism to adopt an egalitarian view:

> "... I'm captain."
> "Girls aren't captains."
> "Then I won't go."

> "I never get to be captain," squeals Billy. "Anthony's always captain."
> "No turns?"
> "No," says Billy, shaking his head. "I'm always crew."
> I should be nice and polite, say "Billy, let's take turns." But if I'm going to risk my life, I want to drown as captain. (34)

This scene shows that Billy and Sugar are able to negotiate an arrangement that is amenable to them both. Billy gets to play with Sugar, who he has long admired for her daring spirit, and he gets to be a captain. Sugar, meanwhile, is able to affirm a sense of authority and insist on her new friend's respect, even if she lacks knowledge of pirates. Both children are open to learning with and through each other, and their education occurs through their modes of play.

Another central support for Sugar's cognitive development, the African-born Mister Beale, contributes to her epistemology of fun and games through his trickster tales. They provide a heroic model of thought and action, rooted in the Black oral vernacular that Sugar embraces and personalizes. Mister Beale's stories foreground the competition between the small, clever rabbit and the predatory, dull-minded hyena, who are often reference points for the African American workers on the Wills plantation. Sugar and the other members of the Black community delight in the rabbit's display of wit and triumph over the more physically powerful, aggressive hyena. And Sugar identifies with Br'er Rabbit's habit of using his wits to overcome his disadvantage. She associates the rabbit with fun, imagination, transgression of social barriers, and departure from the drudgery that she believes consumes the workers' lives. Inspired by his example, she has come to rely on her intellect to find ways to subvert the principal figures of authority in her life, a tendency that Mister Beale sees as dangerous "trouble" (87). Mister Beale's tales are vehicles by which Sugar can transcend the worries of her life: Late in the novel, for instance, when she first shares one of the tales with Billy, Sugar comments, "Me and Billy have left River Road, left Louisiana; together, we're inside Mister Beale's African tale" (185). In addition, the trickster tales provide means for understanding and negotiating her challenges.

The impact of Mister Beale's trickster tales is evident in Sugar's and her neighbors' reliance on them in interpreting and commenting on human tendencies. In criticizing her Black and Chinese friends, for instance, Sugar associates their xenophobia with Br'er Hyena's limited insight and lack of success, thinking "Grown folks are dumber than hyenas" (132). Later she tells Mister and Missus Beale that they are "both acting like Hyena" when they commit to staying on the plantation after it has been sold, explaining, "Hyena wouldn't leave if his village caught fire. But Br'er Rabbit would tell everybody, 'Go.' Turtle, Tiger, and all the animals would leave. Find another home" (268). Sugar realizes that adults settle into habits that prevent them from exploring alternatives that might be more rewarding. To Sugar, her African American friends are like hyena when they limit themselves to a virtual death in life, opting out of fun and growth. This approach to life opposes the rabbit's boldness and her mother's advice to "find joy where you can" and "Do. See. Feel" (39).[21]

Sugar sees her African American friends submitting to an imperative that serves Mr. and Mrs. Wills and the overseer Mister Tom, who are intent on limiting the workers' ability to have lives beyond work. The adults epitomize the hyena's limited thinking by acting as if work were more important than freedom. This is especially obvious when Mister Tom gets his fingers caught in the finger trap that Billy has given Sugar during their first playdate. The cylindrical toy is designed to trap a finger at each end, and to extricate them, the user must relax and bring the trapped fingertips closer together rather than try to pull them apart. Mister Tom becomes enraged when he tries pulling his fingers out, drawing onlookers' laughter and, rather than experimenting with different means of removing the toy from his fingers or taking instruction from others, he destroys it. In foregrounding this failure to engage in thinking that combines play and logic, Rhodes underscores the importance of coming together and not relying only on one's personal resources. Individuals remain stuck when they are not open to new possibilities, fail to use imagination, and do not grow through their connections with others. By the end of the novel, Mister and Missus Beale have fully embraced this ethic of experiment and adventure, which is founded on the spirit of play that the novel suggests needs to infuse even an adult's approach to life.

It can be argued that in embracing trickery as an approach to getting her way, Sugar is not exactly engaged in play. Yet a common way to describe trickery is *playing tricks*, and Sugar's trickery is important to her both as means to an end and for the end itself. Sugar takes pleasure from being a trickster. After a failed attempt to mislead Missus Beale in order to avoid a chore, Sugar concludes, "I shouldn't have tried to trick [her]. It's just more fun acting like Br'er Rabbit" (70). There is definitely some overlap between her more conventional forms of play, such as exploring the shore and climbing trees, and her attempts to manipulate circumstances to achieve a goal, whether it be to spend time with the Chinese workers or to play away from the farm. For Sugar, conventional play and subversion are processes that she associates with freedom: the free expression of her will and the freedom to feel good. Her subversions of authority are usually designed to bring her closer to the realm of play, which for her is the realm of freedom.

Her chief antagonist, in her mind, is Missus Beale, who insists that she do her chores and often blocks her attempts to escape them. Missus Beale's sentences frequently include the word *work*, just as Sugar is often thinking about play. One way that Sugar challenges Missus Beale's authority is by running off before her neighbors have awakened. In a more confrontational display of her subversive ways, Sugar uses a trick to manipulate Missus Beale into breaking the ice with the Chinese workers. When the Black workers are refusing to interact with the Chinese laborers after work, Sugar fools her into sharing some of her biscuits by stoking her ego:

I say, "The Chinese probably think [house servants] Mano and Annie are River Road's best cooks."
　Missus Beale stiffens, her back ramrod straight.
　"They don't know nobody makes corn bread better than you. Outside, all crispy brown. Inside, yellow, soft. *Dee*-licious!"
　Missus Beale brushes the corn bread with cream.
　"But the Chinese aren't really neighbors. I'm going to keep away. Not give them any of your corn bread."
　Missus Beale peers at me. I smile sweetly, then I blurt. "See. I'm a good girl."
　"No, you aren't," says Missus Beale, chuckling. "You just put me in the briar patch." (133).

Missus Beale positions herself in "the briar patch," an apparently troubling place that in the Tar Baby story ultimately proves to be liberating, for it helps the rabbit separate himself from the hyena's trap, the tarred doll (53). She goes on to tell the other African American women, "Can't have our neighbors thinking we can't cook" (133), and walks over to the Chinese laborers, thus initiating the African American adults' friendship with their Chinese peers. This particular trick shows that Sugar is aware of Missus Beale's pride in her cooking skills and is brave enough to try to use it to make positive changes in their community. She wants the workers to be united because she sees their common humanity and their common condition. She sees her Black neighbors' prejudice as an obstacle to a fuller social and intellectual experience, and to a greater range of fun.

　Yet the novel also indicates that Sugar must recognize potentially disorienting illusions that escapist play can engender. Sugar comes to realize that her play and friendship with Billy are ultimately limited by the socioeconomic structures that inform their lives. She cannot maintain and act on an idea of friendship that excludes aspects of reality, like the fact that Billy's father is at least partly responsible for her mother's death from overwork and untreated illness. Instead, she must confront the fact that her status as a Black laborer and Billy's as a white landowner's son creates conflict. Early in the book after Mister Wills threatens to expel Sugar and the Beales if she continues to play with Billy, Mister Beale promises to whip her if she disobeys Mister Wills (88), condemning her pursuit of fun because she transgresses racial and class protocol and boundaries. These rules are in place on planting day, when the Chinese immigrants join the longtime workers. While Sugar works beside the other laborers, Billy assists his father and the overseer Tom, reflecting their perspective and echoing their words. Tom orders the laborers to "Work!" and Billy and Mr. Wills command them to "Earn your pay" (129). And though Billy comes to Sugar later to play, she cannot forget his father's threat to turn her and the Beales out if she and Billy continue to play together. This threat makes her mindful of her responsibility to the Beales and underscores the differences between her and Billy that their play has previously obscured or suspended. Sugar explains to Billy that his father might hold the Beales responsible if she and Billy play together and punish the couple. Where earlier in the novel she followed her desire without thinking of consequences, she becomes more aware of how her decisions and actions may negatively affect others.

Rhodes's novel does not, however, indicate that Sugar must forsake the ways of childhood, including her playful perspective, in order to navigate the challenges of growing up in a stratified world. Instead, she learns that engaging in play is not an escape from her harsh reality, but rather a means of transforming her circumstances to lend them more equilibrium and fairness. The novel indicates that a spirit of play, though associated with childhood, is something that responsible adults should also embrace and express. That is, *Sugar* ultimately suggests that children and adults are parallel in their need for play as a process of invention and release that can orient their creative engagement with the world. In this way, *Sugar* is attuned to Gubar's conception of the kinship between adults and children ("The Hermeneutics" 298, 300). In the novel's application of this model for understanding children and adults, they learn from one another in navigating the challenges of a discriminatory society. This is underscored in Sugar's friendship with Beau, the youngest Chinese laborer, who offers her a model of adulthood that balances hard work and self-discipline, on the one hand, with play and intergenerational empathy, on the other.[22] Beau accepts and respects Sugar for who she is, and she reciprocates. From their first meeting, the pair show their willingness to establish a friendship with each other when others in their respective groups are hesitant because of the groups' racial and national differences. It is true that Sugar learns from Beau, who has reached adulthood, but the novel shows that Beau, like his Chinese and African American elders, learns from her.

Beau's and his compatriots' influence on Sugar's play emphasizes exploration and experimentation, and helps her extend her understanding of the world and her place within it. Although the Chinese workers are defined initially by their capacity to work productively and efficiently, they also represent a balanced way of life that includes relaxation, leisure, and play, in spite of oppressive circumstances (it is notable that the immigrant workers arrive at the Wills plantation in chains). Through Beau and his Chinese comrades, Sugar comes to understand that play need not occasion physical escape from her home and African American friends; she learns that it can be a part of her public, shared life with her community.[23]

In introducing Sugar to kite-flying, Beau exemplifies this approach to maintaining balance in his life, and in the process shows that play, and the possibilities it affords, do not depend on escape; it can occur within the realm of home and surrogate family. One reason he is so sensitive to Sugar's high level of energy and need to run and play may be that his sister, who is deceased, displayed such tendencies. Beau approaches Sugar after a hard week of picking cane, when most of the workers are tired or napping. Billy, who has worked alongside the laborers and served as overseer, is so sore that he is home in bed. As Beau begins to run with the kite and it takes off, Sugar watches the process by which the kite takes flight. Then, she sees the kite's transformation into a living being, comparing it to animals: "its tail wiggling like a captured snake," "*The cotton and sticks are alive*, I think. Like a bird" (207; Rhodes's emphasis). Yet then she sees it as more splendid than "a flock of birds" because of the kite's versatile movements, its "dancing, swirling and spiraling" (207). With the kite aloft, Beau hands her the rope and she realizes that she is transformed by her contact with the kite: "I hold it, feeling the push-pull of the kite and wind. It's tugging me, and I wonder if my feet will lift right off the ground and I'll fly, too" (208). Although Sugar does not literally fly, she does learn to manipulate the kite, guiding its movement with the wind and adjusting her own actions accordingly. In a sense, she fulfills her dream of flight, discovering a new way to move through nature and express her desire for freedom. Unlike the pressure applied by the restraint-minded African American adults, the pull of Beau's kite is freeing. Yet in flying it, Sugar does not have to escape her neighbors and the Wills, for her play is not the private or semi-private experience she has come to associate with freedom. She not only takes turns with Billy, who joins the fun after a while, and has Beau standing ready to assist her, but also shares her joy with an enthusiastic audience. Her Chinese and African American neighbors watch intently and happily; Billy's parents sit together, contentedly taking in the sight of the children at play; and two of the African American adults take turns with the kite, once the children, joined by Beau, move to another activity. Yet before the three retreat to a less public arena for play, in this case, searching for an alligator, Beau fosters an experience of collective joy, like the African American workers' storytelling sessions, in which Sugar takes active part and in which she gives, as well as, receives joy.[24]

In numerous scenes, Beau's words and actions encourage social connection and build community, and in this way he, like Sugar, is central to the novel's exploration of transcultural experience. Beau initiates their relationship soon after the Chinese men arrive, chastened because they have had to travel chained together to keep them from returning to British Guiana. Sugar accompanies Mr. Beale as he walks the line of Chinese men to unlock their chains, and though most are too depressed to acknowledge her presence, Beau speaks to her in Chinese, sharing the greeting, "*Ni hao*," which she echoes, "Knee-how" (101). Although he is proficient in English, Beau will continue to introduce Sugar to the Chinese language. For instance, during one of their earliest meetings, he teaches her the characters for her name, his own, and the Chinese workers' leader Master Liu's. And Beau is receptive to her lesson in American communication when she holds out her hand and asks if they can be friends. After a pause, he answers with actions and words:

> Beau, his rough hand swallowing mine, grips and shakes.
> "First American friend," he says.
> I say, "First Chinaman friend."
> "Chinese. Chinese friend."
> "Chinese." (125)

From this exchange, Rhodes establishes the pair's mutual respect and willingness to learn from each other.

In her most ambitious trick, orchestrating a slowdown of fieldwork, Sugar coaches Beau, in turn, teaching him about the importance of acting in accordance with the needs of the full community of laborers, including the Black field workers. The trick largely illustrates Sugar's growth; she demonstrates her respect for and commitment to her fellow workers, and her resourcefulness in resisting the oppressive system designed to exploit their energies. Yet it also underscores the importance of reciprocity in her relationship with Beau and other workers. Although it might be argued that a work slowdown does not fit within the category of play, Sugar's efforts in this episode are fueled by the same creative spirit driving her other transgressive behavior—her wit, commitment to freedom, and the disruptive influences of Black and working-class vernacular culture. The action caps a narrative trajectory about integrating play and freedom into her complex of allegiances and predilections. In the climactic scene, Sugar is able to bring together the African American and Chinese workers into a mutually beneficial partnership, and she does this by inviting the Chinese workers into the Black vernacular tradition of the work song.

Realizing that her aged Black neighbors, though working intently, will not be able to keep up with the ten Chinese farm workers, Sugar seeks to encourage her longtime friends by singing an impromptu song and trying to set a steady but tolerable pace for their work. Describing the tactic, she mentions the appeal she makes to Beau, "I sing to him, my voice strong. But pleading, too. I'm trying to make him hear, understand the worries of River Road folks" (114). Beau responds by speaking to his mentor, Master Liu, who has words with another Chinese laborer, who in turn speaks to another, until "amazingly, they all slow down" enough for the African American laborers to "catch up" (115). The group, united, works to the music, "All of us moving, in the same rhythm—steady, strong" (115), within a circle of mutual interests. On the next work day, the partnership continues with "everyone working in unison" (131). This interracial group enacts what historian Robin D. G. Kelley calls a classic "slowdown," a labor tactic thought to have been used by many African American laborers who "resisted the conditions of work, tried to control the pace and amount of work, and carved out a modicum of dignity at the workplace" (36). Both groups show their ability to read a situation defined by competing interests and act in ways that are not understandable to the employer and manager, but are clear to their peers.

Playing a trick to benefit the community of workers, Sugar demonstrates the extent to which she has succeeded in revising her idea of freedom, extending it beyond a concern with personal gratification and escape. The slowdown contrasts with her habitual flights from domestic work, as in the chapter "In the Briar Patch," when Sugar tries to escape Missus Beale's watchful eye as they do chores together. Sugar repeatedly says that she hears Mister Beale's call to make Missus Beale, who does not hear his voice, believe she may be suffering hearing loss (66–67). Sugar's trick shows a cruel insensitivity that deviates from the trickster's code of reserving disruptive tricks for real antagonists and respecting and maintaining community (Roberts 45). In exploiting Missus Beale's age to distract her, Sugar recalls the danger of trickery and the example of Curtis's Preacher, for Missus Beale, though a disciplinarian, is a generally kind and sympathetic character (e.g., she is depressed from being separated from her children). Through her relationship with the Beales and other adult associates, Sugar learns that at times she must accept another's authority and consider their teaching, if that person has her welfare in mind. She learns to direct her creative energies to supporting her community, or at least acting on her own and associates' common interests.

In leading the collaborative effort to manage the field workers' pace, Sugar realizes this balance and helps Beau, the Beales, and the other workers demonstrate their agency in a system that demands subordination to its goals and that defines them as beasts of labor, who the farm manager disparagingly calls "Yellow and black monkey men" (201).[25] The workers best this system: Although they serve the employer's interests, they also take care of themselves and take control of the work. They join to channel their energies, control their own bodies, and thus curb the ruling class's control: As Sugar says, "Like Br'er Rabbit, grown folks are tricking Mister Wills and overseer Tom. They're not being lazy, just making sure everyone—young and old, Chinese and African—work the same amount" (132). In tricking the bosses, the workers blur the distinction between work and play in the interest of establishing a more equitable social dynamic. This blurring highlights Sugar's transformative use of play: Her leading her coworkers in this scene is an imaginative, yet pragmatic, way of confronting the obstacles and challenges of an unjust society.

THE SERIOUS BUSINESS OF PLAY

It might be important here to ponder why Sugar, like Dofimae, does not play with dolls, which is a significant denial of a common pastime for nineteenth-century children.[26] This denial underscores her and Dofimae's distance from the model of socialization associated with dolls. As cultural archeologist Lu Ann De Cunzo has noted, "dolls taught not only gendered roles and values but also individuality, and they 'provided an object lesson in the property relations of Victorian society'" (De Cunzo 177). This idea of dolls resonates with Bernstein's conception of toys as "scriptive things" that direct children's responses and interactions as if they were theatrical scripts (ch. 2). The absence of dolls from Dofimae's and Sugar's play distances them from the hierarchies of doll play and the domestic places and racist and classist agendas with which they are associated.[27] The focus on different kinds of liberating play signals the two texts' resistance to neoliberal policies that inform their target audiences' experience. The play opposes neoliberalism's emphasis on prioritizing society's capitalist goals and making leisure activities and other endeavors serve these goals. Intent as *Sugar* and *Mother of the*

River are to challenge property relations, the narratives focus on outdoor adventures, games, and other activities common in narratives about boys and tomboys, such as *Elijah of Buxton*, as well as classics like *Adventures of Huckleberry Finn*, that are associated with physical and cognitive freedom from the constraints of middle-class domestic life.[28] Both girls' narratives highlight aspects of play that challenge abiding standards of work and expectations of material gain, and of Black subordination and self-denial. In the process, the narratives counter longstanding stereotypes assuming that African Americans lack substance and motivation, are incompatible with the Protestant work ethic and require careful management by white persons. In focusing on a range of girls' play, *Mother of the River* and *Sugar* also provide readers with frameworks for analyzing other labor hierarchies and for posing questions about workers' rights.

Furthermore, Rhodes's novel suggests the importance of acknowledging the multiple cultural frames through which it may be necessary to understand Black children's agency within contexts of work and play. *Sugar* appeared at a time when multicultural literature increasingly reflected neoliberalism's tendency to bleach ethnic and racial specificity to fit successful African American experience to a white middle-class model. Countering this tendency, *Sugar* uses realism to invoke traditions in Black, white, and Chinese cultures in characterizing its protagonist and her circumstances: The novel calls on readers to consider the ways in which she embraces and revises inherited and shared traditions, such as that of the trickster and the Romantic child. The novel's focus on Sugar's psychological development and engagement with the world largely shows an optimism about children's capacity to rely on their cultural knowledge as they navigate social challenges. For readers, this emphasis might mean a number of things. *Sugar* encourages young readers to think about how economically disadvantaged and emotionally traumatized children can rely on their imaginations to assert themselves and challenge injustices. Rhodes thus complicates the common narrative about African Americans and laborers as simple victims, requiring rescue, remedy, or remediation by others. The novel *Sugar* presents an ingenious girl and a responsive community that work together to better their situation: If their embrace of play does not lead to lasting changes on the River Road Plantation, the protagonist Sugar nevertheless suggests what one spirited person can achieve with the help of her friends. By helping to institute a more just practice of agricultural labor, Sugar can serve as a model for young readers searching for ways to make positive changes to society. Although Sugar's play does not dismantle the agricultural system that drains workers' energies, she is instrumental to making her adult friends see the importance of resisting an injurious social order. Her disruptions are not contained by the system; instead they alter it. The novel thus contrasts with the comic realism of *Elijah of Buxton*, which suggests that Elijah has to accept the limits of his capacity to create change. Some change is possible within reason, Curtis's novel indicates, but ultimately one has to accept the reigning social order.[29]

Mother of the River provides another alternative to *Elijah of Buxton*'s acceptance of socioeconomic limits. The film's anachronisms, fantasy, and idylls offer viewers a departure from the reasonable and pragmatic messages that emerge from many realist texts; the film's nonrealist features encourage viewers to think imaginatively about the past and present.[30] The film's idyllic scenes of African Americans at leisure and of Dofimae and Cudjoe's reunion with her mother evoke an alternative world in which the beauty of a pastoral place is matched by its inhabitants' elegance, self-possession, and contentment. The ambiguous quality of the ending plays with genre, denying the conventional narrative closure of antebellum narratives, which locate a protagonist in an identifiably American (northern US or Canada) or European space. The film does not clarify if the ending scene is dream, desire, or future occurrence or if it happens in life or an afterlife. Yet it calls on viewers to think about the scene's interpretive possibilities and to question the dominant culture's social classifications of Black people, as drudges and victims under the thumb of white oppressors. The film encourages viewers to think of enslaved persons in a new light, to play against the conventional tales that associate Black persons primarily with oppression and subjection, and, occasionally, with liberation in northern or European locations or through northern antislavery forces.[31]

With Dofimae, Elijah, and Sugar, play is a radical way of indulging and pleasing the self, and in each text, it becomes associated with pursuing knowledge, testing boundaries, and, especially in *Sugar* and *Mother of the River*, strengthening self and community. Although *Elijah of Buxton* critiques the viability of play and imagination alone as ways to secure and maintain freedom and autonomy, each of the texts presents play and imagination as resistant forces that express Black individual energies and American and African American cultural inheritances. If the girl protagonists are more effective at using play to make positive changes, it may be because, in order to survive, they must find ways to resist a dominant white patriarchal culture that denies their wholeness. With Elijah, by contrast, living in a society dominated by Black people, play, especially trickery, is acceptable when it does not upset the balance of the community. In the unequal environments of *Mother of the River* and *Sugar*, Dofimae and Sugar, lacking Elijah's socioeconomic privileges, must rely on games or tricks, which would seem to have no currency in the real world of economic competition and exploitation. Yet these texts suggest otherwise, pointing to the relevance of play as expressions of creative activity that aided Black survival.

It might be argued that in conceiving of play in this chapter, I have defined the term too broadly. Yet through exploring Sugar's, Dofimae's, Elijah's, and their associates' play, I have sought to acknowledge historical narratives' representations of avenues of Black life that are both infused with playful actions and thinking and affected by play's processes, rewards, and limits. Play, of course, is not the only thing that African Americans do in historical narratives about slavery and freedom. As *Sugar* suggests, children's play can suffuse their labor, which may also hold lessons about personal and group creativity. *Sugar*'s scene of Chinese and Black workers united in making their labor their own illustrates the possibilities that work might afford for self- and group expression. Several other texts, which I will explore in the next chapter, depict the relationship between Black children or youth and property, focusing on characters' aspirations to own and maintain land. On the one hand, these aspirations seem to endorse the idea of American opportunity, but on the other, they mark African American writers' play with that idea and insistence that Black socioeconomic aspirations and achievements should be understood through distinct lenses of Black cultures that depart from the exploitative tendencies of American capitalism.

Chapter 6

TENDING TO THE LAND

Challenges of Black Financial Agency and Community in Youth Freedom Narratives

In this chapter, I explore narratives that focus on African Americans' relationship to land as aspiring or actual owners. Admittedly, owning a plot of land or a building may be distant from most contemporary children's concerns, and not all African Americans have aspired to own homes or other real estate.[1] Yet the authors of historical fiction, including freedom narratives, often portray the relationship between real estate, social manners and circumstance, and individual agency to explore an aspiration and reality that large numbers of African Americans have negotiated. In United States history, African Americans had to struggle with society's equating Blackness with object or property status, and narrative portrayals of Black land- or home-ownership examine and critique this equation. Fictional focus on land ownership also resonates with the many ways that owning property, attaining economic security, and sharing it with current family and descendants have historically been challenges for African Americans because of systemic inequities. The pervasiveness of these problems and their effect on Black persons' economic, political, and psychological conditions makes the focus in youth literature important, encouraging readers to interrogate popular conceptions of American opportunity and the accessibility of the American dream. Freedom narratives further the cause of critical multiculturalism, encouraging readers to see both the social structures that have resulted in economic disparities and African Americans' creative efforts to overcome them.

The dream of owning land and the realization of the dream are contemporary with slavery in two books I examine that are set in the North—Joyce Hansen's *Home Is With Our Family* (2010) and Marilyn Nelson's *My Seneca Village* (2015). Both books reimagine a thriving New York City community of Black homeowners and renters that was destroyed in 1857 by the city government to create Central Park. Working and owning southern land are central to Walter Dean Myers's multigenerational novel *The Glory Field* (1994) and Mildred Taylor's Reconstruction-era novel *The Land* (2001). Although each of the four books explores characters' ability to secure land and stake out a claim in a rising regional or national economy, these freedom narratives challenge neoliberalism's touting of the accessibility of the American Dream and the primacy of individualist capitalist achievement in American life. Influenced by late twentieth-century Black Nationalist prioritizing of Black community, economic self-determination, and affluence, all four texts encourage young readers to think critically about the role of property ownership in the African American historical experience. A Black Nationalist focus on communal support and well-being animates the texts, reflecting the optimism in late 1960s and early 1970s social change movements about the possibility of achieving equity for African Americans.[2] The freedom narratives I discuss in this chapter are representative in portraying both the violent effects of US capitalism and African Americans' efforts to counter these challenges by creating spaces through which they can practice communal sustainability and resist the economic inequities systemized within the dominant culture.[3] In each text, African Americans use hard work, ingenuity, and collaboration to create safe places for themselves and their families. Yet these freedom narratives also underscore constraints within US society that threatened Black life, work, enterprise, and property-owning. Although *The Land* and *The Glory Field* show the difficulty of realizing just alternatives to American capitalist pursuits, each text fosters readers' critical engagement with socioeconomic aspects of African American history that are often not addressed in popular culture.

In sum, the four books are representative of freedom narratives' portrayal of the distinctness of Black historical experiences—in focusing on Black aspiration and achievement, the books do less to show African American characters' realization of an American dream of middle-class assimilation and success than to portray the distinct pressures and possibilities of being Black and owning, or aspiring to own, real estate. This refocusing often entails revising the literary or cultural forms the writers draw on to convey Black experience, underscoring its departures from dominant culture myths and assumptions about social success, from the individualist hero to the control of natural resources. In particular, the novels imagine how Black persons of various social standing were able to use their creativity "to bend the means of capitalism to the needs" of African Americans rather than to fit into an existing social standard.[4] They do not portray middle-class status as the gold standard for Black life; indeed, each acknowledges middle-class hypocrisy and classism, along with more edifying aspects of the Black middle class. They also respect African Americans who are working-class and poor, perhaps not surprisingly, given that numerous African Americans have long fit into these classifications. The focus on aspiration, achievement, and the threat or actuality of lost real estate allows each author to uncover underexplored aspects of African American life and thus to offer young readers part of a fuller history of African Americans. This fuller history foregrounds Black cultural imperatives, some of which overlap with, but many of which pointedly counter, dominant American values. The texts' complexities presuppose young readers' ability to understand nuances of Black historical experiences and to reject simplifications of Black identity and culture.

Historically, the possibility and the precariousness of African Americans' control of real estate have been manifest in different ways, from geographical segregation and displacement to redlining and predatory lending. This breadth of negative experience is evident in the range of land- or property-related issues central to recent African American youth narratives. While Renee Watson's *This Side of Home* (2015) explores the effects of gentrification on two Black teenage sisters, Angie Thomas's *The Hate U Give* (2017) presents a conflict between its protagonist's parents over living in a Black neighborhood where the father also owns a business. Interestingly, in Thomas's novel the family moves to a bigger house in a more affluent neighborhood, but in the film adaptation (2018), the family remains in the Black neighborhood. Concerns with property-owning are also prominent in historical narratives. In the realm of children's and young adult fiction, a list of such books would include Taylor's *The Well* (1995) and *Song of the Trees* (1975), Joyce Hansen's *The Heart Calls Home* (1999), Harriette Robinette's *Forty Acres and Maybe a Mule* (1998), and Christopher Paul Curtis's *The Journey of Little Charlie* (2018).[5]

I have chosen *My Seneca Village*, *Home Is With Our Family*, *The Land*, and *The Glory Field* because they allow me to explore issues of economic agency within different social structures and historical periods and to consider how the issue of property-owning works within various thematic schemes. *My Seneca Village* and *Home Is With Our Family* reconstruct Black urban experience before the Civil War from different angles, though both represent individuals' and families' holding of real estate as a foundation for community and a means for positive social action. Through a series of persona poems inspired by actual residents, *My Seneca Village* allows for multiple views of the Black village's development in a thirty-year period, starting before the end of legalized slavery in the state of New York. The book relates to the prose novels by extending beyond the biographical record of historical figures, summoning their responses to everyday lived experience, including errands, labor, entertainment, and antislavery activism. *Home Is With Our Family*, by contrast, focuses on a fictional family whose enterprise, abolitionism, and dedication to community help sustain Seneca Village residents in the area's final years. These books about antebellum Black experience provide an important corrective to popular understandings of African American history, which assume that all slavery was southern, that all African Americans were poor and unlettered, and that white Americans were primarily responsible for the end of slavery. The two Seneca Village books also confront the paradox of Black property-owning at a time when African Americans were often defined in the dominant culture as less than human and valuable mainly as instruments of white American wealth. Both Nelson's and Hansen's books provide an inclusive vision of community, with Seneca Village populated by Black, European immigrant, home-owning, and renting neighbors. In both books, the villagers' sense of community encompasses their efforts to aid fugitives from slavery and to resist and end legalized slavery in the United States. As texts about economic achievement, *My Seneca Village* and *Home Is With Our Family* also provide visions of Black urban development that oppose both stereotypes of the Black ghetto and celebrations of unchecked capitalism.

By contrast, *The Land* and *The Glory Field* explore African Americans' struggle to get and keep land in the South, and though the novels share some important narrative elements, their distinctions provide fertile ground for discussing a range of topics. *The Glory Field*, like *Home Is With Our Family*, shows real estate to be central to a Black family's self-definition over the course of several generations, starting in the late eighteenth century, with a young boy captured in Africa, and continuing through at least the mid-1990s with the struggles of his descendants. This historical breadth allows readers to see the ongoing significance of the family's property amidst societal change, including family members' different ways of surviving slavery, the effects of the Thirteenth Amendment, migration to the North, and the waning and resurgence of Black southern culture's hold on residents of the urban North. In *The Glory Field*, real estate serves as a metonymy for family, a constant on which they rely to affirm their shared experience, their ability to survive social oppression, and their connection to nature's cycles of regeneration. Although southern real estate has a similar thematic value across Taylor's Logan family series, *The Land*, a prequel to the other Taylor novels that are set in the twentieth century, details its biracial protagonist's efforts to establish his financial footing in the racist, postbellum South. The novel's concentration on a relatively short historical span encourages readers to think about the social obstacles the protagonist confronts as a young man, including white power brokers' inconsistency in acknowledging the quality of his work and the effects of class and color differences in Black communities. *The Land* arguably most resembles the *bildungsroman* genre associated with young adult literature, foregrounding its multitalented, alienated young protagonist's journey to selfhood. Yet Taylor's novel sets up the family-oriented world she depicts in subsequent books; its key lessons include the limitations of the protagonist's individualism, the dangers of the New South's capitalist business models, and the necessity for collaboration and restorative agricultural methods.

The Land, The Glory Field, My Seneca Village, Home Is With Our Family, and other freedom narratives about Black real estate foreground Black cultural emphases on collaboration, mutual respect and care, ingenuity, and determination, even as they show the challenges African Americans face in trying to maintain financial security. They recover images and stories from the African American experience that complicate historical pictures of African American people and cultural foundations, moving beyond the association of Blackness with subjection and the equation of Black success with assimilation to white middle-class standards. In sum, the texts constitute the kind of "critical multiculturalism" Melamed has associated with some recent texts, interventions that discourage complacency and that reveal the social structures that perpetuate economic struggles within Black communities (127). The four freedom narratives also provide alternatives to contemporary music and video popular with youth that "glamorize the hard life of poverty and scoff at the ordinances of middle-classdom" associated with whiteness (Pattillo-McCoy 11). The books model economic practices that facilitate achievement, belonging, and progress for a "cross-class" community, not just "a talented tenth," thereby countering negative stereotypes of the Black bourgeoisie that focus on opportunism, capitulation to white social standards, and self-repression.[6] The novels also complicate popular simplifications of working-class life. Nelson's, Hansen's, Myers's, and Taylor's constructions of Black communities emphasize the functionality of the economic practices common in Seneca Village, rural Mississippi, and the Carolina Sea Islands.[7] The narratives challenge capitalism's emphasis on individualism, competition, and exploitation of people and natural resources. In providing alternative concepts of Black economic participation, the novels are representative of the freedom narratives in rejecting assumptions in mainstream commentary about poverty that equate African American financial failures with personal or Black cultural weaknesses.

In two surveys conducted in 1969 and 1980 about financial success, sociologist William Julius Wilson found evidence of such assumptions. Many of the survey-takers saw poverty as a result of individual action or inaction—

"lack of effort or ability, poor moral character, slack work skills" rather than systemic conditions such as "lack of adequate schooling, low wages, lack of jobs" (204). Conservative cultural critics such as Daniel Patrick Moynihan argued that a pathological Black culture was to blame for these individual failures, a belief that many Americans have shared (Franklin 164–66; Wilson 205). Countering these common assumptions about Black social failure, freedom narratives foreground Black creativity, offering young readers distinctly African American histories with real estate that illuminate the inaccessibility of the American dream and provide constructive alternatives to common stereotypes of Black insufficiency and immorality. Moreover, the narratives revise literary and cultural conventions of antebellum slave narratives and domestic fiction to foreground the perspectives and beliefs that facilitated Black survival and success.

AN ANTEBELLUM BLACK URBAN MECCA

In reconstructing Seneca Village, Hansen's *Home Is With Our Family* and Nelson's *My Seneca Village* serve as correctives to limited understandings of antebellum Black life and New York City's development. The two books are part of an effort to reconstruct and reimagine a history of African American life in the northeast, and in New York City specifically.[8] They also confront stereotypes of African American communities as sites of failure and pathology, stereotypes that do not acknowledge the complexity, diversity, and resources of primarily Black neighborhoods. Hansen's and Nelson's portrayals of Seneca Village property-owners acknowledge a long history of African American cross-class culture and resonate with contemporary issues of housing insecurity. The books depict the economic diversity within Black urban neighborhoods. Published after the 2007–2008 housing crisis, which disproportionately impacted African American and Latinx persons, the two books reinforce the idea that African American real estate has had a fraught history, even while underscoring the importance of Seneca Village as a site of beneficent, compassionate economic development.[9] Before turning to Hansen's portrayal of the village's final years, I explore Nelson's careful delineation of differences between the village and downtown Manhattan's more populous residential and business area. In imagining and reconstructing moments in the thirty-year history of the community, Nelson honors the efforts of African American individuals and their churches to use property-owning and community-building, as historian Leslie Alexander has said, to "create a sense of permanence" (24) at a time when African Americans in the North were legally free but subject to racism and legal constraints on their autonomy. *My Seneca Village* balances its concern with Black agency with attention to the lingering forces that oppose Black freedom, promoting readers' cultural awareness and critical thinking about what Melamed has described as a historical pattern of "resistance and containment" (127).

With its use of the conventions of persona poems, *My Seneca Village* necessarily foregrounds the individual—most of its poems affirm an individual African American voice and perspective to counter the cultural tendency to silence and marginalize Black speech and to deny Black interiority ("Persona"). Nelson, in a departure from strict definitions of the persona poem, adds a prose introduction to each of the poems to offer context ("Persona"). These juxtapositions encourage readers to see the villagers in relation to one another and to imagine both the synchronic and diachronic dimensions of village life. Thus, the book's focus on individuality is consistently, and variously, wedded to its insistence on the importance of Black community. In conception and execution, *My Seneca Village* responds to, and even challenges, Edgar Lee Master's *Spoon River Anthology*, whose epitaphic poems have long been part of high-school English curricula: Nelson's poems are spoken by the living, who are engaged in the grand pursuit of building and creating, as opposed to the isolated, lost souls in Master's book. *My Seneca Village* demonstrates the ingenuity and distinctness of African American community building, foregrounding Black agency and communal support systems, and even affording room for the eccentric or unconventional.[10] The poems move chronologically, beginning with early residents' visions for Seneca Village, exploring the workings of its benevolent society, school, and churches, and depicting social experiences, such as courtship, children's play, and work-related travel. Capping this communal story is the poem "Uncle Epiphany," which suggests that the village's success is part of a continuum that includes the hopes of "African ancestors," periodic revelations, and future African American achievements, such as Barack Obama's presidency (Nelson, *My Seneca* 83).

The first three poems in *My Seneca Village*, "Land Owner," "15¢ Futures," and "Saplings," define the ambition of Seneca Village's earliest settlers as an inclusive plan for community, with the village's geographical plot supporting past, present, and future African Americans, including the free and enslaved. Themes of freedom's possibilities are central, but this is freedom charged with social responsibility, as demonstrated by the third poem, "Saplings," in which the speaker Diana Harding is taking stock, claiming her right to herself and to:

two slightly swampy lots, one deeeep well,
one one-room palace, and opportunity.
In honor of generations denied the right to roots,
I plant saplings. We'll harvest the future's fruits. (Nelson, *My Seneca* 7)

Harding dedicates her work in the present to predecessors and contemporaries who have been forced to live cut off from their origins. The poem affirms her self-possession ("myself the owner of one me"), and demonstrates her willed and imagined connection to others through the labor of planting trees, which represent life, longevity, and strength (7). She ends the poem by invoking the collective to which she belongs and balances her personal accomplishment with the promise of a "harvest" she will share with others.

Preparing such a "harvest," according to the book's opening poem, "Land Owner," involves complicated negotiations of freedom and subordination that suggest both the possibilities and constraints of Black freedom. With the speaker Andrew Williams both bending to shine shoes and capitalizing on economic opportunities he hears about while doing so, the poem offers a rich characterization of an ambitious man's ability to gain profit and autonomy in a socioeconomic system that runs on exchanges of information, money, and power. For even free African Americans, interracial financial exchanges often involve Black subordination to white persons, and though Williams acknowledges this, he also shows how he takes advantage of the arrangement. The first two quatrains of the poem present Williams speaking about the service for which affluent white New Yorkers pay him downtown, in lower Manhattan. In cleaning and shining the men's boots, Williams emphasizes the need to "keep his head down," a physical attitude that seems to oppose the common hope that work not get in the way of personal dignity, which is associated with being upright and looking up. Yet Williams's bent, downward-looking demeanor allows him access to potentially valuable information: "I listen when rich folks talk. / The finer the leather, the wiser the financial sage" (Nelson, *My Seneca* 3). Here Williams reveals that he uses his senses—listening, touching, seeing—as well as his reasoning and evaluative powers to prepare to conduct his own business. This is not to discount the significance of shining shoes, a job that is indicative of the kinds of reliable service work many African American men engaged in to provide for themselves and, in many cases, family members (L. Harris 75, 80–81). In Nelson's poem, polishing shoes is the most obvious part of the transactions that make Williams's affluent clients into servants of his interests as a financial risk taker and property owner.

These negotiations underscore the ways African American middle-class standing encompasses both gestures and aspirations commensurate with popular conceptions of white American middle-class identity and attitudes, pressures, limitations, and possibilities of Black working-class identity. This combination attunes the portrayals of nineteenth-century African American urban experience with still recognizable elements of the Black experience, thus countering the equation of middle-class with whiteness and countering the tendency within contemporary Black culture to conceive of middle-class African Americans as sellouts. The poem thus underscores the ways that middle-class and working-class experiences have often overlapped in Black American culture, complicating, but certainly not obviating, issues of intraracial class division.[11] Accordingly, in "Land Owner," Nelson's speaker Williams provides a lesson about his work ethic, asserting "There ain't nothing shameful about good, honest work" (*My Seneca* 3).

The poem's second half portrays his entrepreneurial spirit, showing William's actions and identity as a bold, ingenious Black businessman: "I deal merchandise shipped in on the Erie Canal. / Buy low, sell high. Then buy land, for the right to vote" (Nelson, *My Seneca* 3). Underscoring Williams's control and rationality, the lines' isocolons ("Buy low, sell high. Then buy land"), along with the three short, straightforward declarative sentences within the two lines of iambic verse, lend equilibrium to Williams's statements. His financial agency enables his political participation, another kind of social power that can benefit him and his community. By the poem's close, his reasonable, assertive voice reaffirms the link between his labor as a bootblack, his confidence, and his home ownership, which are informed with a spiritual power:

> Thanks to dropped tips, I'm a bootblack with his own place.
> I may bow at their knees, shushing with the horsehair brush,
> but I buff with spit on a rag to a mirrored face
> aflame with pride, blazing like a burning bush. (Nelson, *My Seneca* 3)

Williams's pun on "dropped tips," the extra money that is "dropped," rather than handed to him, and the information he overhears, again points to his humored acceptance of the social system of imbalances. Moreover, the image of the burning bush suggests that Williams's work and property acquisition and his work ethic compare to the biblical Moses's challenge to Egypt's Pharaoh and slavery: a path that expresses allegiance with God and serves God's people. Williams's people, like the Jews of the Old Testament, are God's chosen, and Williams's life not only challenges a status quo that holds many African Americans in bondage, but also serves to inspire and model a way to a new society of freedom and opportunity. As fellow founder Epiphany Davis asserts in the book's second poem, "15¢ Futures," "we all scrimped and saved / to own this stony swamp with its fetid air, / to claim the dream for dreamers yet enslaved" (Nelson, *My Seneca* 5). Nelson alludes to Dr. Martin Luther King Jr.'s and Obama's dreams of social justice, in presenting the speaker's hopes for the future. Along with other founding Seneca Villagers, Davis, Williams, and Harding act in the early years of the village to create a promised land for themselves and others, including the many who are still enslaved.

In Nelson's Seneca Village, African American social success is not designed for personal glory. Instead, it becomes a means of maintaining and building Black community for the benefit of the group, even those not present within the village perimeters. Several poems highlight the difference between the Seneca Villagers' community ethos and lower Manhattan's very different values that are indicative of the white dominant culture. "Hand-Me-Down Petticoat," which features live-in domestic worker Ada Thompson as speaker, associates the lower Manhattan of the mid-1830s with indulgence, plenty, and privilege. Ada sees it as a "Babylon," in which her presence is "silent, invisible" (Nelson, *My Seneca* 29). Like the biblical Babylon, the Manhattan of robber barons, who are alluded to through the poem's reference to John Jacob Astor's daughter, is morally and physically dangerous—a place in which wealthy persons' self-indulgence can prove destructive to others. Although the focus of the poem is Ada's insistence to her "prideful" daughter that receiving Miss Astor's used gown is a blessing, the Astor reference establishes a subtext that reinforces the differences between Seneca Village and lower Manhattan. Epitomizing the baseness of capitalist enterprise, John Jacob Astor, the family's patriarch, was known for his ruthlessness in making money. Astor took advantage of the Panic of 1837 to buy the mortgages of financially insecure persons at low cost, only to gain a big profit when the economy improved. He used bribes and intimidation to take over others' property: For instance, if his renters were not able to keep up with payment, he would claim their other property by way of compensation. Although the reference to the Astors is brief, it is important to Nelson's portrayal of the Seneca Village community as a refuge from and alternative to such cutthroat practices.

Yet the reference to the Astor clan is not the only indication of troubling trends in lower Manhattan. Another poem set in the 1830s, "Fire, Ice, Kiss," indicates that the corrupt economic practices of lower Manhattan extend beyond the practices of its wealthiest families, thereby suggesting the commonality of greed and exploitation. The poem presents the burning financial center of Manhattan as a "distant apocalypse" (Nelson, *My Seneca* 33), which one Seneca Villager sees as punishment for New Yorkers capturing and returning fugitives from slavery (33). Presenting Maria W. Stewart's powerful words and social criticism, the poem "Babylon," uses the metaphor of an intemperate, domineering queen to describe, not only lower Manhattan, but also America more generally, as insensitive, exploitative, and cruel: "America has boasted in her heart, / 'I shall see no sorrow, for I am The Queen!'" (43). The United States' power is manifest in its cruel merchandising of "human bodies and souls" (43), and its status as "an open mart," diction which signals the dominant culture's greed, corruption, and disrespect for African Americans. By contrast, in *My Seneca Village*, African American cultural institutions are designed to edify residents intellectually and spiritually and to extend support to those in need, as suggested by the banners listed in "Across the Parade," with each representing an organization defining Black America's, especially Black New York's, humanitarian emphasis. Among those the poem lists are:

> MOTHER BETHEL CHURCH A.M.E. ZION,
> AFRICAN THEATRE COMPANY OF NEW YORK,
>
> NY MANUMISSION SOCIETY, THE NY
> AFRICAN FREE SCHOOL, MASONIC LODGE NO 1 (9)

Beginning with one of the several Black Methodist Episcopal churches in the city and including several others institutions, the list suggests a range of cultural supports that associate Black America with efforts to develop, balance, and sustain Black individuality and community.

Although focused primarily on the rhythms of life among village residents, Nelson's *My Seneca Village* relies on the opposition between downtown Manhattan and Seneca Village to suggest America's lost opportunities—its destruction of Seneca Village can be understood as a rejection of the village's model of fair trade, sustainability, and social inclusion.[12] In its focus on the particularities of Black (and German and Irish immigrant) lives and its insistence on substantive, definitive distinctions between minoritized and dominant cultures, *My Seneca Village* shows the influence of the Black Nationalist commitment to honoring Black persons' and groups' histories.[13] This is no less true of Hansen's *Home Is With Our Family*, which also portrays Seneca Village as a fulfilment of a Black Nationalist dream of community in documenting its adolescent protagonist's developing moral and cultural awareness in the village's last year. Originally intended as the opening novel of a trilogy about members of an African American family, the Peters, the novel juxtaposes the village with less privileged terrain in other parts of New York City, indicating that the American dream of plenty and individual fulfillment is out of reach for many. On their drive from church to her grandmother's house in downtown Manhattan, the protagonist Maria Peters's family customarily passes through an area with white residents that appears as "a cluster of small shacks, where dogs and pigs scavenged among the garbage. The land was damp and swampy, and children with thin jackets and coats and worn, turned-over boots roamed with the pigs and dogs, looking for animal bones to sell to the bone-boiling plants" (Hansen, *Home* 12). Another section of the city is more developed, but squalid nevertheless: "Two- and three-story rickety wooden houses and saloons looked as if they had just been thrown against one another. Drunks staggered in and out of alleys, and women hung out of windows" (16). In contrast to these areas, Seneca Village represents functionality and inclusion, a refuge not only to homeowners, but also to renters, including Maria's friend Anna Holmes and her parents, and to African Americans and immigrants.[14]

Hansen's representation of Seneca Village and its residents emphasizes the villagers' fruitful participation in financial exchanges that counter the competitive, exploitative aspects of the capitalist system taking root in the United States in the mid-nineteenth century and recent capitalist systems that disempower many African Americans. For many Seneca Villagers, owning land and making money is part of a complex mission with practical, financial, and moral benefits, a mission aligned with the community's spirit of reciprocity, which is founded on intergenerational support and mutual respect. Proximity to Black institutions is essential to village life: The petition Mrs. Peters drafts for the villagers mentions the importance of the Colored School Number Three, which provides schooling to the young, and Zion Church, with its worship opportunities and burial grounds (Hansen, *Home* 83).[15] Although Hansen acknowledges the community's racial diversity, she concentrates on its status as a resourceful, majority Black world. Maria's family not only lives in their house in Seneca Village but also uses part as a store to sell the homemade goods, used clothing, and books that Mr. Peters, Papa, trades for downtown. The family's sense of enterprise acknowledges the reality for many African Americans—that a family's economic welfare depended not only on a patriarch, but also on the whole family (L. Harris 80). The store's wares attest to the Peters's understanding of their neighbors' material needs and ability to satisfy them, and this extends to the community's need for a place where villagers can meet to talk and fight for their rights. Moreover, the Peters have established a reputation beyond the village based on Mrs. Peters's buttermilk, for which there is regular demand. Mr. Peters sells or trades it and his wife and daughters' needlework, with the oldest child Moosa assisting him by driving their wagon to areas outside Seneca Village and helping with loading and unloading it. Papa Peters assiduously avoids participating in the ready market of stolen goods through which some New York vendors make their living. In addition to trading, Papa, like Andrew Williams in Nelson's book, has a viable business as a bootblack, which shows how service work was instrumental to many African Americans' success. The novel suggests that these practices allowing the Peters family to thrive also support the village's well-being.

To chronicle Maria and her family's experience, Hansen adapts the nineteenth-century domestic novel: In particular, the genre's focus on a young female protagonist in and around domestic spaces is relevant, as is the genre's centering on the conflict within the protagonist between a desire to express her agency and a need to conform to social expectations and find a viable social place for herself. Moreover, Hansen plays with the domestic novel's tendency to grant a protagonist opportunities to experiment with and subvert prescribed social roles (Tate 65–66). In *Home Is With Our Family*, such generic elements are filtered and transformed through Hansen's concern with the possibilities and limits of Maria's experience as a young Black middle-class Seneca Villager in a context defined both by legacies of racism and African American survival.

Home Is With Our Family suggests that the conflict between possibility and constraint is part of Maria's inheritance as a free Black New Yorker, a condition with which many young (and older) readers may be unfamiliar. Her mother, Mama Peters, comes from a Black family that has not been enslaved and that has had long experience with home-owning; indeed, her own mother (Maria's Grandma Isabella) often tells of an earlier city annexation project that took their ancestors' land without compensation (Hansen, *Home* 21). This earlier loss certainly resonates with the villagers' current concerns about the city's plan for their land, but the novel focuses on possibilities of life more than on past losses, balancing a focus on self- and group actualization with acknowledgement of the negative impact of the city's economic shifts and development. Within this historical context, Mama and Papa Peters expect their son Moosa to attend college and become a well-compensated, respectable professional, either a lawyer or doctor, and they expect their daughters to develop the domestic skills that will prepare them for responsible roles as middle-class women. As Grandma Isabella tells Maria, "If you sew real well, you'll help keep a roof over your head" (20). In addition to skills like sewing, a girl needed to learn how to manage a household, including its social dynamics and physical upkeep.[16] In portraying antebellum Black middle-class Seneca Villagers, Hansen presents attitudes about femininity, respectability, and accomplishment that are very similar to those prominent in popular domestic novels like Susan Warner's *The Wide, Wide World* (1850).[17] Yet the Peters and other middle-class Seneca Villagers are not intent on assimilating into a white world, even though in many respects their world parallels that of middle class white Americans. One difference is Black Seneca Villagers' vulnerability to socioeconomic and political change, as when the city exercises its right to lay claim to Seneca Village's land. Yet even before this, Maria and her Black family and neighbors have been dedicated to remaining connected to and supporting less affluent Black persons. In this respect, they demonstrate mid-nineteenth-century Black Nationalist emphases that incorporated Protestantism and acceptance of white middle-class standards of respectability, along with "the feeling on the part of black individuals that they are responsible for the welfare of other black individuals, or of black people as a collective entity, simply because of a shared racial heritage and destiny" (Moses, *The Golden Age* 20–22). *Home Is With Our Family* emphasizes the distinctness of a Black middle-class family and their commonalities and alliance with poor African Americans, though it does acknowledge some villagers' middle-class bias, as when Maria's mother expresses her disapproval of street people dancing on Sunday and of the violence in "Tailypo," a southern folktale circulating among the children; however, this is partly countered by Papa Peters's delight in hearing the account.[18]

As in much nineteenth-century domestic fiction, Maria must learn to adjust her perspective and gain a fuller understanding of her social place, but this is not the place of a white middle-class New York girl. Maria's education is infused by codes of Black gentility, and she must learn to overcome her resistance to sewing and temper her pride about her exceptional academic performance, as well as practice patience and tolerance with those who uphold the gender protocols she flouts. Yet Maria's moral education entails developing keener insight into matters of social injustice, a deeper commitment to Black people across lines of class, and a realistic sense of how she can effect social change. The novel not only portrays how Maria commands her considerable energy and intelligence to help Seneca Villagers fight annexation, but it also shows how she comes to contribute to the fight against slavery. In the process, she lays claim to genteel expectations in ways that allow her to be herself, thus mining the domestic novel's tendency to grant a protagonist opportunities to reshape inherited traditions and social roles (Tate 65–66). Maria learns how to exercise her power within and outside her home in fighting social injustice. In foregrounding Black characters and their sensibilities and experiences, Hansen revises conventions of domestic fiction and early African American literature about Black girlhood. She emphasizes the connections between Maria's self-development and issues of property and ownership, encouraging young readers to think about how her thoughts and actions are important to local, regional, and national debates about individual power and property management.

Although Maria's social position is more privileged than those of similarly aged characters in nineteenth-century African American narratives, such as Frado in Harriet Wilson's *Our Nig* and Linda Brent in Harriet Jacobs's *Incidents in the Life of a Slave Girl*, Nazera Sadiq Wright's descriptions of these two characters as "youthful and unknowing" with a "capacity to undergo transformation through intellectual agency and achievement" resonates with Hansen's portrayal of her protagonist (61). Maria does not experience the emotional and physical abuse that Frado endures or the sexual predation and manipulation Linda faces, but like them, she is initially "unknowing" about the ways society disempowers African Americans and about the most viable ways of asserting her power. Maria's "unknowing" is manifest in her smug intolerance for a talkative elder and a ladylike classmate and her certitude about the right way to do antislavery work. Paralleling the portrayal of the willfulness or waywardness of the female protagonists of domestic novels, the book-smart, ambitious Maria resists the expectation at her school and in her family that she develop proficiency in sewing and presses her parents to let her attend to the ostensibly more weighty work of attending antislavery meetings. Although her desire to join the fight for African American freedom is admirable, her assumptions, paralleling Elijah Freeman's in Curtis's novel, convey her innocence about slavery and viable ways to challenge it.

From the novel's first scene, Maria shows how moved she is by Sojourner Truth's activism, which looks more ambitious and transformative than domestic tasks like sewing. Present for a talk by Truth at the family's church in lower Manhattan, Maria "felt the power of God in the woman's voice," and later longs to attend other meetings at which Truth lectures so she can again experience the strong feeling of possibility Truth has ignited (Hansen, *Home* 8). This response calls to mind Wright's point about the empowering influence of one of Truth's contemporaries, Maria Stewart, whose "speeches contribute to a trope of black girlhood in the nineteenth century in which black girls develop traits of early awareness, self-sufficiency, and resilient willfulness as preemptive weapons against their victimization" (Wright 6). Maria is inspired by

Truth's story about rescuing her son from slavery: Truth tells the congregation that "I walked from county to county. I harassed anyone who would listen. I walked to the Quakers. I walked to the constable. . . . I walked to the Grand Jury. I walked to and fro—all day" (Hansen, *Home* 7). Truth's determination, which is signaled by the passage's tautologies, will ultimately inspire Maria to accompany her friend Anna Holmes, a fugitive from slavery, out of Seneca Village on a long walk to Grandmother Isabella's neighborhood in lower Manhattan, where Anna will find sanctuary at the family church. From the initial encounter with Truth, however, Maria focuses less on what she can do within her current circumstances to create change than on the excitement and inspiration she feels when she remembers Truth's speech. And later, when she aims to help Anna, she initially tries to assume the role of savior, discounting Anna's knowledge and power. For example, Maria pressures Anna to get Mr. Holmes to speak at an antislavery meeting in order to draw support, disregarding the Holmeses' efforts to not draw attention to themselves. In establishing the sewing and craft society and in helping Anna get to a safe space in lower Manhattan, however, Maria is able to adapt Truth's model of determination and resistance to fit her own and Anna's situation, addressing both the need to raise money to help fugitives and to operate in secret.

The presence of the Holmes family in Seneca Village facilitates Maria's growth and keeps the book from being an idealized portrait of middle-class life. Through her thinking and rethinking strategies for interacting with and helping Anna, Maria grows both more radical and less self-centered. Initially, however, Maria does not understand the Holmeses' status, beyond their obvious poverty, which is manifest in Anna's ill-fitting, donated clothing. Maria tries to understand various clues that signal Anna's difference and that suggest she is not being fully open about her personal history. These clues include indications that the Holmes are not long-time New Yorkers and may be from the South, as well as Mrs. Holmes's vigilance in conducting Anna to and from school, and Anna's unfamiliarity with many of the games popular among village children. Such clues suggest the Holmes family's distance from the comfort and security that Maria's family have realized, and weighing what she sees of Anna's circumstances broadens Maria's perception of African American social conditions. By the novel's midpoint, Anna tells Maria that Mr. and Mrs. Holmes have recently attained their freedom legally and that, Anna, according to US law, is still owned by their former enslaver and subject to being repossessed. The Holmes do not accept this classification, for as Anna explains to Maria, her father "always say we free our own selves," and her mother makes a similar assertion (Hansen, *Home*

159). Committed to the entire family's freedom, Anna's parents have refused to let her follow the trajectory prescribed by their former Virginia enslaver, who has planned to exploit Anna's skill at sewing and training for elite domestic service by hiring her out. Defiant, Mr. and Mrs. Holmes have moved to a part of New York City where public education is open to Black children and where they can foster Anna's multifaceted development. The cost for this defiance, according to Anna, is guardedness. With the novel set in the years after passage of the Fugitive Slave Act, African Americans in the North, whether escaped from slavery or legally free, were vulnerable because the law supported enslavers' rights and rewarded people who were willing to exploit opportunities of capturing African Americans who were not carrying free papers (L. Harris 272). Indeed, when Maria accompanies Anna to a hiding place in lower Manhattan, already aware of Anna's vulnerability, she realizes that without the legal papers documenting her free status, she is also vulnerable to being taken into slavery.[19] This realization shows not simply Maria's self-concern, but also her awakening into a fuller understanding of the dominant culture's classification of Black persons as tradeable objects in the United States' socioeconomic system.

Maria's antislavery thoughts and efforts comprise the central narrative thread that illuminates the issue of economic agency and personal power more generally; in the novel, her grappling with the obstacles to self-possession, or individual autonomy, and familial integrity take precedence over the Seneca Villagers' attempts to maintain their right to real estate. African Americans' status as actual or potential property in mid-nineteenth-century US society impacts the Seneca Villagers' right to real estate, whether owned or rented. The system of slavery affects Black people whether they have free papers or not, circumscribing freedoms and opportunities, even in Seneca Village and among its residents. Maria takes part in the community's petition drive, helping to copy the document that will be presented to city officials, and she and Anna express concern about the planned annexation. Yet Maria has a revelation during one of the village meetings that the problem of African American enslavement is more pressing and immediate than the planned annexation of land. At a meeting about organizing to fight the planned park, Maria notes that "Everyone was concerned with holding on to their property, but Anna was being treated as if she herself were a piece of property" (Hansen, *Home* 165). The loss of land, for which owners will receive a deflated price, is certainly consequential, and stands to destroy at least some residents' economic standing. And this threat affects the Irish and German immigrants who reside in the village, as well as African American renters and home-owners. But as the Peters parents repeatedly state, a physical home and legal title to land are less important than family: Home is family. Obstacles to maintaining personal autonomy and keeping family intact were the most dangerous threats to African Americans in the 1850s. According to the historian Leslie M. Harris, this was a time in which many black New Yorkers, not just Seneca Villagers, gave up on the city because of the judicial system's complicity with economic discrimination and southern enslavers searching for fugitives (275).

As it progresses, *Home Is With Our Family* devotes just as much, if not more, attention to the ways Maria and Anna act in defiance of systemic objectification and navigate racial and class injustice than to efforts to preserve Seneca Village. From their first meeting, the two girls establish an easy intimacy based on mutual respect and a shared sense of fun. After Anna is corrected by the teacher for using "ma'am" rather than "Miss James," Maria seems to realize that affirming rather than rejecting Anna's speech will reinforce her confidence. Maria does not know that Anna is from the South, that she has lived all her life in slavery until recently, and that "ma'am" is a token of servility and deference. What matters is honoring her new friend's particular way of speaking and seeing the world. Showing her independence and inventiveness, Maria declares, "I like the sound of the word. . . . Sounds like a bleating lamb, almost. . . . I don't see anything wrong with you saying it" (Hansen, *Home* 32). In accepting Anna's speech, she shows her respect for Anna and her particular personal history. The girls' use of "ma'am" in addressing each other flouts standard usage that reflects one speaker's subordination to another, for Maria and Anna are recognizing each other's authority. The girls' use of "ma'am" also shows fluency in the Black vernacular communicative practice of signifying, a form of wordplay that indirectly critiques the teacher's preferred usage, which signals her bourgeois status (Smitherman 118). The girls' equity is expressed further through their parallel, but distinct, talents: Whereas Maria is an accomplished student in academic subjects, Anna is a skilled seamstress. After Maria tutors her in writing letters of the alphabet, Anna tries to help Maria with a sewing assignment. When the two girls stay inside during lunch recess, in part because Anna does not know most of the games, Maria's younger sister volunteers to read from Hawthorne's *Tanglewood Tales*, and Anna declares she will tell a story instead. This exchange emphasizes that Anna and the Peters sisters have notable, but different, skills: The Peters sisters are proficient readers and writers, and Anna is a gifted storyteller. Moreover, the girls' embrace of Anna's storytelling reflects the Black Arts Movement's celebration of Black orality as a foundation for Black culture.

The story Anna tells the Peters girls, "Tailypo," ingratiates her with them, and eventually goes viral in their peer group, further signaling the abiding creative energies of the southern Black vernacular within the African American diaspora and extending Maria's awareness of Black culture. Anna's story also resonates with the novel's examination of personal power and property, offering a negative model of self-reliance that opposes and underscores the novel's emphasis on the benefits of community. "Tailypo," with which the other girls are unfamiliar, is a classic cautionary tale told by many Black and white southerners (Petro 118, 125). Although details vary, generally, the story's main character is a loner who survives from hunting and gathering. In some versions of the tale, the man has dogs, but Anna's version includes no dogs, accentuating the man's isolation and individualism. The encounter with the creature may occur outside during a hunt or, as in Anna's telling, in the man's house, which the creature enters unbidden. Once the man encounters the creature, he cuts off, cooks, and ingests its tail; the creature returns, repeatedly demands its tail ("Tailypo, tailypo. Give me back my tailypo"), and soon avenges the dismemberment by killing the man.

On an obvious level, the story cautions against self-isolation and shows how nature does not guarantee a person's survival. One way of surviving its challenges might be to join with others to guard against the desperate hunger that drives the story's protagonist to eat the creature's tail. At another level, given Anna locating the action in the man's house, the story comments on its penetrability and the man's lack of control. This dimension resonates with the Seneca Villagers' situation: They, too, will lose control of their real estate, but unlike the man in "Tailypo," they will survive the loss and continue to maintain their sense of community. By the end of the novel, with many residents dispersed and Maria and Anna to go in different directions. The teacher Miss James will keep track of residents and provide updates so that Seneca Villagers can maintain contact.

Anna's version of the story points to the presumption of believing that the place you occupy or own is only yours, denying the power of property ownership in which families like the Peters have largely put their faith.[20] Yet if real estate is an inconstant register of African American social power in *Home Is With Our Family*, it continues to inspire the Holmes and Peters as they imagine their futures. In addition to relying on the adage associating home with family rather than with a physical place, the Peters plan to move to Kansas, a state where the parents believe their possession of land will be better honored.[21] Anna tells Maria that her family may also proceed to Kansas, because "My father say that he want to get his own land" (Hansen *Home* 278). Maria accepts her parents' plan, though the oldest child Moosa is not sure about Kansas, favoring a journey further west to prospect for gold. Readers do not know if the Peters will reach Kansas and realize the parents' dream of acquiring and maintaining a homestead, for Hansen's plan to depict the Peterses' later history in subsequent volumes of a trilogy was ultimately not supported by her publisher. *Home Is With Our Family* does end with the Peters family together, and with Maria, one year older and much more empowered through her education in and out of school. She has learned how to finish a sewing project competently, to use the products of her and other girls' domestic industry to help secure African Americans' rights, and to remain attuned to other persons' needs in fighting for justice. Through the novel's representation of Maria's progress and her and the family's uncertainty, Hansen urges readers to ponder the idea that Black freedom is possible but contingent, and that Black community, in spite of its demands and contradictions, can be a foundation for thinking and acting freely, even within the context of disruptive, destructive social change.

BLACK LAND AND PERSONAL DEVELOPMENT IN THE POSTBELLUM SOUTH

Unlike *Home Is With Our Family*, Taylor's *The Land*, in keeping with the conventions of the bildungsroman, follows its protagonist's growth over several years, from childhood to manhood. *The Land* conforms to Roberta Seelinger Trites's influential definition of the young adult novel as bildungsroman; it follows a protagonist "who self-consciously sets out on a quest to achieve independence" (11). The novel also reflects the tendency of the African American bildungsroman "to use personal experience in order to make a viable protest ... about race, slave history, and the White establishment" (LeSeur 1). Indeed, the novel focuses on its biracial protagonist Paul-Edward's estrangement from his childhood acceptance of whiteness as standard and his development of a critical intelligence informed by his experience as an African American (M. Harris 95–96). In detailing Paul-Edward's developing awareness as African American, *The Land* encourages readers to weigh his choices and learn from his changing relationship to the dominant culture and to African American culture. This process is indicative of the critical multiculturalism that May and Sleeter have theorized, for the novel carefully renders Blackways of being and thinking that are historically and geographically specific (9). Reckoning with Paul-Edward's fictional experience encourages the kinds of nuanced cultural and historical awareness that can combat longstanding racial stereotypes.

The novel relies on common motifs in American literature, such as the conquering of apparently undeveloped land and the assumption of American exceptionalism, to show the limitations of the individualism Paul has inherited from his white upper-middle-class family. In some respects, Paul-Edward parallels Hansen's Maria in that his innocence is gendered and classed, as is his path to knowledge and self-actualization. As with Maria's "unknowing," Paul-Edward's naiveté threatens to become an entrenched, destructive self-justification and self-assurance that prevent responsible social awareness.[22] Taylor uses conventions of the bildungsroman to expose the inadequacy of Paul-Edward's assumptions, including his unquestioning faith in Jeffersonian agrarianism. *The Land* both dramatizes Paul-Edward's struggles in ways that indict the racism that often controls or cancels out Black labor and creativity, and underscores the importance of collaborating with other African Americans and reinforcing the ties of Black community. His efforts to claim his own land, though ultimately successful, come with grave losses and expose the need to act on a model of Black creativity and achievement that is opposed to the white dominant culture's valuing of individualism over collaboration and community. Paul-Edward's embrace of the collective also involves growing attuned to his own family history and to the larger history of social inequity in the American South, suggesting that cultural and historical awareness is indispensable in working responsibly to realize personal goals.

Taylor's *The Land*, like other narratives about the fictional Logan family, such as *Roll of Thunder, Hear My Cry*, and *Song of the Trees*, is derived from her own family history. Paul-Edward is based on one of her great-grandfathers, who was the child of a former enslaved woman with Indigenous and African American roots and of a Euro-American planter. Although Paul-Edward is born enslaved on his father's spacious Georgia farm, he grows up during Reconstruction with a sense of freedom and entitlement akin to that of his white brothers. The novel explores his losing trust in his white family, taking heed of his mother's admonition that he "get something of his own," and running away with his African American friend Mitchell to achieve independence. Away from his father's influence and land, Paul-Edward relies on his skills with carpentry, horse training, and jockeying to make a living, but he also bumps up against a system sustained by corrupt and complacent white businessmen who suppress or punish Black self-assertion. Though inclined to rely on himself, Paul-Edward ultimately accepts help from Mitchell, Mitchell's widow Caroline, his own sister Cassie, and other trustworthy Black and white members of his community to gain title to the Mississippi land that will be a central setting for other works in the Logan family series.

The title of Taylor's novel refers to this large plot of land, which Paul-Edward falls in love with at first sight, but it also may refer to the hilly, woody forty acres, which they call "the forty," that he and Mitchell must clear before they can legally own any Mississippi land, or it refers to the Georgia estate where both young men grew up. From Paul-Edward's childhood, land has been an important register of personal and familial power. His individualism and freedom are first connected to the openness and freedom of his father's land, a kind of Eden that has allowed him, his sister Cassie, and their half-brothers the freedom to explore and play within nature during their childhoods. Growing up, he has felt a strong connection to his father's land (35), which is conveyed by the text's repetition of the phrase "my daddy's land" or close variants such as "my daddy's forest."[23] The land's beauty, spaciousness, and topographic diversity inspire Paul's curiosity, awe, and confidence: "I knew every bit of the place. I knew every bit of lowland, every rise and knoll, every cave and watering place, every kind of plant and tree" (35). Here Taylor associates Paul-Edward's connection to the land with knowledge, repeating the phrase "I knew," and cataloguing the land's features as a kind of claiming. Like the biblical Adam, Paul-Edward is able to name the contents of an Eden, but his knowledge is incomplete, for land like his father's is unlikely to be owned by a man of color in the postbellum South.

The land is also a realm of unsustainable interracial familial bonding and of inequality among the farm's residents. The first section, entitled "Mitchell," concerns Paul-Edward's difference from the other Black boys on the property, including Mitchell, who becomes his best friend when they are young men. Another early section focuses on Paul-Edward's dawning awareness of his difference from his white family members, including his longtime best friend and youngest white brother Robert.[24] Mitchell and other Black youth are the children of sharecroppers, and Paul-Edward, with his light skin and straight hair, stays away from them whenever he can, playing with his white brothers and reading books the other African American boys cannot read or even own because of their illiteracy and poverty. The contact he does have with Mitchell and the other African American boys takes the form of them harassing or hitting him. After he realizes that Mitchell cannot read and would be willing to accept lessons in reading in exchange for lessons in self-defense, things begin to change in their relationship. Their friendship grows gradually as Paul-Edward's relationship with his half-brother Robert becomes a casualty of the postbellum South's rigid racial stratification. When conflict arises between Paul-Edward and two white supremacist sons of a horse dealer, Robert sides with the latter, and the relationship between the Logan half-brothers never recovers.

Mining the bildungsroman's capacity to detail a protagonist's growth, Taylor uses Paul-Edward's relationship to the Logan family land to reveal his limited understanding of social dynamics and history before he recalibrates his vision of himself, takes the measure of the position postbellum society will allow him to fill, and creates a position that will allow him to thrive. On a trip home to attend his mother's funeral, Paul-Edward goes out to look at this father's property, and after cataloguing aspects of the land, such as the contiguous house, gardens, barn, animal stock, and pastures, the narrator, Paul-Edward, adds,

> Beyond the pasturelands where the horses and cattle grazed were the forests. The cotton fields could not be seen. They, along with all the sharecropping shanties and the people in them, were on the other side of the woods, hidden from view. So was my mam's house. It was mid-spring, and all the grasses were emerald green and all the plants were in bloom. There was *only beauty* before me. (98, emphasis added)

The young Paul-Edward focuses on the parts of his father's property that he finds beautiful, comforting, and orderly at a time of distress, when his beloved mother has died. Although his vision of his father's estate is empowering, it is founded on a willful rejection of the land's complicated history and present social inequalities. The older Paul-Edward's narration presents the more complete reality, including sharecroppers' huts, which once served as enslaved person's huts, and his formerly enslaved mother Deborah's house. Before the white Logans had acquired the land, members of an Indigenous group, the Nation, (most likely the Creek) had occupied it and given it up to avoid war with encroaching white settlers. Signs of such troubling socio-historical and contemporary displacements and denials are "hidden" from view, but as he grows up, Paul-Edward cannot ignore them and the ways in which his own racial difference from his father and brothers matter. He nevertheless keeps his father's manhood and landed success as the standard by which he measures himself, though he will revise his concept of the gentleman farmer in light of his years confronting the systematic denial of African American success. Through plot and character development, *The Land* encourages young readers to learn with Paul-Edward and engage with a history of loss and displacement that southern and US cultural mythology obscure.

Paul-Edward becomes aware of the social weight of his and Cassie's Blackness not from reading the landscape, but from the changing dynamics within his family, which he has long idealized. Although Paul-Edward mostly feels included in his father's family, he chafes at his exclusion from the dinner table when the family has white guests. He breaks from his white family after it becomes clear to him that his father's plan for his future differs from those he has marked out for his white sons. Mr. Logan's plan for Paul-Edward's education is determined by and reinforces the circumscription of his status as African American. Although Mr. Logan sends Robert to an academic institution, he has Paul-Edward apprentice with a master carpenter, in spite of the boy's bookish tendency. And the father does not plan to leave Paul-Edward the Logan real estate holdings, having chosen Robert as the future manager of the estate. Although Mr. Logan believes he is taking a pragmatic course in preparing for Paul-Edward's future economic security, his plan ties them both to a racial status quo. This social order allows opportunities to a small subset of the Black population who can train as artisans or other skilled laborers and attain middle-class standing, but it limits the idealist Paul-Edward's sense of possibility. In the father's opinion, supporting Paul's gift for rearing and racing horses and funding his apprenticeship as a furniture-maker will permit him to maintain a middle-class life. These skills ultimately do help him secure a foothold after he has left his family, but these vocations do not satisfy his spiritual nature in the way overseeing the land of his choice would (Taylor, *The Land* 325).

Paul-Edward's development into a self-possessed man involves him facing and learning how to navigate the Jim Crow restrictions that limited African American power. Although in one scene he passes as white to circumvent white intruders' threat to him and the darker-skinned Mitchell, he is habitual in making sure that people know he is a "man of color." He is insistent that he wants his success to be on his terms, to stem from his abilities, and to express his identity as a gifted African American. R. W. B. Lewis's concept of the American Adam is relevant to Taylor's portrayal of Paul-Edward's growth, for he strives to be a new man and set himself apart from the racist regime that diminishes him. Associated with nineteenth- and twentieth-century literature largely written by white American authors, the American Adam, like the claiming of the West, is associated with a popular version of the American dream that emphasizes freedom, individualism, achievement, and exceptionalism. These motifs help convey the idea of the United States as a free society in which hard work, individual initiative, and ingenuity yield success. The Adamic protagonist who tries to command the American landscape is associated with whiteness, usually a white man's struggle and achievement; the motifs often obscure Indigenous, Chicano, Asian American, and Black histories or subordinate them to the quest for white American preeminence. *The Land* challenges this mythologizing by foregrounding a Black man who is in the process of growing attuned to social experiences that African Americans share across lines of socioeconomic class. Tending to historical and current conditions and reckoning with Jim Crow restrictions and violence, Paul-Edward remakes an American icon of individual exceptionalism into an African American creative, collaborative force.[25]

Taylor's use of comedy in parts of *The Land* does not completely mitigate the seriousness of this purpose, though it does invite young readers into a part of the novel that focuses on Paul-Edward's break from his family and awkwardly absurd attempts to assert his autonomy. Taylor presents Paul-Edward and Mitchell's independence from their families and growing mutual dependence initially as a burlesque of escape that acknowledges but ironically diminishes the threat they face in navigating the possibilities and challenges of the New South. The novel's handling of the pair's early adventure in independence stands in stark contrast to later episodes in which Taylor abandons comedy to show that Black self-assertion can incur horrible consequences. In the section entitled "East Texas," however, Paul-Edward, about fifteen years old, defies his father's authority by agreeing to ride an unfamiliar horse in a race; he uses the opportunity to commit to being on his own and not having a parent advocate for him. When the racehorse owner delays paying Paul-Edward and then grows angry when he demands his pay, the young men choose to run away rather than to seek help from Mr. Logan. Mitchell confronts the horse dealer and forcibly takes money from him to compensate Paul-Edward. Obviously, given the racial dynamics of the time, this act of defiance could result in severe punishment, even lynching, but Taylor accentuates the scene's humor by having the two teenagers hide behind barrels and under a woman's and her daughters' skirts to avoid the father and the racehorse owner. The scene highlights Paul-Edward's lack of control of circumstances, for he is not prepared for Mitchell's defiance; the pair's hiding under a train seat opposes their efforts to stand tall and assert their maturity. Yet the two friends do escape, and their benefactress, the Louisianan gentlewoman who hides them on the train, proves to be an employer who grants them considerable autonomy. The racehorse episode and its aftermath suggest that individual success will be a challenge, but is not impossible and that some social structures may accommodate Black individual spirit. Yet the long section that follows, in which comedy is far less frequent, focuses on the difficulty Paul-Edward has participating in a southern economy in ways that will permit him to fulfill his desires for property.

As the novel progresses, Taylor's portrayal of Paul-Edward's growing comfort with his Blackness complicates the common myth of American self-realization, suggesting, on the one hand, that Black persons' success may be manifested in various ways, and, on the other, that the failure to achieve success needs to be contextualized. After his and Mitchell's two-year stay with the benefactress from the train, Paul-Edward works periodically as a carpenter and teacher, but he and Mitchell, for the most part, are immersed in a working-class existence of physical labor, a modality that Mitchell prefers. Although working at logging camps is physically demanding, Mitchell, a large, exceptionally strong man, finds the work manageable and delights in socializing outside of work hours. The smaller, capable Paul-Edward meets the challenges posed by the labor, but faces discrimination because his appearance and manners differ from those of the other workers: His light skin and tendency to read books and write letters, rather than to socialize in his free time, alienate coworkers. The friends also have very different plans for their lives. In contrast to Paul-Edward, who has his eye on the possibility of farming his own land, Mitchell explains, "All I want is what I'm doin' right now" (153). When Paul-Edward pushes him to explain what he has to show for his labor, his friend remarks, "Freedom t'move and freedom t'be. That's all I want" (153). Mitchell's desire to move and feel free is a way of affirming selfhood and personal desire without becoming ensnared by obligations to others. Though he is loyal to Paul-Edward, helping him escape a worksite where he faces abuse, Mitchell works, and then tries to live as fully as possible, day to day, preferably in a Black social milieu, whether it's Miz Mary's bar or his fiancé Caroline Perry's church-going family. Once he decides to give in to his romantic feelings for Caroline, he changes his mind about the need for land, seeing it as a means to provide for family. For both men, land is a practical investment, but for Paul-Edward, land can have aesthetic and spiritual value that Mitchell does not embrace. The larger plot Paul-Edward longs for inspires emotional transport that brings him into contact with the divine: "My heart soared, higher than any mountain I'd ever imagined, up to God's own perfect clouds, and I felt a peace come over me" (159). The land offers the possibility of transcendence that enables Paul-Edward to feed and use his imagination and step into the role of creator. The vastness and sublimity of land serves as a metonym for the landowner's power and authority, which Paul-Edward cannot realize by racing a horse or making a dresser.

 As a novel about the creation of the Logan family's landed legacy in Mississippi, Taylor's novel acknowledges the little-known history of Mississippi's rate of Black landownership after the Civil War and relates this history to Paul-Edward's and Mitchell's economic agency and model of collaboration. Although Mississippi has long been known for its racist regime and customs, the decades after the Civil War, according to historian John C. Willis, held much promise for African American farming and landowning and for interracial economic connections, with partnerships between white planters and merchants and aspiring Black farmers driving the number of Black landowners to record heights (in the Mississippi Delta, two-thirds of landowners in 1900 were African Americans, but this level of Black landownership was not sustained) (1–3). By the early years of the twentieth century, white stakeholders' priorities changed and they introduced a system of tenant farming into the Mississippi Delta that negatively impacted the number of Black landowners (3). For a few decades after the Civil War, however, African American farmers, in concert with white planters and a white mercantile class, transformed the densely wooded area into land that farmers could gain profit from. *The Land* presents Paul-Edward and Mitchell as part of this generation. The two characters' tolerance for each other's differing relationships to land sends a message to readers about friendship and collaboration. Their alliance shows that Black persons do not all think the same way, and that when there are differences of opinion, cooperation and respect are still possible. When Paul moves on an opportunity to buy land in Mississippi, his plan depends on and stands to benefit himself and Mitchell, who is both independent-minded and trusting in Paul's ambition and business sense.

By pushing against the prevalence of individualism in the American cultural imagination, the novel offers a sustained examination of the power of collaboration. Acting on his mother's advice that he "watch out for [himself] and get something of [his] own," Paul-Edward reaches out to Mitchell to help him realize his goal (90). The friends' collaboration counters the individualism of many iterations of the American dream and contrasts with the hierarchical southern social structure in which they have been groomed. The collaboration is largely among African Americans, which reflects the Black Nationalist commitment to Black communal sufficiency. The two agree to work together to clear a forty-acre plot in a deal that will give them ownership if they finish cutting all the larger trees in two years.[26] They plan to divide the land evenly, sharing food and lodging as they work. And they rely on the labor of other African Americans, especially Nathan Perry, the younger brother of Caroline. Clearing the forty acres within two years proves to be trying, but it enhances the workers' mutual dependence and respect. The community of workers ultimately includes Caroline, once she and Mitchell marry. She insists that the men clear land for a garden, which she manages, selling its produce, along with eggs from her chickens. When Mitchell is killed, a pregnant Caroline joins the logging effort. The group's work on the forty acres constitutes a form of Black enterprise that runs on hard work, dedication, and efficiency (a mix of dreaming, hoping, and rational planning and acting). And although it includes Nathan's carpentry apprenticeship with Paul-Edward, the arrangement avoids the hierarchical, exploitative relations that Mr. Logan's land encodes.

The site is not, however, the separate African American preserve that Paul-Edward and Mitchell would prefer, suggesting the difficulty of creating a space that they can completely control. The owner of the acreage also employs white workmen who regularly come to the tract to pick up the cut lumber, though they are not individuated and do not interact with Paul-Edward and Mitchell, who accept their presence as part of Paul-Edward and the owner's agreement. More troubling to Paul-Edward and Mitchell is the presence of Wade Jamison and John Wallace, two white boys who are attracted to the logging project and who offer assistance. Paul-Edward and Mitchell are wary of the boys' involvement, for they increasingly see the land as their refuge from the infringements of white society. Wade, who is solidly middle-class and liberal-minded, comes to the property both to help and to play with Nathan. John, who is poor and estranged from family, has bonded with an African American laborer who Paul-Edward and Mitchell employ. The two boys represent a physical mobility and metaphysical freedom that Black boys and men lack in the larger society, and the prerogative and privilege that Paul-Edward assumed as a boy. Although neither Wade nor John directly upsets Paul-Edward's plan, and Wade's father proves helpful when Paul-Edward finalizes a deal on his preferred tract, John draws a family member, Digger, who kills Mitchell.[27] As a white man who lacks means, Digger is angered by both Mitchell's and Paul-Edward's self-confidence, competence, and economic promise. He represents a deadly form of the racism that manifests itself in other ways in the pair's everyday lives, and always calls on the two men to restrict their self-expression and ambition.

Mitchell has sought to limit the damaging effects of the white gaze by immersing himself in a Black world, except for the necessary, brief interactions with white bosses. It is significant, then, that he is killed on what he and Paul-Edward have come to call "the forty," but the novel suggests that the power of white supremacy can overwhelm Black efforts at self-preservation. Mitchell is punished for not following Digger's command to retrieve his little brother, for resisting a threatened whipping, and finally for witnessing Digger's fearful, undignified response to his firmness. Paul-Edward's self-confidence also threatens the white power structure and imperils his plans for land. Unlike Mitchell, Paul-Edward acts on the realization that he must maintain some connections to white society, but their efficacy is tenuous because of the prevalence of white supremacism. Only rarely does a white person actually acknowledge and support Paul-Edward's full abilities, and not just those skills that serve the status quo. A white banker, for instance, who praises his furniture-making is reluctant to grant him a loan and advises him to become a share-cropper. The owner of the forty acres, Filmore

Granger, lies that Paul-Edward and Mitchell, either as a result of deceit or incompetence, have not complied with the terms of contract so that he can renege on his promise to transfer ownership to them. The narration's emphasis has detailed their proficiency and care, delegitimizing these doubts about their work and providing readers with examples of the kinds of explanations often used to account for Black people's absence from certain kinds of jobs and other kinds of socioeconomic opportunities.

The Land also counters the concepts of individualism and anti-Black patriarchy, reflecting a Black feminist emphasis on community, collective action, Black women's creative contributions, and antiracism (The Combahee River Collective 235; D. King 312). Once Paul-Edward's sense of his Black selfhood is secure, he can accept help from others without sacrificing his integrity. Paul-Edward's ability to carry through on his plan to own the superior, larger plot of land he longs for depends not only on his and Mitchell's hard labor, but also on him accepting assistance from a Black matriarchal network and from socially progressive white men like Wade's father, Charles Jamison, and Luke Sawyer, a white storekeeper. Each of these men is willing to establish relationships with Paul-Edward through which they build mutual respect. Sawyer sells Paul-Edward's furniture, and Paul-Edward depends on Sawyer's tools, salesmanship, and community standing and contacts; notably, Sawyer recognizes that Paul-Edward is a better carpenter than he is, but he respects the young man's ability rather than denying or feeling threatened by it. Paul-Edward, while still in his teens, negotiates a fifty-fifty split in the profit on the furniture he makes for Sawyer to sell. Jamison, already a holder of many acres, agrees to hold off from buying the portion of an estate that Paul-Edward has chosen. He risks asking Jamison to accompany him when he goes to buy the tract. These partnerships do enable Paul-Edward to succeed in purchasing the land he prefers, and they offer young readers a message about the possibilities of cross-racial alliances that do not serve an unjust status quo, but that lay a foundation for a more just and inclusive society. Whereas Jamison and Sawyer see and accept Paul-Edward on his own terms, most white persons that he encounters are not willing.

The novel opposes anti-Black patriarchy by showcasing Black women's creative contributions. In addition to trusting these white powerbrokers, Paul-Edward also gains financial support to buy the superior land because he reaches out to his family to explain what he needs and they work together to heed his call for help. His sister Callie, who is of Black, white, and Indigenous descent like Paul-Edward, sells their mother's land to help finance the purchase and provides him with money the mother had put aside for him. She also advocates for Paul-Edward with their white family members. Callie's, their deceased mother Deborah's, and Caroline's inputs are indispensable, further underscoring the communal nature of his achievement. That Paul-Edward depends on Black and Indigenous women, and not simply on powerful white men, sends a powerful feminist message that challenges the individualism of the dominant culture's conceptualizations of achievement. Moreover, Paul-Edward and Caroline's marriage ensures that he will not be able to settle into complacency, for she is highly attuned to power imbalances and injustices and active in addressing them.[28] At least within *The Land*, Taylor suggests that addressing systemic racism entails concerted efforts by an alliance of African American men and women, with strategic interracial partnerships.

Because of Mitchell's death, Paul-Edward's two hundred acres will not be a mirror copy of his father's land, just as he will not be able to wield the same kind of authority his father carries. Paul-Edward's and Mitchell's experience with land in Mississippi underscores the precarious nature of African Americans' command of real estate, even as it portrays the ingenuity and determination that led some African Americans to acquire and maintain it. Paul-Edward's acreage will include Mitchell's grave, not as an obscured sign of slavery and sharecropping, but as a reminder of African Americans' dangerous struggle to establish their autonomy. This emphasis sends a message to Taylor's audience that African American successes cannot be divorced from sacrifice and loss, and that these successes and losses must be acknowledged and remembered. The large plot of land becomes the basis for another phase of Paul-Edward's life, for he begins a family with Mitchell's widow Caroline, who gives birth to her and Mitchell's child and who brings her own communitarian vision to their family.[29] Caroline reasons that Paul-Edward needs to preserve and share his story in its fullness, and though she assumes the audience will be their children, her insistence that he write about his life reinforces the idea that stories of everyday struggles and achievements are essential for understanding history. Paul-Edward's story combines an emphasis on his self-interest with his interdependence with family and community members, reflecting a balance struck in many African American children's books. It is also notable that his story highlights the destructive forces of the larger society, as well as its fragile supports for positive change. As an embodiment of enterprise and innovation, Paul-Edward is a Black Adam who, with the help and sacrifice of loved ones, cocreates a world he can share with his family, a home that is not completely removed from the dangers of a white supremacist society, but one that proves to be an inspiration and refuge for current and subsequent generations of the family.

Although *The Land* might be read as an attempt to incorporate an African American man into a standard narrative of American promise and success, its revelations about the injustice of the New South's agrarian economy complicate such an interpretation. The novel provides young readers with a sense of the challenges Black rural laborers faced during the Reconstruction era. And the novel's nineteenth-century trials resonate with the many burdens and obstacles African Americans have faced in their efforts to get or maintain property in the twentieth and twenty-first centuries. Indeed, assaults on African American autonomy, including land ownership, continue for subsequent generations of the Logan family. In *The Well*, which comes next in the family's history, Caroline, now a mother of four children, confronts envious, angry white persons resentful about the bounty of the family's land. Threats to the family's possession of land are central to many books in the Logan series, as is the family's spirited defense of their, and other Black community members', rights. Given the persistent racism in American society, the Logan land represents a communal effort to claim and sustain a safe space over generations, and this entails engaging in agricultural and social practices that benefit family and a wider community in a context in which violent anti-Black sentiment persists. Paul-Edward's individualist drive and vision in *The Land* are certainly central, but they are enmeshed with Mitchell's, Caroline's, and other family members' and community helpers' generative energies.

The Land also provides contemporary readers with a message about the need to care for the land, rather than to exploit it, perhaps a surprising emphasis given the role of logging in Paul-Edward's and Mitchell's lives. Their work clearing "the forty" and their itinerant labor at logging camps and, more rarely, at turpentine camps, reflects the New South's tendencies to shape the land for profitability, rather than to respect its integrity. Yet Paul-Edward in particular expresses concern about the extent to which turpentine mining damages trees, a concern through which Taylor acknowledges many African Americans' difficult history with "woods work," which involved exploiting not only the land's resources, but also African American laborers (Johnson and MacDaniel 52, 54, 56). His preference for the larger plot of land may stem from its pristineness and from the promise that its riches are available to him without dramatically altering the landscape. Of course, it may be that this land, which summons memories of his father's land, is attractive because the historical signs of former occupants, including Indigenous persons, have been destroyed. The narrative does not provide a history of the land. Instead, it suggests that going forward, Paul-Edward, Caroline, and their descendants will be loving caretakers; within the novel, gaining access to the land allows

Paul-Edward to pursue his preferred way of interacting with nature. This is perhaps best demonstrated in his relationship with horses. His talent with horses stems from his ability to become attuned to their character in order to build trust; he lets the horses know him. Although this process is designed to allow him to ride the horses and arguably, exploit the relationship, he sees himself as working with each horse, respecting its peculiarity, and not imposing his needs to the detriment of the horse. Similarly, his plans for the land involve responsiveness to the land's features. *The Land* does not go into any detail about the development of sustainable farming, a field in which George Washington Carver had a leading role. Yet Taylor suggests that Paul-Edward and Caroline tend to the land in ways that protect and enrich it, and thus provide resources for their family, and in times of hardship, members of the larger community.

SPIRIT LAND

The Glory Field, Myers's multigenerational saga, also insists that Black personal achievement depends on community and intergenerational connections, including the continuing influence of Black ancestors. Examining the lives of the African American Lewis family of Curry Island, South Carolina, *The Glory Field* presents tending to the past and tending to family as necessary for orienting African Americans to live fruitfully in the present and future. Like other freedom narratives, *The Glory Field* acknowledges the abuse and trauma of living in racist, stratified societies, even as it shows African Americans' ability to create opportunities to express their autonomy. More than the other texts discussed in this chapter, Myers's novel portrays African sources of Black American cultural practice and cognitive frameworks. It also highlights familial and community connections between historical eras, facilitating young readers' thinking about how past responses to social injustice matter to subsequent generations, providing hope, insight, and models of active engagement. The novel's balancing of synchronic and diachronic representations of Black historical experience shows how cultural influences and familial character manifested themselves at different times in response to historically specific challenges and pressures. This narrative structure encourages readers to consider how history remains important within their own lives and communities. *The Glory Field* epitomizes the freedom narratives' emphasis on communal supports for confronting and navigating racism. In variations on this theme in different phases of history, the novel is indicative of the "critical multiculturalism" that Melamed sees as an important antiracist intervention (102): Repeatedly, Myers shows societal structures that disadvantage African Americans and demonstrates how young protagonists navigate these obstacles by carefully thinking about and observing the world, drawing on their historical awareness to make decisions, and gaining insight and support from nurturing elders and peers.

Myers's novel consists of six sections, each of which follows one or more youths who are in the process of learning how to act with integrity and force given the constraints of racism.[30] Sections are set during the Civil War, the turn of the twentieth century, the Great Migration, and the civil rights movement, with the action in each case foregrounding a young protagonist's "freedom dream" or connection to the "glory field," family land in coastal South Carolina where their ancestors are buried. The final section presents two teen cousins from the urban North who journey to the area for a reunion at which the family discusses its plan to transform the land into a resort. The first and briefest episode, however, set in July 1753, focuses on the founder of the Lewis family, Muhammad, who has been captured in Africa. Muhammad's episode, set on the ship that takes him away from Africa, explores the emotional and physical hardship of his displacement, including his uncertainty about his beloved parents. The section ends with him shackled but "trying to think of being free again" (8). This will to be free is central to his legacy, as is his West African birth. Although the next sections are increasingly distant from Muhammad chronologically, each presents him or the burial ground, as a source of remembrance and regeneration for later members of the Lewis family.

As the title *The Glory Field* suggests, land is not simply a place that marks Black exploitation and suffering, but also a locus of generative experiences that need to be preserved and passed on. In a Sunday sermon at the gravesite, Moses, one of Muhammad's great-grandsons, explains that the land is "precious" because it holds the spirits of the community's ancestors: "Lord, we have raised up from this ground and have lain down in it for nearly one hundred and fifty years. . . . And we know we might not be able to hang on to it. But Lord, everybody we ever loved is buried here" (78). The land holds Moses's and his people's history, a long history of turning the soil and reaping a harvest for white persons, but also of using the land for their own self- and group actualization. If the land that Paul-Edward Logan loves is a source of wonder and awe that writes him into the literature of American Romanticism, the Lewis family's land taps the spirit of bravery and resilience that defined an African-born ancestor, Muhammad Bilal, and others of his generation who, even in slavery, tended their "freedom dream" (31).

Coming into a productive relationship with both Muhammad and his burial ground is instrumental to establishing personal authority as a Lewis. His descendants associate him and his burial site with various powers that support their ability to survive with dignity. In the nineteenth century, for instance, the plot, though still owned by the white Lewis family, becomes the site for marriages between Black Lewis family members and their romantic partners and for naming ceremonies for babies born into the family. These rituals defy the dominant class's conception of enslaved persons as tools that do not require social institutions that affirm choice and future possibilities. The rituals and the land offer affirmations of selfhood and collectivity, and acknowledge the Black community's desire to act on their choices. The site offers "direction from the elders," whose spirits confer blessings on the living as they embark on new phases of their lives (13). The novel suggests that the place's ceremonial function is veiled from the white owner of the property, but is knowledge shared within the enslaved community. Long before they own the land, the family uses it in ways that express their will and counter the enslaver's wishes, as when they bury community members there who have fought or otherwise defied the enslaving class. The land, though associated with their enslavement, also signifies their power to express their desire for ongoing connection to the dead and to act on their desire for some control of their lives. By the novel's third section, which is set in 1900, the Black Lewises own land that has previously been part of the plantation on which they were enslaved, including the burial plot, showing the ongoing importance of their family's history and the spirits of the dead. Until the late twentieth century, the land proves to be a resource for strengthening themselves and reinforcing self-confidence and familial ties, which the novel suggests are interdependent.

The parts of the novel set in 1864 and 1900 both demonstrate ways that Myers portrays the empowering forces of Muhammad's memory and the land. In each case, freedom and achievement are circumscribed or limited, bound as they are to the legacy of slavery, but young protagonists use their ingenuity to press against confinement and assert their rights to freedom. In 1864, the fourteen-year-old Lizzy, an adopted member of the family, shows her allegiance with Muhammad's model of leadership when she rejects her peer's opinion that the stories about Muhammad are outdated and ponders what he would have said about his great-great- grandson Lem's attempt at escape. Lizzy, though fearful, shows courage and a commitment to her friendship with Lem when she visits him to provide water and offers encouraging words "so he wouldn't feel so all alone" (34). She ends up running away, too, after the overseer catches her with Lem, and the two youths, along with an older Black fugitive, defend themselves against the man. The episode ends with Lizzy at some distance from the plantation and the glory field, but she is still animated by the spirit of defiance and commitment to freedom she associates with the land. She joins a company of Black Union soldiers to support their efforts to win freedom for enslaved persons.

The land is more central in the 1900 narrative, in which Elijah, the section's main character, a sixteen-year-old descendant of Muhammad and son of Lizzy, commits himself to maintaining the burial ground. Early in the episode, an elder assigns him the task of keeping it tidy, but Elijah goes on to extend this responsibility to include helping keep the land in the family when they are confronted with a required tax that seems designed to discourage or terminate Black landownership. The glory field serves as a metonymy for the family, as well as a means by which they express their extended family's culture. During a talk with the elder, Elijah asks about the graves' decoration with glass and shells, which relate the site to West African burial practices. Traditionally, such decorations signaled survivors' ongoing care for the dead and the dead person's continued journey in the afterlife, which was associated with water (Vlach 143). Elijah's fight to save the family's land symbolizes the family's efforts to maintain its autonomy in the Jim Crow South. When a white child from a wealthy family goes missing during a storm, Elijah, recalling Paul-Edward in *The Land*, bargains with the child's father to raise the reward to an amount that would allow his elders to cover the tax.[31] His boldness in negotiating the increase and his exceptional skill at navigating waters around the Sea Islands inspire anger and anxiety among the white men interested in the reward. Yet Elijah remains firm and proves successful, along with his cousin Abby, in saving the child and claiming the reward. Myers suggests that Elijah's courage and poise, whether in navigating storm-tossed waters or racist social policies, are informed by his efforts to preserve his family and to respect their values. The novel also shows that Elijah's dedication to family and to self-expression carries danger and occasions sacrifice. Because of his effectiveness and bravery, Elijah is threatened with punishment and, heeding his family's advice, decides to travel to the North.

Through the experiences of Elijah's children and grandchildren, *The Glory Field* represents the geographical diversity of African American life and abiding connections between the Black North and Black South. The novel also demonstrates, however, that these connections can be tested, and require a full, conscious engagement with the land and the history so that their connection remains manifest and important. This is evidenced in the section dated 1994, in which two young New Yorkers, the now deceased Elijah's great-grandsons, journey to Curry Island for a reunion. Malcolm, the main character, is given the responsibility of ensuring that his cousin Sheppard, who is addicted to crack, attends. Their journey back to their family includes one trial after another, from Shep using his plane fare on drugs to getting motion sickness on a train. After they are left behind at a rest stop, they accept a ride from a trucker who has room for them in a trailer holding hides. Barely able to breathe in the hot, smelly, dark trailer, Malcolm reckons with the misery that traveling with Shep has caused, realizing "Shep was an anchor that made moving on hard" (340). Feeling trapped, he nevertheless understands that Shep's entrapment is greater: "The chains could rattle, but they weren't broken," which is manifest when Shep struggles with withdrawal from cocaine and Malcolm witnesses his suffering and tries, unsuccessfully, to provide succor. Though the circumstances are vastly different, the cousins' wrenching experience recalls Muhammad's confinement in the slave ship, and serves as part of their initiation into a fuller, empathetic understanding of their family history. This initiation continues when they reach Curry Island and must help harvest its last crops.

Myers does not provide many scenes of farm labor in the earlier parts of *The Glory Field*, but he renders Malcolm's work beside an elder, Planter, the great-grandson of Moses, in some detail to underscore not only the gifts of the land, but also the nurturing and guidance the older generation offers the young as they learn to act responsibly and creatively. Planter goads Malcolm to rise to the challenge of the land, which entails reaping the crop and not simply doing the work he feels comfortable with. Although the harvest is important, Planter urges him to think about how past farmers in the family must have felt: "Just think how it must've been working out here before we got our freedom. . . . Working out here all day for nothing but the right to get up and do it the next day" (356). In addition to inviting Malcolm to think about the injustice of this hard, forced labor, Planter speaks with him about the change that emancipation allowed: "cold water to a thirsty soul" (357)—a metaphor that resonates with Malcolm's recent draining travel by trailer. Being able to use the land as free people was empowering, and Planter wants Malcolm to be mindful of this empowerment and the more frustrating, painful experience of forced and uncompensated labor. This history lesson involves Malcolm using his mind and body to envision the past. It also is shaped by Planter drawing Malcolm into call and response, a traditional form of African American communication that depends on hearing and affirming a speaker. Myers's choice of this rhetorical structure reinforces the pair's psychological connection and sets a standard for teaching history experientially and empathetically, for Malcolm is called on to be responsive to the subject matter.

In focusing on Malcolm's reckoning with familial history, this penultimate section of the novel also has him witness the family's embrace of Shep, who continues to suffer from the effects of cocaine withdrawal. Malcolm watches from a distance as Shep tries to work in the field and falters. Planter responds to Malcolm's appraisal that Shep needs assistance with the authoritative, "his help starts from within himself" (367). Yet this self-care is enveloped by the family's supportive energies. As Planter and Malcolm work, for instance, they watch Planter's daughter-in-law kneel beside Shep, patiently allowing him to rise to a standing position, regroup, and resume work. Malcolm is consumed by the hope that his cousin will continue his healing, which he understands will be a gradual process. He also sees that as the field work continues, it is not a mindless activity, but one bursting with the spirit of hope, rejuvenation, and belonging: "He wanted with all of his heart for Shep to make it through just this one reunion, maybe just this one day, maybe just one more row of sweet potatoes. Malcolm looked around and saw that the work had picked up again. They were all glad to see Shep on his feet" (366). Here, as elsewhere in *The Glory Field*, healing is supported by the life-affirming powers of the family and its land. Like the earlier focal characters, Malcolm realizes that as life continues, and its many demands and challenges remain, the land and the family are resources through which selfhood can be empowered and expressed.

As the twentieth century progresses in Myers's novel, more of the Lewis family live in the urban North and engage in nonagricultural labor, but the glory field retains its importance. In deciding to convert their land on Curry Island into a resort, the elders are acknowledging their desire both to keep ownership and to transform the land in light of demographic shifts, including the marginalization of the family farm and the growth of the hospitality industry. The conversion will allow the family to continue, and even spread, its power and influence by entering a sector of the American economy, the hospitality industry, that has long been controlled by corporations run by non-Black persons. In South Carolina, as in other parts of the southern United States, the hospitality industry long exploited Black labor as it catered to white customers and promulgated a myth of caring service that often excluded African American patronage (Szczesiul 180). In creating a resort owned and managed by the family, the Lewises are challenging that system, continuing to exert their freedom, and opening parts of their rich, transformative land to an inclusive customer base. The land carries the pain and sacrifices of their past, as well as the healing and community that have helped the family survive. The elderly Luvenia Lewis, daughter of Elijah and a successful Chicago businesswoman, points out, the family "can look forward, and we can look back, too" (368), indicating that the Lewis family's and the land's legacy, will continue to be honored. Although the resort will locate its tennis courts where enslaved persons' quarters once stood, it will maintain the glory field where the family ancestors are buried.

Although my focus has largely been on stories about life in the eighteenth and nineteenth centuries, *The Glory Field* acknowledges that African Americans' fight for freedom is not specific to these earlier eras. Myers's novel provides multiple portrayals of Black youth defining themselves in an American society, which in spite of demographic and political changes, has maintained structures that demand African American conformity, silence, and subordination. In various manners, the novel shows that protagonists' self-definition involves being responsive not only to their developing selfhood but also to familial tradition, which encourages an active, creative response to society's injustices. In factoring land ownership into this process of identity formation and self-expression, Myers, like Nelson, Hansen, and Taylor, recognizes the important role of real estate in measures of individual agency and group power. Acknowledging African Americans' socioeconomic struggles and achievements, *The Glory Field*, like *The Land, Home Is With Our Family*, and *My Seneca Village*, insists on telling African American stories that do not reinforce dominant cultural narratives that foreground individual success, transcend ancestry, and equate success with the power to consume America's, or the world's, bounty. Accordingly, the books support critical multicultural initiatives that balance attention to systemic problems that impact African Americans and to modes of resistance. Each text encourages young readers to see Black success in ways that depart from stereotypical ideas of American social success: for instance, through Shep finding the inner strength to stand on his family's land as they provide support and encouragement, or through Maria recognizing her ability to organize an antislavery crafts group, or through Paul-Edward and Caroline gazing in awe at land they will own (and share with others).

Arguably, some narratives bear a complicated relationship to neoliberalism, not simply questioning or critiquing capitalism and its inequities, but also echoing popular celebrations of capitalism and glossing over its problems. Such mixed messages can foster readers' critical thinking about the difficulty of creating and maintaining alternatives to flawed, inequitable systems, but they may dilute a text's radical edge. *The Land* is critical about the role of Paul-Edward and Mitchell's logging and turpentine extraction work within the New South's economic rehabilitation, which benefited industrialists more than ordinary workers and the landscape. And the novel shows how carpentry, which Paul-Edward likes to do and at which he excels, can be a trap: it is the work an affluent class of white southerners expects him to do to help them display their economic power. Yet this revelatory aspect of the novel coexists with Paul-Edward training Caroline's brother Nathan in carpentry so that he can contribute to the elite market for well-made consumer goods. Perhaps more problematically, the plan in *The Glory Field* to establish a vacation resort can be seen as imitating white ventures that capitalize on consumers' desires for leisure and escape on southern, coastal plantations. Joining the ranks of resort owners in the late twentieth-century hospitality industry would seem a clear example of assimilating to a capitalist system that runs on exploitation, escapism, and cultural erasure. By ending on a business-friendly note, Myers's novel reflects a tendency of some, but not all, freedom narratives from the early 2000s. Although narratives like *The Land*, *The Glory Field*, and *Copper Sun* challenge the practices of the dominant culture, the novels show characters seeking to express their freedom through its channels, which can lead to readers' complacency about socioeconomic disparities and the intractability of racism. It is notable, however, that these forms of assimilation resonate with the phrase W. E. B. Du Bois uses to describe Frederick Douglass's leadership: "assimilation *through* self-assertion" (126; emphasis added). When applied to the freedom narratives' concentration on Black selfhood that is infused by Black culture, assimilation is not a mere capitulation to the dominant culture's structures and expectations; instead, the process entails negotiating the differences between cultures, and being creative in maintaining one's allegiances and standing up for oneself.

Whether radical, more muted, or ideologically mixed, freedom narratives insist on Black protagonists' confrontation with social challenges. They encourage readers, in turn, to confront the difficulties of the past and the present. The power of Black creativity is central, and this power is expressed through endeavors that demonstrate the need for collaboration, mutual respect, and intergenerational alliance, important Black cultural values. In stories about aspiring to own or keep land, Black youth show their agency in numerous ways, but the common thread, as in other freedom narratives, is the complementarity of self, community, and culture. Black community and culture have their rules and traditions, but provide structure for both maintaining the ways of the past and embracing change and innovation. They foreground learning, growth, partnership, innovation, and remembrance. The relationship between self and community is rich and fluid, allowing room for young and older characters' growth, self-awareness, partnership, and innovation. The narratives do more than offer information about the past; they open up spaces for readers and viewers to think about the challenges of the past and the present, and to experiment, along with protagonists, with ways of surviving alone and together with integrity and creativity.

AFTERWORD

Research methods that explore the experiences and perspectives of everyday Black people became more central to professional historians' work in the second half of the twentieth century. This historiography also acknowledged and examined the continuity of Black resistance to racist cultural practices and social structures. Yet as E. James West has observed, these scholarly developments were met with corporate America's, conservative politicians', the mainstream media's, and many Americans' embrace of a commemorative historicizing that focused on select Black heroes who embodied individualism and exceptionalism. Commemorative projects can be balanced and thorough, offering keen insight into a historical figure's contributions and contexts. Yet commemorative African American history, according to West, often disengages Black historical achievements from systematic analysis of economic oppression and racism (112).

As an example, West cites the Seagram Company's 1970s "Negro achievement calendar," which highlighted a different great African American each month (97). He also argues that in the commemorative approach to history, Dr. Martin Luther King Jr. appears as "a champion of colorblind individualism" (114), rather than a searching activist who fought systemic economic and racial injustices (114). And King is not alone. Frederick Douglass has also been pressed into serving as a heroic embodiment of American individualism and freedom (Kennedy). Focusing on African American triumphs can lead away from the particular challenges that figures like Douglass and King faced and diminish the contributions of networks of their supporters. The process inscribes acceptable leaders into a cultural narrative that validates the United States' exceptional status as a nation that facilitates self-realization and social success such as theirs. As West has observed, the dominant culture has tolerated and even embraced versions of Black history that serve and reinforce the myth that the United States is a progressive nation that grants opportunities to all. Yet books that show African Americans' struggles with systemic racism remain subject to challenges and bans, as the last couple of years have indicated.

Education scholar Jarvis R. Givens has argued that suppressing African American voices and perspectives has been one of the constants in American life ("The Fugitive Life"). And African Americans' resistance to this suppression has been one of the constants in the African American and American experience ("The Fugitive Life"). Freedom narratives are part of this resistance. These narratives resist cultural amnesia and myopia, African American stereotypes, and other forms of cultural suppression that penalize African American racial and cultural differences. While acknowledging the pain and suffering many Black persons experienced historically, freedom narratives portray many Black people's ability to survive and, in some cases, thrive, in spite of social oppression. In the texts, Black power is manifested in various generative ways: through staying attuned to Black ethnic or national roots, through learning, through establishing and preserving community, through working and playing on one's own terms, and through acting on Black tradition in creative ways. These pursuits are grounded in Black epistemologies, and do not function to validate the idea of the American way as one of justice and inclusion. If freedom narratives reconstruct young Black persons' powers, and seek out the joys and successes of their everyday lives, they expose a dominant US culture that touts the myth of equal access to social freedom, even as it exploits, defunds, and otherwise oppresses and kills Black people. The narratives show how African American achievement too often occurs in spite of the dominant culture and its agents, rather than because of them.

As revelatory stories about Black history, freedom narratives are not about indoctrination. The freedom narratives I explore in this book are representative of the genre in showing how Black authors have been able, as Morrison has observed of her own work, to find "ways to free up the language from its sometimes sinister, frequently lazy, almost always predictable employment of racially informed and determined chains" (*Playing* xi). The narratives free young readers to engage critically with history and encourage them to think about alternatives to longstanding myths of American individualism and colorblind opportunity. They interpret the past, using historical sources that suggest ways ordinary Black persons saw the world and lived in it. Building on a Black aesthetic that respects Black perspectives and approaches to life, particularly those not overly influenced by opposing white cultural values, the narratives provide a necessary refutation to historical portrayals that deny Black interiority and experience, rely on stereotypes of Blackness, or gloss over systemic obstacles that impacted African Americans. The narratives counter commemorative accounts that obscure the workings of Black cultures that fostered many individuals' and groups' achievements. Insisting on the importance and distinctiveness of Black cultures, freedom narratives provide readers with frameworks for constructing for themselves an inclusive understanding of history as a complex, contingent set of stories, experiences, orientations, images, messages, and other phenomena. The narratives, I argue, are essential parts of the rich, diverse body of African American children's literature that fosters young audiences' critical thinking about the powers of selfhood within particular contexts of nurture and oppression, and about the contours and legacies of past injustices. I hope that *Tending to the Past* inspires more scholarly attention to the texts' dynamics and to actual readers' engagement with their interpretations of historical Black power.

NOTES

INTRODUCTION

1. I regularly taught Frederick Douglass's, Harriet Jacobs's, Henry Bibb's, and Booker T. Washington's narratives, as well as contemporary fiction about slavery by Morrison, Butler, Charles Johnson, Sherley Anne Williams, and other Black authors.

2. Throughout this book, I follow the *New York Times* and several other news organizations' style guidelines in capitalizing Black, but not white. See Coleman. As she explains, the word "Black" parallels other descriptors that refer to persons who share a culture. When relevant, I use Black synonymously with African American. I do not capitalize "white," because it does not designate a shared culture; also, hate groups often capitalize the word to express white supremacism.

3. I borrow the phrase, "group victimization," from C. Johnson, who is focusing specifically on longstanding patterns within African American literature for adults. Yet much popular culture that has represented Black history has relied on the assumption that Black persons were only victims of slavery, except for those who were able to liberate themselves or benefit from the efforts of abolitionists, who are often assumed to be white.

4. Gates ("Who Really") offers useful information about the myths of the Underground Railroad and gives estimates of the number of escapes, though the webpage's language is outdated. The webpage refers to excellent scholarly resources on the topic of Black self-emancipation. Add to these Hudson, which is an invaluable resource for young researchers.

5. Freedom narratives in these other categories arguably include such picture books as Nikole Hannah-Jones, Renée Watson, and Nikkolas Smith's *The 1619 Project: Born on the Water* (2021), Schele Williams and Tonya Engel's *Your Legacy: A Bold Reclaiming of our Enslaved History* (2021), Carole Boston Weatherford's *Freedom in Congo Square* (2016), and Ashley Bryan's *Freedom Over Me: Eleven Slaves, Their Lives and Dreams Brought to Life* (2016).

6. For further consideration of the auteur theory, including critiques, see Mast "The Film Artist."

7. Bolden's *Crossing Ebenezer Creek* and Hansen's *The Heart Calls Home* are two examples.

8. Also, see D. Johnson 3–9, for a thoughtful discussion of the importance of Black authorship.

9. Rizzuto's essay "'Good Cause for Living': Environmental Justice in Virginia Hamilton's *M.C. Higgins, the Great*" drew me back to this quotation. Austin relates Hamilton's work to the Black Arts Movement, noting that it "expands and challenges scholarly conceptions of the BAM by reworking hegemonic white myth-making and story-telling tropes, challenging the BAM's focus on mythic representations of Africa, presenting a non-misogynist reading of black masculinity, and contributing to the sociopolitical awareness of child readers while building a positive image of black identity and black culture" (263–64).

10. K. Alexander's book also recognizes that fighting against slavery may take many forms. The mentor who speaks in this scene kills herself after attacking enslavers aboard the ship carrying her and Kofi to America.

11. Though award-winning, the project has attracted attacks from both liberal and conservative critics. See Serwer's overview of debates surrounding the project.

12. James Berry's *Ajeemah and His Son* (1992) and Kwame Alexander's *The Door of No Return* (2022) are examples that refute this.

CHAPTER 1. FREEDOM NARRATIVES, HISTORY, AND BLACK AGENCY

1. Collins and Crawford 7–8.

2. For a fuller discussion of the intellectual and political foundations for neo-slave narratives, see Rushdy chapter 3.

3. Martin 50 mentions other African American authors and illustrators of Lester's and Hamilton's generation, including Tom Feelings, Jerry Pinkney, Eloise Greenfield, and Leo Dillon, whose work bears the influence of the social change movements of the 1950s and 1960s.

4. Although there is no simple correlation between college attendance and salaried, middle-class labor, economists have long acknowledged that those who attend and graduate from college are more likely to get higher-paying jobs.

5. According to Melamed's timeline, Curtis's novel bridges two different kinds or phases of multicultural engagement: "liberal" and "neoliberal." The latter supports a new world order that centers on the market and tries to make everything serve it (41).

6. For a discerning discussion of the Black Arts Movement's enduring influence on picture books, see Martin 73–81.

7. This is not to deny the efforts of earlier writers of children's literature that was shaped by a Black orientation. See Tolson "The Black Aesthetic within Children's Literature"; Smith; Capshaw; Roethler 57, 63–67.

8. This emphasis informs BAM literature and post-BAM literature. Baraka's provocative poem "Black Art," a signal BAM statement, ends with the affirmation of "a Black Poem and a Black World" and declares "Let the World be a Black Poem, / And let all Black people speak this Poem / Silently or LOUD." As Smethurst has pointed out, Morrison, whose literary career largely occurred after the end of the BAM, was greatly influenced

by its nationalist commitments and spoke eloquently about her work's foregrounding of Black worldviews: "I've spent my entire writing life trying to make sure that the white gaze was not the dominant gaze in any of my books" (*Toni Morrison*). Morrison also edited *The Black Book*, a compendium of documents about Black historical experience.

9. This concern with reaching an inclusive racial audience resonates with Langston Hughes's conception of the audience for his and coauthor Milton Meltzer's *A Pictorial History of the Negro*, first published in 1956, with new editions appearing in the 1960s and beyond.

10. Dubey 25–27 contrasts BAM men's reliance in their writing on a linear progress from oppression to liberation with BAM women writers' reliance on cycles that relate a narrative present with past economic and social oppression.

11. The interplay between adult and child reading and sources of information can be complicated. Butler, Book-in-Common Lecture, identified Lester's *To Be a Slave* as an important source for *Kindred*.

12. Loewen's "Slave Narratives" focuses on studies by Blassingame, Escott, Genovese, Gutman, and Rawick, and reflects his perspective as a sociologist. Faust, a historian, offers a more recent appraisal of these and other authors' histories of slavery. See Stevenson for a discussion of earlier historiography that uses slave narratives.

13. Nichols's *Many Thousand Gone* (1963) was a key forerunner that Lester acknowledges in his bibliography. Nichols's book also presents many enslaved persons' testimony about a range of experiences and includes Nichols's scholarly voice.

14. Narratives originally published before 1865 that were republished in the 1960s include *Narrative of Events in the Life of William Green, (Formerly a Slave.), Written by Himself* (1853) and Samuel Ringgold Ward's *Autobiography of a Fugitive Negro: His Anti-Slavery Labours in the United States, Canada and England* (1855).

15. D. Johnson 5 also points out that publication of African American authors became more common with the Black Power movement's emergence.

16. Bishop's *Free Within Ourselves* provides an excellent history of African American children's book writers and illustrators. Especially pertinent to this discussion are her sections focusing on the 1960s and afterward. See, 133–48, for instance, her examination of the expansion of subject matter in Black picture books during the 1990s' push for multiculturalism.

17. For a nuanced examination of the racial power dynamics in neo-abolitionist fiction for young readers, see Connolly 173–78.

18. Together the McKissacks wrote several nonfiction titles about persons or experiences in the nineteenth and early twentieth centuries. Yet their purview was actually broader, including books about later twentieth-century figures. I realize that my wording here alludes to Lawrence Levine's groundbreaking *Black Culture and Consciousness*.

19. See, for instance, Hamilton's discussion of her imagining of the historical figure Anthony Burns's life ("Boston Globe-Horn Book Award" 172–73).

20. See Nelson, Interview.

21. Crossover literature is read by children and adults. For a helpful discussion of the concept, see Beckett. In nineteenth-century culture, crossover literature was common, and

children and adults often read together. For more on nineteenth-century intergenerational reading among African Americans, see Gardner and DeLombard. For an informative survey of scholarship on early African American literature for young black readers, see the introduction to Capshaw and Duane's collection. Plato's *Essays*, Brown's *The Black Man: His Antecedents, His Genius, and His Achievements*, and William Still's *The Underground Railroad* are examples of collections that may have reached young readers. Frederick Douglass, reviewing Brown's book, recommended it for school and family libraries (Greenspan 388).

22. For a study of the magazine's biographies as sites of resistance against racist history, see VanderHaagen. I received the book that includes her essay too late to fully engage with her argument.

23. In discussing teaching Taylor's *Roll of Thunder, Hear My Cry*, Martin 86 explains that she also has students read Feelings's *Middle Passage*, Paulsen's *Nightjohn*, and a second Logan family narrative that each student can choose. The purpose of this approach is to provide students with a deeper sense of the social structures affecting African Americans. Schwebel 129 recommends that children read multiple narratives about an event or experience to better grasp how different writers have interpreted it.

CHAPTER 2. RETAINING AFRICAN SELFHOOD AND CULTURE IN AMERICAN SLAVERY

1. Arna Bontemps's *Story of the Negro* (1948) stands out from early twentieth-century African American children's literature about slavery for its straightforward representation of Black African agency on both sides of the Atlantic and during the Middle Passage. For insightful discussions of the book, see D. Johnson 49–51 and Connolly 164–67. Although D. Johnson notes that aspects of the book betray a classist perspective, she praises Bontemps for presenting "the humanity of African peoples" and "the richness and diversity of this humanity" (51).

2. The phrase "school of slavery," which appears in the postbellum slave narratives of dressmaker Elizabeth Keckley and educator Booker T. Washington, is a productive metaphor for the socialization of Draper's and Hansen's protagonists. Keckley's and Washington's use of the term is problematic, downplaying slavery's horror in order to promote the idea that it afforded enslaved persons skills that made them self-reliant and thus prepared for the challenges of postbellum life (Keckley 19–20, Washington 37). See Schwebel 100 and F. Foster, *Witnessing* 118–19 for discussions of the commonality of the assumption that slavery was a training ground. Yet their metaphor can be adapted to encompass the wide range of lessons that African American slaves encountered. Although formal education was not provided for most enslaved children during the antebellum era, enslaved persons had to learn agricultural, domestic, artisan, mechanical, or "unskilled" tasks, lessons about social place and self-abnegation, and the often competing, empowering teachings of the Black vernacular.

3. In K. Alexander's *The Door of No Return*, the protagonist Kofi is shielded from knowledge about the slave trade, but he has begun to ask questions.

4. For an informative discussion of West African spiritual writing, see Gundaker 33–46.

5. In this manner, Amari's experience recalls that of protagonists in a tradition of African American women's writing, including Harriet Jacobs's *Incidents in the Life of a Slave Girl*, Zora Neale Hurston's *Their Eyes Were Watching God*, and Toni Morrison's *A Mercy*.

6. See, for instance, his Rituals of Blood: The Consequences of Slavery in Two American Centuries.

7. Although by the late seventeenth century the Spanish colony of Florida was a relative haven for enslaved persons who fled the British colonies, slavery was a common practice in other Spanish colonies.

8. Draper's novel has had much success, winning the 2007 Coretta Scott King Award and since then having been used in an exhibit at the National Underground Railroad Museum, and chosen by the US State Department for an international reading program (Draper *Official Website*.). *The Captive*, a CSK Honor Book in 1995, has been out of print at least since 2006, when I purchased a used copy.

CHAPTER 3. TENDING TO MEMORY AND AFRICAN AMERICAN CULTURE

1. See Hinton 94–95 for Draper's description of her inspiration for *Copper Sun*. Like Hamilton and Lester, Draper describes being moved to write by the spirits of enslaved persons.

2. Walter Dean Myers and Virginia Hamilton were among the many African American writers who grappled with the issue of erasing Black history. See, for instance, Hamilton's *Sweet Whispers, Brother Rush*.

3. Faulting Pierre Nora 284–87 for condescension towards oral accounts of memory, as opposed to written history, Dixon lays claim to their importance in Black culture, including Black American literary culture. See Dixon 18–19.

4. See Giroux "Schooling," for a discussion of the late twentieth-century disregard for history, 270–71. See Baldwin for one of the most eloquent popular critiques of cultural amnesia.

5. See Schwebel 97, 129–30 on the importance of reading multiple historical narratives about the same historical period or issue.

6. Moore and MacCann 206.

7. Harriet's Christianity is manifest in her kindness to her enslaver Chelsea, her care for Nat and Ellen, both of whom she has raised, and her forgiving nature. By the end of the book, she has forgiven Ekundayo for possessing her grandson's body; she has also forgiven Gabriel. Harriet also sees common ground between her Christian faith and the rituals Ekundayo introduces.

8. This focus on community connections is present in several antebellum narratives, including Frederick Douglass's *My Bondage and My Freedom* and Harriet Jacobs's *Incidents in the Life of a Slave Girl*.

9. Though there has been attention to the closing of this gap in recent years, with statistics indicating that rates of mortality for all African American youths have decreased, Black teenagers aged fifteen to nineteen have continued to die at higher rates (15–26.6 more deaths per 100,000 persons) than white teens ("Infant, Child, and Teen Mortality").

10. This emphasis on characters' emotional response to Black mortality resonates with recent social justice initiatives and cultural criticism inspired by anti-Black racist violence. The scholar Karla F. C. Holloway and poet Claudia Rankine have both, for instance, theorized about the centrality of mourning in African American cultural life. Holloway has identified "mourning stories," which explore and lament the fragility of Black lives, as definitive of Black culture (32). And in examining the distinction of the Black Lives Matter Movement, Rankine has explained that it demands public mourning for African Americans who have died as a result of anti-Black racism and performs necessary work of reforming the ways the larger American public deals with living African Americans (Rankine).

11. Admittedly, stereotypes of African Americans, like those of other racial and ethnic groups, are often contradictory, but easy emotion and inconstancy were often attributed to Black Americans and have buttressed arguments about our moral deficiency. See Fredrickson 57–58 for an influential discussion of nineteenth-century stereotypes, many of which resonate with more recent US conceptions of Black people.

12. Lester's memory of being possessed resonates with instances in African American literature in which living fictional characters, like Sethe in Morrison's *Beloved* and Tree in Hamilton's *Sweet Whispers, Brother Rush*, interact with the dead.

13. See Eakin for a discussion of the fictive nature of life-writing. See Fields for her reflection on the subjective nature of life-writing.

14. "Hold'em Down, Brer Fox," for instance, turns on Brer Rabbit's deceptive use of language and Brer Fox's naïve acceptance of his lies, in spite of past experience.

15. In the novel's afterword, Lester explains "The story is perhaps one of the most autobiographical I've ever written" (*Time's Memory* 228–29).

16. For more on the issue of African Americans' resistance to him and his work, see Atkinson 67–68.

17. The scene recalls Fields's discussion of her co-composition with her grandmother Mamie Garvin Fields of *Lemon Swamp and Other Places: A Carolina Memoir*, a process that involved more questions and tensions than the writing partnerships Lester portrays. Although both Fields were highly literate, Karen Fields was challenged to adjust some of her professional methodology to honor her grandmother's oral storytelling and explanations of written artifacts. See, for instance, Fields 152–54. Fields 153 also acknowledges her grandmother's reliance on communal supports for personal memory, which relates to Dixon's point about the communal nature of orality.

18. See Baker 27–52 and Gates, *Signifying* 127–69.

19. Clifton memorably makes this call in her poem "at the cemetery, walnut grove plantation, south carolina, 1989," after a guided tour that has yielded no mention of enslaved persons: "tell me your names / tell me your bashful names" (13–14). And like Lester, she positions herself to "testify," to affirm the existence of these hidden lives (15). Her poem concludes with a repetition of "here lies," without offering the lost names and

identities of enslaved persons, and ends with a pun on "here"—"hear," which again emphasizes the importance of voice (31–35).

20. "Black People Don't Read" was part of the title of a 2006 call for papers posted on the website of the University of Pennsylvania's English department.

CHAPTER 4. STEALING LETTERS: FREEDOM NARRATIVES, LITERACY, AND BLACK VERNACULAR TRADITIONS

1. Ann Rinaldi's historical novel about Phillis Wheatley, *Hang a Thousand Trees with Ribbons* (1996), presents a morning ritual reflecting Wheatley's West African heritage, but it does not connect the poet's writing with a West African epistemology as scholars like John Shields were doing in the 1990s. Also, the popularization of Black radical thought through publishing ventures aimed at a general Black readership was evident much earlier than the 1990s, as E. West has shown in his study of *Ebony* magazine.

2. Marie Bradby and Chris Soentpiet's *More than Anything Else* (1995) is an excellent example of a picture book biography that conjoins literacy and the Black vernacular. For an interpretation of the text, see my "Reading for Success: Booker T. Washington's Pursuit of Education in Two Children's Books."

3. Representations of the convergence of print and folk cultures in Black boys' or teens' narratives are not unusual. Hansen's *The Heart Calls Home* (1999), set during the Civil War, presents a young African American man and woman's exchange of letters. Yet I have found more examples of this convergence in Black girls' narratives, whether historical or contemporary fiction, such as Renee Watson's *Piecing Me Together* (2018).

4. Many recent studies of elementary and secondary education show that achievement gaps between white Americans and African Americans have been narrowing, but they also show that disparities persist in test performance and graduation rates. When gender difference is noted in such studies, researchers have found that African American girls have tended to do significantly better than many African American boys. Such statistics should not suggest that African American girls have overcome obstacles to academic and social success. If they live in areas where schools are underfunded and jobs are scarce, African American girls' (and others') potential for success is still precarious. See Casserly and "Status and Trends in the Education of Racial and Ethnic Minorities."

5. See, for instance, Capshaw and Duane's collection of scholarship *Who Writes for Black Children?*

6. See Carby's critique of scholars' canonizing of folk-based texts to the exclusion of alternatives.

7. F. Foster's analysis of slave narrative conventions and textual address in *Witnessing Slavery* is very instructive. She reminds us that "slave narratives were rigidly patterned, didactic works. Their generic conventions made it necessary that all characters—including to some extent the protagonist—be types. The narrator was a symbol, the one who by God and good luck got away, the spokesperson for the thousands remaining in the wilderness. It was the narrator's life with which the narrative was specifically concerned. The lives of other slaves were noted as supplementary evidence" (xxx).

8. Although Burnett has generally written the screenplays for films he has directed, he joined the production team for *Nightjohn* after Cain had completed its script (Dauphin 107). Cain, a white Jesuit priest, also created and wrote for the Peabody-Award-winning series *Nothing Sacred*.

9. Hubler offers an insightful discussion of the ways McKissack's and Kathleen Lasky's entries in the series relate their protagonists' personal experiences to larger social currents of the era under investigation. Hubler does not discuss Hansen's contribution to the series, but she examines volumes by Rinaldi and Osborne that seem characteristic of the series' obscuring of societal structures and focus on individual problems and achievements.

10. Wheatley's poetry has long come under attack because it seems to cater to prejudices against Blackness, but over the last thirty years scholars have argued that it offers more complex messages, including concerns with resistance. For an influential negative appraisal, see Redding. For a more balanced one, see Shields. For a discussion of diaries as alternatives to literary conventions associated with white male authors, see Braham. Braham and Shields, in their discussions of diaries and Wheatley's poetry, respectively, focus on metaphor as a means of countering accepted male-dominated discourse.

11. This dual focus on print and Black folk cultures did not transfer to ancillary products Scholastic sold to supplement the Dear America novels, especially its CD-ROM and website. (The low-budget film adaptation of *A Picture of Freedom* does adhere to the novel.) The CD-ROM, Dear America: Friend to Friend, promoted literacy, not folklore, and emphasized self-development. Communal exchanges were restricted to the computer user's relationship to the CD's fictional characters, including the protagonist Clotee. A major goal of the CD was to foster girls' awareness and valorization of their own experience of the world. To encourage computer users to keep a diary, the CD offered many brainstorming ideas to spark young writers' imaginations. Among the prompts featured in Clotee's section were the question, "Why not write a story about the first time you felt truly free?" and the suggestion to "write about your secret place," a place secure enough to write and act freely. Similarly, girls were advised to go to the dictionary, find a word "you've never seen before," and "write down a paragraph where you say what kind of pictures, tastes, and smells that word gives you." Literacy was here a means of self-knowledge, self-documentation, and self-authorization.

12. Chesnut's description of an African American man praying before a group of worshippers betrays a complicated web of responses, but it is important to note that no matter how moving she finds the prayer, it is ultimately ineffectual, a mere safety valve:

> Jim Nelson, the driver—the stateliest darky I ever saw. He is tall and straight as a pine tree, with a fair face—not so very black, but full-blooded African. His forefathers must have been of royal blood over there.
>
> This distinguished gentleman was asked to "lead in prayer." He became wildly excited. Though on his knees, facing us, with his eyes shut, he clapped his hands at the end of every sentence, and his voice rose to the pitch of a shrill shriek. Still, his voice was strangely clear and musical, occasionally in the plaintive minor key that went to your heart. Sometimes it rung out like a trumpet. I wept bitterly. It was all sound, however, and emotional pathos. There was literally nothing in what he said. The words had no meaning at all. It was the devotional passion of voice and manner which was so magnetic. The negroes sobbed and

shouted and swayed backward and forward, some with aprons to their eyes, most clapping their hands and responding in shrill tones, "Yes, my God! Jesus!" "Aeih! Savior! Bless d Lord, amen—&c." (213–14)

13. I appreciate Carol Mattingly's helpful questions as I weighed the significance of Patsy's writing.

14. The girls' initiative in learning to read and write and then teaching others represents a historical tendency in Black communities, in which those with the most formal education tended to share their knowledge with others (Brandt 127–29).

CHAPTER 5. LET'S PLAY: BLACK CHILDREN'S AGENCY AND THE PURSUIT OF FUN

1. See Hurston 53–56 for an artful illustration of this idea.

2. Around the same time that the controversy over *A Fine Dessert* arose, another picture book, *A Birthday Cake for George Washington* provoked debates on the same issues. Authored and edited by persons of color, the book was withdrawn from publication. For information and commentary about this case, see Older.

3. For a compilation of critiques and defenses of the book, see Reese.

4. According to an account of the study,
The researchers presented 64 White college students with two images that flashed on a monitor in quick succession. The students saw the first image—a photograph of a child's face—which they were told to ignore because it purportedly just signaled that the second image was about to appear. When the second image popped up, participants were supposed to indicate whether it showed a gun or a toy, such as a rattle. The photographs of children's faces included six images of Black five-year-old boys and six images of White five-year-old boys. The data revealed that the student participants tended to be quicker at categorizing guns after seeing a Black child's face than after seeing a White child's face. ("Faces")
This tendency to associate Black children and guns was paralleled in a second part of the study, in which pictures of toys were mistaken for weapons, when juxtaposed with images of Black children ("Faces").

5. In many freedom narratives for young audiences, like *Second Daughter*, an enslaved child's play underscores the idea that she is not completely deprived of means to express her agency and Black cultural orientation. Child's play in these books is continuous with other expressions of agency, such as communal gatherings of enslaved Africans Americans, parties, conversations, etc., that suggest many Black persons established tight communities in which they could express themselves, relax, and otherwise make choices about their use of time and space even in the midst of slavery. Adding an additional conflict, Woods's *My Name Is Sally Little Song* concerns a protagonist who tries to maintain her ties to African American culture after her family takes refuge in a Seminole community. Sally's play is influenced both by her position as an enslaved Black girl and a member of her adopted Seminole society.

6. In exploring this manipulation of adult roles, Argenti challenges the theories of Piaget and Freud that emphasize play as an escape from the real world: "I therefore

explore the folktales I recorded in Oku between 1992 and 2005 for their potential to enable children not to escape, but rather to address and express their lived experience of the world" (228).

7. Elijah's experience differs markedly from that of children in other historical narratives in which "work is central" (Nikolajeva 313).

8. For a fuller exploration of the effects of Elijah's naïve perspective, see Barker.

9. The film won several awards, including the 1995 Children's Jury Award, Best Film/Video, at the Chicago International Children's Film Festival; the 1995 Best Short Feature Award at the New England Children's Film and Video Festival; and the 1996 Jurors Choice award at the Charlotte Film and Video Festival.

10. The film is partly inspired by a Haitian folktale that is called "The Mother of the River." For a version of the tale, see Wolkstein. See G. Foster for more about Davis and the film.

11. These anachronisms are one feature of Davis's Afrocentric aesthetic and resonate with a tendency that Spaulding sees in postmodern African American historical fiction. Emphasizing parallels between the past and present and the continuation of past problems within the present, such fiction, according to Spaulding 29, encourages readers to think critically about history and contemporary society in ways that can foster transformative improvements to society.

12. Monique Coleman, who plays Dofimae, also lends an air of artifice to the film, though her performance is more naturalistic ("Monique Coleman"). The actress, who was fourteen or fifteen when the film first aired, is playing a character who acts younger. This disjunction has the Brechtian effect of discouraging viewers from forgetting they are watching a constructed narrative.

13. Schwebel discusses the shift in historiography and children's literature to representations of African American agency, even using the term "the world slaves made" (119).

14. Proverbs are concise assertions conveying cultural beliefs and vernacular knowledge (Okpewho 226). See Jirata for an examination of actual children's play with riddles in Ethiopian society.

15. Many of the tales in Virginia Hamilton's *The People Could Fly*, for instance, present this lesson: Not being observant and reading the possible threats and opportunities within one's immediate environment can leave an individual or a group more vulnerable. "Bruh Lizard and Bruh Rabbit," in the Hamilton collection, features a rabbit who observes a lizard using a magical sword, which he steals and gets to work on its own by using a phrase he has heard the lizard use in commanding the tool. Yet the rabbit's observation has been limited, for he has not learned the phrase to make the sword stop working and it destroys his crop.

16. Davis uses cross-cutting and setting brilliantly in the sequence that includes this riddle. At one point, she presents footage that suggests Mistress Anne's sway over the land, presenting her on her porch and walking on a path surrounded by the mansion's big lawn. While Mistress Anne strolls slowly down a path from her mansion, the girls occupy less visible areas of the plantation—in woods and near the river—for their transgressive play.

17. At one point Emma does order Dofimae to play with her, but the film suggests that this is more an act of desperation than a full-scale acceptance of her superior social

ranking. Dofimae reminds her that Mistress Anne has banned their play; in expressing her obedience to this proscription, Dofimae engages in signifying, using ironic commentary to stress the inadequacy of another person's speech or writing (Smitherman 118–19). In this instance, she alludes to the similarity between the order-giving Mistress Anne and Emma. In refusing to play, Dofimae is not just following the mistress's command but also refusing to submit to her friend, and thus destroy the balance of their friendship.

18. This bears comparison to the dream sequences of an African American pastoral in *Mother of the River*, though the latter lack any reference to work or commerce, emphasize the beauty of Black persons, and suggest an Afrocentric world.

19. This passage is often discussed in the criticism on Douglass's autobiographies. For examples, see Levine 104 and Andrews 143–44.

20. The loss of a family member is not exactly equivalent: Billy's older brother is away at school; Sugar's mother has died and her father has disappeared from her life.

21. Sugar's mother Sarah chose to remain on the plantation, hoping for an eventual reunion with her husband, who was sold away before the Civil War. In staying, she emphasized the importance of holding on to dreams that exceeded one's current reality. Sarah also put into practice the methods of Br'er Rabbit, though to her detriment, when she tricked Mister Wills into letting her work, even though she was ill (40). Sugar seeks to act on this legacy of trickery and imaginative aspiration, though she eventually foregoes her mother's optimism about the absent father's imminent return.

22. As Naomi Lesley pointed out to me, this blend challenges the stereotype of Chinese persons as one-dimensional over-achievers.

23. Like the African American workers, Beau, Master Liu, and the other Chinese men insist through their actions that they are more than workers—at least, work, as important as it is for their livelihood, does not completely define them. Just as the African Americans use their time to tell stories, cook, make handicrafts, and play games, the Chinese men engage in similar activities, albeit ones that are specific to their national and ethnic culture. For instance, they introduce the game of Chinese checkers and a dragon dance to their Black neighbors.

24. See C. West 129–30 for his distinction between pleasure and joy. It is operative here in that much of Sugar's trickery is about pleasing self but in this scene she is sharing her happiness with others and contributing to the community's joy.

25. Contrasting with the farm manager Tom's use of "monkey, the Chinese workers' leader Master Liu sees Sugar as a "Metal Monkey," "smart," "strong," "fighting," a "Great spirit" (123, 124), thus acknowledging her drive and astuteness. Rhodes shows the Chinese and African American workers relying on their own storytelling traditions for understanding some of Sugar's methods and ambitions. The monkey of Chinese legend is not the same as the rabbit of African American folktales (or Anansi from Ashanti oral traditions). Yet for the African American and Chinese workers, their traditional stories serve as touchstones for interpreting aspects of their everyday lives, including issues of social inequity and community members' efforts to overcome disadvantage to find freedom and contentment. Although the reliance on the monkey and rabbit may suggest that long popular forms of imaginative play and entertainment are universal, transcending cultural differences, the novel's emphases respect cultural distinctions in demonstrating how

people from different traditions can find points of connection through which they can establish understanding. The association of Sugar with the monkey hero also counters longstanding stereotypes of African Americans as apish and subhuman. In this way, too, Rhodes plays with our expectations of cultural revision, nodding toward a problematic stereotype and refuting and retooling it.

26. The exception to this tendency is the tar baby doll in one of the folktales shared among the Black workers.

27. According to Bernstein, black rubber-dolls scripted violence (*Racial* ch. 2). She also cites Tavia Nyong'o's arguments about black ceramic dolls that figured "blackness as a hardened form of subjectivity" (*Racial* ch. 2).

28. See Tribunella 35–36.

29. *Elijah of Buxton* conforms to a key convention of realism: avoiding excess and staying within the realm of the reasonable and verifiable. A young boy rescuing more than one captured Black fugitive would probably exceed the realist standard.

30. See Spaulding 28–29 for a discussion that distinguishes between uses of anachronism in postmodern African American and Euro-American literature.

31. See chapter 1 of Asim's *The Road to Freedom* for a fictional reconstruction of a Union regiment's freeing of enslaved persons during the Civil War. Asim portrays African Americans' vibrant, resourceful community on a southern plantation, juxtaposing it with both the enslaver class's paternalism and Union soldiers' disrespect toward Black persons and theft of their property. The chapter pointedly conveys the Union soldiers' racism and doubts about the appropriateness of Black freedom.

CHAPTER 6. TENDING TO THE LAND: CHALLENGES OF BLACK FINANCIAL AGENCY AND COMMUNITY IN YOUTH FREEDOM NARRATIVES

1. See, for instance, Allen's illuminating examination of millennial African Americans' ambivalence about home-ownership (139–45). Allen also offers some historical perspective for this ambivalence (145–50).

2. Black economic welfare was also important to the Poor People's Campaign, coordinated by the Southern Christian Leadership Conference and Dr. Martin Luther King Jr. and designed to begin to address widespread economic inequities, including those among non-Black Americans. According to Wideman, such social change initiatives expressed a "dream of better, not more. Truly better. Not more pigs slopping at the trough, not a larger bit of a rotten pie, not more, but better. For everyone, and everyone meaning really everyone."

3. In discussing mid-nineteenth-century concerns about economic disparity, Stuckey uses "land monopoly," a term used often through the beginning of the twentieth century to refer to the control of much of a country's land by a small percentage of the population ("A Last" 142).

4. Stuckey, "A Last" 143. This quotation refers to nineteenth-century Black Nationalist minister and activist Henry Highland Garnet's economic vision, which resonates with the novels' portrayals of Black economic behavior.

5. Anxieties about claiming, controlling, or owning land or a home are common in African American literature and film, ranging from Lorraine Hansberry's *Raisin in the Sun* and August Wilson's award-winning play *Fences* (1985) and the recent film adaptation (2016) to the independent film *The Last Black Man in San Francisco* (2019), based on a story coauthored by Euro-American director Joe Talbot and African American actor Jimmie Falls. Although these texts have different thematic emphases and situations, they all concern the tenuous search for a home, the legal, economic and social obstacles to African American property-holding, and the creative means by which African Americans acquire and maintain real estate.

6. I borrow the term "cross-class" from L. Harris, who offers a nuanced examination of tensions and distinctions between working- and middle-class African Americans, focusing on New Yorkers, but also considering them within national and regional contexts. See, for instance, 119–21 and especially 217–19. Hansen's novel reflects the "cross-class" alliance African Americans maintained in the antebellum period. The novel also reflects some middle-class Black New Yorkers' identification with enslaved southern Black persons and minimizes concerns about Black working-class morality. Many abolitionists and proponents of slavery saw working-class behavior and attitudes, including those of enslaved African Americans, as manifesting Black persons' unfitness for freedom and citizenship. Hansen acknowledges this pattern through Mama Peters's bias.

7. Nelson's and Hansen's books acknowledge that Seneca Village included immigrants, as well as renters.

8. Hansen and Nelson have contributed to this reconstruction effort in various ways. Hansen's nonfiction book *Breaking Ground, Breaking Silence* (1998), for instance, explores the 1991 discovery of the African burial site in lower Manhattan. *Fortune's Bones: The Manumission Requiem* (2004) and *The Freedom Business* (2008), along with the coauthored *Miss Crandall's School for Young Ladies and Little Misses of Color* (2007) are among the "lyrical histories" Nelson has written about African Americans in early Connecticut (Voigt).

9. Black persons' home foreclosures began in large numbers as early as 2004 ("Report Shows").

10. Freddy Riddles appears as something of a Transcendentalist in "Under the Fathomless" (15).

11. See, for instance, Pattillo-McCoy 2, 10 on late twentieth-century African American socioeconomic status, and Kelley, introduction, on African Americans', and most Americans', status as working class.

12. Nelson's and Hansen's books portray Seneca Village as interracial communities.

13. Nelson has written about her respect for Black Arts Movement revolutionary writing, but explains that she has taken a more measured approach to writing that claims rather than rejects white literary models. See Waniek.

14. The novel acknowledges the presence of German immigrants through the character of Farmer Gruner, a landowner who helps draft the petition the villagers present to city officials.

15. Nelson's portrait of Seneca Village presents several religious institutions as settings for poems, including the African Union Church, which includes the village school,

All Angels (Episcopalian) Church, where Frederick Douglass speaks, the New Hope Missionary AME Church, and the Convent of the Sisters of Mercy, which provided support to the growing population of Irish immigrants.

16. This gendered training reflects patterns prescribed in an early-nineteenth-century periodical directed at African Americans, the *Colored American* (Wright 48–49).

17. Adapting the domestic novel is not uncommon among African American authors and often involves a complex negotiation of gender and narrative conventions and racial justice concerns. As Claudia Tate has explained, writers such as Frances Ellen Watkins Harper and Pauline Hopkins adopted domestic fiction as a way of ostensibly portraying African Americans' emergence from slavery, embracing assimilation as a means of showing African Americans' fitness for US citizenship and social integration (56). Yet the texts also present Black female agency through domesticity (68). Twentieth-century novels such as Paule Marshall's *Brown Girl, Brownstones* and Alice Walker's *The Color Purple* also draw on domestic fiction's formulas to explore the limits and possibilities of Black feminine agency.

18. Tate has explained that late nineteenth-century African American domestic fiction adheres to an assimilationist philosophy. According to Tate, "With emancipation, African Americans marginalized slave culture with the adoption of dominant values, as schools and churches taught them that the survival codes of slavery and strategies for racial advancement often stood in mutual opposition" (56). She points out that "individual willful self-advancement" became a defining value, and that white standards of beauty became key (56–58). Moreover, enslaved persons' culture was associated with social disadvantage, including economic hardship and stasis (57). Tate also observes, however, that the process wasn't either or—staying true to Black culture or assimilating: "African Americans became bicultural; that is, they deliberately acquired dominant bourgeois constructions of individual and collective success, while retaining to various degrees the folk wisdom of slave culture" (57).

19. For a sound historical discussion of the vulnerability of New Yorkers in the 1850s, see L. Harris 265–67, 270–75.

20. Also relevant is the tense scene in which Anna and Maria retreat to the Holmes residence as a catcher of fugitives pursues them. They barricade the door to prevent him from entering.

21. Kansas did have a small population of African Americans by the 1850s, and its state constitution, from 1859, indicated that it did not discriminate against persons on the basis of race or ethnicity. Yet with the increase in the African American population in the 1860s, anti-Black rhetoric and violence intensified (Campney 17).

22. Their innocence recalls poet and memoirist Cathy Park Hong's statement that "Innocence is both a privilege and a cognitive hardship, a sheltered unknowingness that, once protracted into adulthood, hardens into entitlement" (ch. 3).

23. See, for instance, Taylor 3, 4, 11, 35, 36, 47, 51, and 97.

24. In her talks with Paul-Edward, the older Cassie has spoken about her own coming into awareness of her liminal status in the family.

25. I am grateful to Jesus Montaño for his question about race and the myth of the Adamic hero at the "Theorizing Race" panel at the 2018 Children's Literature Association Conference.

26. The agreement specifies that Paul-Edward will clear the land of all the trees with a diameter of sixteen inches or greater. The land's owner, Filmore Granger, plans to sell the lumber.

27. The man also shoots Paul-Edward's thoroughbred, which he was hoping to sell to gain the means of securing the other plot of land.

28. Paul-Edward and Mitchell fall in love with Caroline around the same time, but Paul-Edward is only poised to declare his romantic interest once Mitchell and Caroline are engaged. The first time Paul-Edward meets Caroline, he hears her first—intervening when a group of white boys torment a Black child. She is out-spoken, discerning, and questioning.

29. Caroline's dedication to community is also important to the next volume in the family's history, *The Well*, in which she and her husband allow Black and white neighbors to use a well on the Logan property during a drought.

30. Each section is headed by a family tree with members' dates of birth. Among the many interesting details in the trees is the absence of the years family members die. Also, though each tree shows marital partnerships for many family members, Muhammad, who is listed as having two sons, does not have a wife listed. Another interesting detail is that Muhammad's younger son, Yero, is married to Sarah, or, as she is called by African Americans, Saran, which was the name of Muhammad's mother. Whether Yero's wife Saran is biologically related to Muhammad, the use of the traditional West African name may show deference to him and to his or other community members' West African roots.

31. Elijah and his cousin Abby are not only motivated by the reward; like many in the community, they are concerned about the child's welfare, they know their grandmother is especially attached to the child, and Elijah, who loves sailing, is drawn to the challenge of working in the water during a heavy storm.

WORKS CITED

PRIMARY SOURCES

Alexander, Kwame. *The Door of No Return*. Little, Brown and Company, 2022.
Asim, Jabari. *The Road to Freedom: A Story of the Reconstruction*. Jamestown, 2000.
Butler, Octavia. *Kindred*. Beacon, 2004.
Chesnut, Mary. *Mary Chesnut's Civil War*. Edited by C. Vann Woodward, Yale UP, 1981.
Clifton, Lucille. "at the cemetery, walnut grove plantation, south carolina, 1989." *quilting: poems, 1987–1990*. BOA Editions Limited, 1991, pp. 11–12.
Clifton, Lucille. "I am accused of tending to the past." *Reflections: The Future of Race*, spring 2013. www.reflections.yale.edu/article/future-race/i-am-accused-tending-past.
Curtis, Christopher Paul. *Elijah of Buxton*. Scholastic, 2007.
Dear America: Friend to Friend. CD-ROM. Torrance: Knowledge Adventure, 2000.
Douglass, Frederick. *Narrative of the Life of Frederick Douglass, an American Slave, Written by Himself*. Boston: Anti-Slavery Office, 1845, docsouth.unc.edu/neh/douglass/menu.html.
Draper, Sharon. *Copper Sun*. Atheneum, 2006.
Giovanni, Nikki. "Ego-Tripping (there may be a reason why)." *Hip Hop Speaks to Children: a celebration of poetry with a beat*, edited by Nikki Giovanni, Sourcebooks, 2008, pp. 42–43.
Griffin, Emily. *A Fine Dessert*. Illustrated by Sophie Blackall, Random House, 2015.
Hamilton, Virginia. *The Magical Adventures of Pretty Pearl*. Harper, 1986.
Hansen, Joyce. *The Captive*. Scholastic, 1994.
Hansen, Joyce. *Home Is With Our Family*. Jump at the Sun, 2010.
Hansen, Joyce. *I Thought My Soul Would Rise and Fly: The Diary of Patsy, a Freed Girl*. Scholastic, 1997.
Hansen, Joyce. *Out From This Place*. Avon, 1992.
Keckley, Elizabeth. (1868). *Behind the Scenes, or Thirty Years a Slave and Four Years in the White House*. Carlton, 1868, docsouth.unc.edu/neh/keckley/keckley.html.
Lester, Julius. "Thirty Years of 'To Be a Slave.'" *To Be a Slave*, pp. 3–11.
Lester, Julius. *Time's Memory*. FSG, 2006.

Lester, Julius. *To Be a Slave*. 1968. Puffin, 1998.
McKissack, Patricia. *A Picture of Freedom: The Diary of Clotee, a Slave Girl*. Scholastic, 1997.
McKissack, Patricia, and Fredrick McKissack. *Let My People Go: Bible Stories Told by a Freeman of Color*. Atheneum, 1998.
Mother of the River. Directed by Zeinabu irene Davis, performances by Monique Coleman, Michael Nesbit, and Joy Vandervort-Cobb, ITSV, 1995.
Myers, Walter Dean. *The Glory Field*. Scholastic, 1994.
Nelson, Marilyn. *My Seneca Village*. Namelos, 2015.
Nightjohn. Directed by Charles Burnett, performances by Carl Lumbry, Allison Jones, Lorraine Toussaint, Beau Bridges, and Bill Cobbs, Disney, 1996.
Paulsen, Gary. *Nightjohn*. Bantam, 1993.
A Picture of Freedom: The Story of Clotee, a Slave Girl. Directed by Helaine Head, performance by Shadia Simmons, Scholastic Entertainment, 1999.
Rhodes, Jewell Parker. *Sugar*. Little, Brown and Company, 2013.
Taylor, Mildred. *The Land*. Scholastic, 2001.
Taylor, Mildred. *The Well*. Penguin, 1998.
Walter, Mildred Pitts. *Second Daughter: The Story of a Slave Girl*. Scholastic, 1996.
Washington, Booker T. (1999/1901). *Up from Slavery*. *Three Negro Classics*, edited by John Hope Franklin, Avon, 1999, pp. i-157.
Wolkstein, Diane. "Mother of the Waters." *The Magic Orange Tree and Other Haitian Folktales*. Schocken Books, 1997, pp. 152–56.
Woods, Brenda. *My Name Is Sally Little Song*. Putnam, 2006.
Yates, Elizabeth. *Amos Fortune, Free Man*. Puffin, 1989.

SECONDARY SOURCES

Abrahams, Roger D. *Singing the Master: The Emergence of African-American Culture in the Plantation South*. Penguin, 1992.
Alexander, Leslie M. "Community and Institution Building in Antebellum New York: The Story of Seneca Village, 1825–1857." *"We Shall Independent Be": African American Place Making and the Struggle to Claim Space in the United States*, edited by Angel David Nieves and Leslie M. Alexander, UP of Colorado, 2008, pp. 23–46.
Allen, Reniqua. *It Was All a Dream: A New Generation Confronts the Broken Promise to Black America*. Nation, 2019.
Anderson, Carol. *White Rage: The Unspoken Truth of Our Racial Divide*. Bloomsbury, 2016.
Anderson, Melinda D. "What Kids Are Really Learning about Slavery." *The Atlantic*, 1 Feb. 2018. www.theatlantic.com/education/archive/2018/02/what-kids-are-really-learning-about-slavery/552098/.
Andrews, William L. *To Tell a Free Story*. U of Illinois P, 1986.
Argenti, Nicolas. "Things That Don't Come by the Road: Folktales, Fosterage, and Memories of Slavery in the Cameroon Grassfields." *Comparative Studies in Society and History*, vol. 52, no. 2, 2010, pp. 224–54.

Atkinson, Yvonne. "The Cadence of Language; Interview with Julius Lester." *Ethnic Literary Traditions in American Children's Literature*, edited by Yvonne Atkinson and Michelle Pagni Stewart, Palgrave Macmillan, 2009, pp. 65–69.

Austin, Sara. "Two Separate Hearts: Virginia Hamilton and the Black Arts Movement." *The Lion and the Unicorn*, vol. 40 no. 3, 2016, p. 262–79. Project MUSE, doi:10.1353/uni.2016.0024.

Baker, Houston. *The Journey Back: Issues in Black Literature and Criticism*. U of Chicago P, 1980.

Baldwin, James. "The White Man's Guilt." *Ebony*, 1 Aug. 1965.

Barker, Jani. "Naïve Narrators and Double Narratives of Racially Motivated Violence in the Historical Fiction of Christopher Paul Curtis." *Children's Literature*, vol. 41, no. 1, 2013, pp. 172–203. Project MUSE, muse.jhu.edu.echo.louisville.edu/article/508933/pdf.

Batho, Nick. "Black Power Children's Literature: Julius Lester and Black Power." *Journal of American Studies*, vol. 55, no. 1, 2021, pp. 25–47.

Beckett, Sandra L. "Crossover Literature." Nel, Paul, and Christensen, pp. 47–50

Berlin, Ira. "Foreword: The Short Course for Bringing Slavery into the Classroom in Ten Not-So-Easy Pieces." Jay and Lyerly, pp. xi–xx.

Bernstein, Robin. *Racial Innocence: Performing American Childhood from Slavery to Civil Rights*. New York UP, 2011.

Bishop, Rudine Sims. *Free Within Ourselves: The Development of African American Children's Literature*. Heinemann, 2007.

Bishop, Rudine Sims. "Mirrors, Windows, and Sliding Doors." *Reading is Fundamental*, 3 Jan. 2015, www.readingrockets.org/sites/default/files/Mirrors-Windows-and-Sliding-Glass-Doors.pdf.

Blassingame, John. "Using the Testimony of Ex-Slaves: Approaches and Problems." *The Journal of Southern History*, vol. 41, no. 4, Nov. 1975, pp. 473–92.

Bontemps, Arna, editor. *The Great Slave Narratives*. Beacon, 1969.

Bradford, Clare. *Unsettling Narratives: Postcolonial Readings of Children's Literature*. Wilfred Laurier UP, 2007.

Braham, Jeanne. "A Lens of Empathy." *Inscribing the Daily: Critical Essays on Women's Diaries*, edited by Suzanne Bunkers and Cynthia Huff, U of Massachusetts P, 1996, pp. 56–71.

Brandt, Deborah. *Literacy in American Lives*. Cambridge UP, 2001.

Brison, Susan J. "Trauma Narratives and the Remaking of the Self." *Acts of Memory*, edited by Mieke Bal, Jonathan Crewe, and Leo Spitzer, UPNE, 1999, pp. 39–54.

Brooks, Wanda, and Jonda C. McNair. "'But This Story of Mine Is Not Unique': A Review of Research on African American Children's Literature." *Review of Educational Research*, vol. 79, no. 1, 2009, pp. 125–62.

Brown, Anthony L. "Counter-Memory and Race: An Examination of African American Scholars' Challenges to Early Twentieth-Century K-12 Historical Discourses." *Journal of Negro Education*, vol. 79, no. 1, winter 2010, pp. 54–65.

Burnett, Charles. "Inner City Blues." *Questions of Third Cinema*, edited by Jim Pines and Paul Willemen, BFI, 1989, pp. 223–26.

Burton, Tara Isabella. "The Insidious Cultural History of Kanye West's Slavery Comments." *Vox*, 2 May 2018. www.vox.com/2018/5/2/17311148/kanye-west-slavery-choice-harriet-tubman-quote-comments-trump.

Butler, Octavia. Book-in-Common Lecture. 25 Feb. 2005, University of Louisville.

Campbell, Edi. "The Dessert, By the Way, Is Blackberry Fool." *Crazy QuiltEdi: Promoting Literacy for Teens of Color One Book at a Time*, www.edicottonquilt.com/2015/11/04/the-dessert-by-the-way-is-blueberry-fool/.

Campney, Brent M. S. *This Is Not Dixie: Racist Violence in Kansas, 1861–1927*. U of Illinois P, 2015.

Capshaw, Katharine. *Civil Rights Childhood: Picturing Liberation in African American Photobooks*. U of Minnesota P, 2014.

Capshaw, Katharine, and Anna Mae Duane, editors. *Who Writes for Black Children? African American Children's Literature Before 1900*. U of Minnesota P, 2017.

Carby, Hazel. "Ideologies of Black Folk: The Historical Novel of Slavery." *Slavery and the Literary Imagination*, edited by Deborah McDowell and Arnold Rampersad, The Johns Hopkins UP, 1989, pp. 125–43.

Casserly, Michael. "Beating the Odds IV: A City-By-City Analysis of Student Performance and Achievement Gap on State Assessments, Results from 2002–2003 School Year." Mar. 2004. www.files.eric.ed.gov/fulltext/ED485517.pdf.

Chandler, Karen Michele. "Reading for Success: Booker T. Washington's Pursuit of Education in Two Children's Books." *Literary Cultures and Twentieth-Century Childhoods*, edited by Rachel Conrad and Brown Kennedy, Palgrave, 2020, pp. 129–45.

Cheng, Anne Anlin. *The Melancholy of Race*. Oxford UP, 2000.

Clark, Eric L. "Folklorist Virginia Hamilton tells the tale." *The Crisis*, Jan. 1996, 28–29, 32.

Coleman, Nancy. "Why We're Capitalizing Black." *The New York Times*, 5 July 2020, www.nytimes.com/2020/07/05/insider/capitalized-black.html.

Collins, Lisa Gail, and Margo Natalie Crawford. "Introduction: Power to the People! The Art of Black Power." *New Thoughts on the Black Arts Movement*, edited by Collins and Crawford, Rutgers UP, 2008, pp. 1–19.

The Combahee River Collective. "A Black Feminist Statement." Guy-Sheftall, pp. 232–40.

Connolly, Paula. *Slavery in American Children's Literature, 1790–2010*. U of Iowa P, 2013.

Crawford, Margo Natalie. *Black Post-Blackness: The Black Arts Movement and Twenty-First-Century Aesthetics*. U of Illinois P, 2017.

Crawford, Margo Natalie. *What Is African American Literature?* Wiley Blackwell, 2021.

Dauphin, Gary. "Above It All: Charles Burnett Puts Black Power in Subtle Films." *Charles Burnett: Interviews*, edited by Robert E. Kapsis, UP of Mississippi, 2011, pp. 106–8.

De Cunzo, Lu Ann. *A Historical Archeology of Delaware: People, Contexts and the Cultures of Agriculture*. U of Tennessee P, 2004.

DeLombard, Jeannine. "African American Cultures of Print." *The Industrial Book, 1840–1880*, edited by Scott Casper et al. U of North Carolina P, 2007. Vol. 3 of *A History of the Book in America*, pp. 360–73.

Diouf, Sylviane A. *Slavery's Exiles: The Story of America's Maroons*. New York UP, 2014.

Dixon, Melvin. "The Black Writer's Use of Memory." Fabre and O'Meally, 18–27.

Draper, Sharon. *Official Website of Sharon Draper*. 2016. sharondraper.com/.

Duane, Anna Mae. "Introduction: When Is a Child a Slave?" *Child Slavery Before and After Emancipation: An Argument for Child-Centered Slavery Studies*, edited by Anna Mae Duane. Cambridge UP, 2017, pp. 1–22.
Dubey, Madhu. *Black Women Novelists and the Nationalist Aesthetic*. Indiana UP, 1994.
Du Bois, W. E. B. *The Souls of Black Folk. The Oxford W. E. B. Du Bois Reader*. Edited by Eric Sundquist, Oxford UP, 1996, pp. 97–239.
Eakin, Paul John. *Fictions in Autobiography: Studies in the Art of Self-Invention*. Princeton UP, 1985.
Ezra, Kate. *The Art of the Dogon*. The Metropolitan Museum of Art and Abrams, 1988.
Fabre, Genevieve, and Robert O'Meally, editors. *History and Memory in African-American Culture*. Oxford UP, 1994.
"Faces of Black Children as Young as Five Evoke Negative Biases." *Association for Psychological Science*, 8 Feb. 2016.
Faust, Drew Gilpin. "The Scholar Who Shaped History." Review of *The Problem of Slavery in the Age of Emancipation*, by David Brion Davis. *The New York Review of Books*, 20 March 2014. www.nybooks.com/articles/2014/03/20/scholar-who-shaped-history/.
Fielder, Brigitte. "Before *The Brownies'* Book." *The Lion and the Unicorn*, vol. 43, no. 2, 2019, pp. 159–71.
Fields, Karen. "What One Cannot Remember Mistakenly." Fabre and O'Meally, pp. 150–63.
Finn, Patrick. *Literacy with an Attitude: Educating Working-Class Children in Their Own Self-Interest*. State University of New York P, 1999.
Foster, Frances Smith. *Witnessing Slavery: The Development of Antebellum Slave Narratives*. U of Wisconsin P, 1994.
Foster, Gwendolyn Audrey. *Women Filmmakers of the African and Asian Diaspora: Decolonizing the Gaze*. Southern Illinois UP, 1997.
Franklin, Donna L. *Ensuring Inequality: The Structural Transformation of the African-American Family*. Oxford UP, 1997.
Fredrickson, George. *The Black Image in the White Mind: The Debate on Afro-American Character and Destiny, 1817–1914*. Oxford UP, 1971.
Gardner, Eric. "Remembered (Black) Readers: Subscribers to the Christian Recorder, 1864–1865." *American Literary History*, vol. 23, no. 2, 2011, pp. 229–59.
Gates, Henry Louis, Jr. *Figures in Black: Words, Signs, and the "Racial" Self*. Oxford UP, 1987.
Gates, Henry Louis, Jr. "Lifting the Veil." Zinsser, pp. 141–58.
Gates, Henry Louis, Jr. *The Signifying Monkey: A Theory of African-American Literary Criticism*. Oxford UP, 1988.
Gates, Henry Louis, Jr. "Who Really Ran the Underground Railroad?" *African Americans: Many Rivers to Cross With Henry Louis Gates Jr.*, PBS, www.pbs.org/wnet/african-americans-many-rivers-to-cross/history/who-really-ran-the-underground-railroad.
Gee, James Paul. "Orality and Literacy: From The Savage Mind to Ways with Words." *Journal of Education*, vol. 171, no. 1, 1989, pp. 39–60.
Gilroy, Paul. *The Black Atlantic: Modernity and Double Consciousness*. Harvard UP, 1993.
Giroux, Henry. *On Critical Pedagogy*. 2009. Bloomsbury, 2020.

Giroux, Henry. "Schooling and the Culture of Positivism: Notes on the Death of History." *Educational Theory*, vol. 29, no. 4, 1979, pp. 263–84.

Givens, Jarvis. "The Fugitive Life of Black Teaching: A History of Pedagogy and Power." The Anne Braden Institute's Virtual Black History Month Talk, 2 Feb. 2022, University of Louisville.

Graff, Harvey. "The Legacies of Literacy." *Language and Literacy in Social Practice*, edited by Janet Maybin, Multilingual Matters, 1994, pp. 151–67.

Greenspan, Ezra. *William Wells Brown: An African American Life*. Norton, 2014.

Gubar, Marah. "The Hermeneutics of Recuperation: What a Kinship-Model Approach to Children's Agency Could Do for Children's Literature and Childhood Studies." *Jeunesse: Young People, Texts, Cultures*, vol. 8, no. 1, 2016, pp. 291–310.

Gubar, Marah. "Innocence." *Keywords for Children's Literature*, edited by Phil Nel and Lissa Paul, New York UP, 2011, pp. 129–35.

Gundaker, Grey. *Signs of Diaspora, Diaspora of Signs*. Oxford UP, 1998.

Guy-Sheftall, Beverly, editor. *Words of Fire: An Anthology of African-American Feminist Thought*. New Press, 1995.

Hacker, Andrew. *Two Nations: Black and White, Separate, Hostile, Unequal*. 1992. Scribner, 2003.

Hall, Jacquelyn Dowd. "The Long Civil Rights Movement and the Political Uses of the Past." *Journal of American History*, vol. 91, no. 4, 2005, pp. 1233–63.

Hamilton, Virginia. "Ah, Sweet Rememory!" 1981. *Speeches*, pp. 93–101.

Hamilton, Virginia. "Boston Globe-Horn Book Award Acceptance Speech." 24 Oct. 1988. *Speeches*, pp. 172–75.

Hamilton, Virginia. "Reflections: The Marygrove College Contemporary American Authors Lecture, April 1997." *Speeches*, pp. 284–93.

Hamilton, Virginia. *Speeches, Essays and Conversations*. Edited by Arnold Adoff and Kacy Cook, Blue Sky, 2010.

Hamilton, Virginia. "The Spirit Spins: A Writer's Revolution." *Speeches*, pp. 114–30.

Hamilton, Virginia. "Together: Virginia Hamilton and Arnold Adoff." *Speeches*, pp. 203–14.

Harris, Leslie M. *In the Shadow of Slavery: African Americans in New York City, 1626–1863*. U of Chicago P, 2003.

Harris, Marla. "'A History Not Then Taught in History Books': (Re)Writing Reconstruction in Historical Fiction for Children and Young Adults." *The Lion and the Unicorn*, vol. 30, no. 1, 2006, pp. 94–116.

Harris, Trudier. *Saints, Sinners, Saviors: Strong Black Women in African American Literature*. Palgrave, 2001.

Harris, Violet. "African American Children's Literature: The First One Hundred Years." *Journal of Negro Education*, vol. 59, no. 4, 1990, pp. 540–55.

Harvey, David. *A Brief History of Neoliberalism*. Oxford UP, 2005.

Hinton, KaaVonia. *Sharon M. Draper: Embracing Literacy*. Scarecrow, 2009.

Hinton, KaaVonia. "Virtual Erasure: Ntozake Shange, Black Spaces, Wealth, and Children's Biographies." *International Research in Children's Literature*, vol. 16, no. 3, 2023 (forthcoming).

Holloway, Karla F. C. "Cultural Narratives Passed On: African American Mourning Stories." *College English*, vol. 59, no. 1, Jan. 1997, pp. 32–40.
hooks, bell. "'When I was a Young Soldier for the Revolution': Coming to Voice." *Landmark Essays on Voice and Writing*, edited by Peter Elbow, Hermagoras, 1994, pp. 51–58.
Hong, Cathy Park. *Minor Feelings: An Asian American Reckoning*. Random House, 2020.
Hubler, Angela E. "Girl Power and History in the Dear America Series Books." *Children's Literature Association Quarterly*, vol. 25 no. 2, 2000, p. 98–106. Project MUSE, doi:10.1353/chq.0.1657.
Hudson, J. Blaine. *Encyclopedia of the Underground Railroad*. McFarland, 2006.
Hunter, Karen. "Kwame Alexander Talks *The Door of No Return*: #WhattoRead." *The Karen Hunter Show*, 2 Jan. 2023, www.youtube.com/watch?v=RSmok1K5_c8.
Hurston, Zora Neale. *Mules and Men*. 1935. Harper and Row, 1990.
"Infant, Child, and Teen Mortality." *Child Trends*, 2018, www.childtrends.org/indicators/infant-child-and-teen-mortality.
Jirata, Tadesse Jaleta. "Learning through Play: An Ethnographic Study of Children's Riddling in Ethiopia." *Africa: The Journal of the International African Institute*, vol. 82, no. 2, 2012, pp. 272–86.
Johnson, Cassandra V., and Josh McDaniel. "Turpentine Negro." Glave and Stoll, pp. 51–62.
Johnson, Charles. "The End of the Black American Narrative." *The American Scholar*, 1 June 2008, www.theamericanscholar.org/the-end-of-the-black-american-narrative/.
Johnson, Dianne. *Telling Tales: The Pedagogy and Promise of African American Literature for Youth*. Greenwood, 1990.
Jordan, A. C. *Towards an African Literature: The Emergence of Literary Form in Xhosa*. U of California P, 1973.
Katz, William Loren, editor. *Five Slave Narratives*. Arno, 1968.
Kelley, Robin D. G. *Race Rebels: Culture, Politics and the Black Working Class*. Free Press, 1996.
Kennedy, Randall. "The Confounding Truth about Frederick Douglass." *The Atlantic*, Dec. 2018, www.theatlantic.com/magazine/archive/2018/12/the-confounding-truth-about-frederick-douglass/573931/.
King, Deborah K. "Multiple Jeopardy, Multiple Consciousness: The Context of a Black Feminist Ideology." Guy-Sheftall, pp. 294–317.
King, LaGarrett J. "'A Narrative to the Colored Children in American': Lelia Amos Pendleton, African American History Textbooks, and Challenging Personhood." *The Journal of Negro Education*, vol. 84, no. 4, 2015, pp. 519–33.
King, LaGarrett J. "The Status of Black History in U.S. Schools and Society." *Social Education*, vol. 81, no. 1, 2017, pp. 14–18.
King, Wilma. *Stolen Childhood: Slave Youth in Nineteenth-Century America*. Indiana UP, 2011.
Kraamer, Malika. "Ghanian Interweaving in the Nineteenth Century: A New Perspective on Ewe and Asante Textile History." *African Arts*, vol. 39, no. 4, 2006, pp. 36–53, 93–95.
Landers, Jane. *Black Society in Spanish Florida*. U of Illinois P, 1999.
"The Largest Slave Auction, March 3, 1859." *Library of Congress*, 2000, www.americaslibrary.gov/jb/reform/jb_reform_slaveauc_1.html.

LeSeur, Geta. *Ten is the Age of Darkness: The Black Bildungsroman.* U of Missouri P, 1995. *EBSCOhost*, search-ebscohost-com.echo.louisville.edu/login.aspx?direct=true&db=nlebk&AN=46740&site=ehost-live.

Lesley, Naomi. Personal exchange via email, 12 July 2016.

Lester, Julius. *On Writing for Children and Other People.* Dial, 2004.

Lester, Julius. "Hold'im Down, Brer Fox." *The Tales of Uncle Remus: The Adventures of Brer Rabbit.* Dial, 1987. pp. 6–8.

Levine, Robert. "The slave narrative and the revolutionary tradition of American autobiography." *The Cambridge Companion to the African American Slave Narrative*, edited by Audrey Fisch, Cambridge UP, 2009, pp. 99–114.

Lewis, R. W. B. *The American Adam.* U of Chicago P, 1955.

Loewen, James W. *Lies My Teacher Told Me: Everything Your American History Textbook Got Wrong.* Simon & Schuster, 2007.

Loewen, James W. "Slave Narratives and Sociology." *Contemporary Sociology*, vol. 11, no. 4, 1982, pp. 380–84.

Lorde, Audre. "The Master's Tools Will Never Dismantle the Master's House." *Sister Outsider: Essays and Speeches.* Crossing, 1984, pp. 110–13.

Martin, Michelle H. *Brown Gold: Milestones of African American Picture Books, 1845–2002.* Routledge, 2004.

Masolo, Dismas. *African Philosophy in Search of Identity.* Indiana UP, 1994.

Mast, Gerald. "The Film Artist." Mast and Cohen, *Film Theory and Criticism*, pp. 637–41.

Mast, Gerald, and Marshall Cohen, editors. *Film Theory and Criticism: Introductory Readings.* U of Chicago P, 1979.

May, Stephen, and Christine Sleeter. Introduction. *Critical Multiculturalism: Theory and Praxis*, edited by May and Sleeter, Routledge, 2010, pp. 1–16.

McHenry, Elizabeth. "Rereading Literary Legacy: New Considerations of the 19th-Century African-American Reader and Writer." *Callaloo*, vol. 22, no. 2, 1999, pp. 477–82.

McKissack, Fred, and Patricia McKissack. Interview. *Reading Rockets*, www.readingrockets.org/books/interviews/mckissack.

McNair, Jonda C., and Rudine Sims Bishop. "'To Be Great, Heroic, or Beautiful': The Enduring Legacy of *The Brownies' Book*." *The Horn Book*, vol. 94, no. 3, pp. 28–34.

Melamed, Jodi. *Represent and Destroy: Rationalizing Violence in the New Racial Capitalism.* U of Minnesota P, 2011.

Mellix, Barbara. "From Outside In." *The Fourth Genre: Contemporary Writers of/on Creative Nonfiction*, edited by Robert L. Root Jr. and Michael Steinberg. Allyn and Bacon, 1999, pp. 112–20.

Mikkelsen, Nina. "But Is It a Children's Book? A Second Look at Virginia Hamilton's *The Magical Adventures of Pretty Pearl.*" *Children's Literature Association Quarterly*, vol. 11, no, 3, 1986, pp. 134–42.

Mikkelsen, Nina. *Virginia Hamilton.* Twayne, 1994.

Mitchell, Angelyn. *The Freedom to Remember: Narrative, Slavery, and Gender in Contemporary Black Women's Fiction.* Rutgers UP, 2002.

"Monique Coleman." *Internet Movie Database*, www.imdb.com/name/nm0170912/?ref_=ttfc_fc_cl_t3.

Moore, Opal, and Donnarae MacCann. "The Uncle Remus Travesty II: Julius Lester and Virginia Hamilton." *Children's Literature Association Quarterly*, vol. 11 no. 4, 1986, p. 205–9.

Morrison, Toni. *Playing in the Dark: Whiteness and the Literary Imagination*. Vintage, 1992.

Morrison, Toni. "The Site of Memory," Zinsser, pp. 83–102.

Moses, Wilson Jeremiah. *Afrotopia: The Roots of African American History*. Cambridge UP, 1998.

Moses, Wilson Jeremiah. *The Golden Age of Black Nationalism, 1850–1925*. Oxford UP, 1978.

Mullen, Harryette. "African Signs and Spirit Writing." *Callaloo*, vol. 19, no. 3, 1996, pp. 670–89.

Myers, Christopher. "The Apartheid of Children's Literature." *The New York Times*, 15 Mar. 2014.

Neal, Larry. "And Shine Swam On." *Black Fire: An Anthology of Afro-American Writing*. Edited by LeRoi Jones and Larry Neal, William A. Morrow, 1968, pp. 638–56.

Neal, Larry. "The Black Arts Movement." 1968. Bracey, Sanchez, and Smethurst, pp. 55–66.

Nel, Phil, Lissa Paul, and Nina Christensen, editors. *Keywords for Children's Literature*. New York UP, 2021.

Nelson, Marilyn. Interview. C-Span, 22 May 2005, www.c-span.org/video/?187039-1/a-wreath-emmett-till.

Newkirk, Vann R., II. "The Great Land Robbery." *The Atlantic*, Sept. 2019, www.theatlantic.com/magazine/archive/2019/09/this-land-was-our-land/594742/.

Nichols, Bill. "*Auteur* Criticism." *Movies and Methods*, edited by Nichols, U of California P, 1976, pp. 221–23.

Nichols, Charles H. *Many Thousand Gone: The Ex-Slaves' Account of Their Bondage and Freedom*. Brill, 1963.

Nielsen, Aldon Lynn. *Black Chant: Languages of African-American Postmodernism*. Cambridge UP, 1997.

Nikolajeva, Maria. "'A Dream of Complete Idleness'; Depiction of Labor in Children's Fiction." *The Lion and the Unicorn*, vol. 26, no. 3, Sept. 2002, pp. 305–21.

Nodelman, Perry. *The Hidden Adult*. The Johns Hopkins UP, 2008.

Nora, Pierre. "Between Memory and History: *Les Lieux de Mémoire*." Fabre and O'Meally, 284–300.

O'Connor, Roison. "John Legend appears to condemn Kanye West after slavery comments." *The Independent*, 2 May 2018, www.independent.co.uk/arts-entertainment/music/news/john-legend-mel-west-slavery-tmz-interview-comments-twitter-criticism-retweet-a8332096.html.

Ogunleye, Foluke. "Transcending the 'Dust': African American Filmmakers Preserving the 'Glimpse of the Eternal.'" *College Literature*, vol. 34, no.1, 2007, pp. 156–73.

Okpewho, Isidore. *African Oral Literature: Backgrounds, Character and Continuity*. Indiana UP, 1992.

Older, Daniel José. "The real censorship in children's books: smiling slaves is just the half of it." *The Guardian*, 29 Jan. 2016, www.theguardian.com/books/2016/jan/29/smiling-slaves-the-real-censorship-in-childrens-books.

Osofsky, Gilbert, editor. *Puttin' On Ole Massa: The Slave Narratives of Henry Bibb, William Wells Brown, and Solomon Northup*. Harper & Row, 1969.

Owens, Ann. "Income Segregation between School Districts and Inequality in Students' Achievement." *Sociology of Education*, vol. 91, no. 1, 2018, pp. 1–27.

Patterson, Orlando. *Rituals of Blood: Consequences of Slavery in Two American Centuries*. Basic Civitas, 1998.

Patterson, Orlando. *Slavery and Social Death: A Comparative Study*. Harvard UP, 1982.

Pattillo-McCoy, Mary. *Black Picket Fences: Privilege and Peril among the Black Middle Class*. U of Chicago P, 1999.

Paul, Lissa. "Enigma Variations: What Feminist Theory Knows about Children's Literature." *Signal*, vol. 54, 1987, pp. 186–201.

"Persona." *Academy of American Poets*, www.poets.org/glossary/persona-poem.

Petro, Pamela. *Sitting Up with the Dead: A Storied Journey through the American South*. Arcade, 2002.

Pratt, Mary Louise. *Imperial Eyes: Travel Writing and Transculturation*. Taylor & Francis, 2008.

Price, Danielle. "Heteropic Nightmares and Coming of Age in *Elijah of Buxton*. *Jeunesse*, vol. 8, no. 1, 2016, pp. 202–26. *Project MUSE*, www.muse.jhu.edu.echo.louisville.edu/article/629403/pdf.

Price, Richard. "Maroons: Rebel Slaves in the Americas." *Creativity and Resistance: Maroon Cultures in the Americas*, Smithsonian Institute, 1992, www./folklife.si.edu/resources/maroon/educational_guide/table_of_contents.htm.

Radano, Ronald M. *Lying Up a Nation*. U of Chicago P, 2003.

Rankine, Claudia. "The Condition of Black Life is One of Mourning." *The New York Times Magazine*, 22 June 2015, www.nytimes.com/2015/06/22/magazine/the-condition-of-black-life-is-one-of-mourning.html.

Redding, J. Saunders. *To Make a Poet Black*. U of North Carolina P, 1939.

Reese, Debbie. "Not Recommended: *A Fine Dessert* by Emily Jenkins and Sophie Blackall." *American Indians in Children's Literature*, 29 Oct. 2015, americanindiansinchildrenslit erature.blogspot.com/2015/10/not-recommended-finedessert-by-emily.html.

"Report Shows African Americans Lost Half Their Wealth Due to Housing Crisis and Unemployment." *National Low Income Housing Coalition*, 30 Aug. 2013, www.nlihc.org/resource/report-shows-african-americans-lost-half-their-wealth-due-housing-crisis-and-unemployment.

Rizzuto, Lauren. "'Good Cause for Living': Environmental Justice in Virginia Hamilton's *M. C. Higgins, the Great*." *International Research in Children's Literature*, vol. 16, no. 3, 2023 (forthcoming).

Roberts, John W. *From Trickster to Badman: The Black Folk Hero in Slavery and Freedom*. U of Pennsylvania P, 1989.

Roethler, Jacque. "Three Phases of the Black Aesthetic—Ann Petry's *Tituba of Salem Village*, Eloise Greenfield and Lessie Jones Little's *Childtimes* and Patricia McKissack's *Sojourner Truth: Ain't I a Woman*." *Journal of African Children's & Youth Literature*, vol. 6, 1994/95, pp. 56–73.

Royster, Jacqueline Jones. *Traces of a Stream: Literacy and Social Change Among African Americans*. U of Pittsburgh P, 2000.

Rudd, Thomas. "Racial Disproportionality in School Discipline: Implicit Bias is Heavily Implicated." The Ohio State University, The Kirwan Institute for the Study of Race and Ethnicity, Feb. 2014, kirwaninstitute.osu.edu/racial-disproportionality-in-school-discipline-implicit-bias-is-heavily-implicated/.

Rushdy, Ashraf. *Neo-Slave Narratives: Studies in the Social Logic of a Literary Form.* Oxford UP, 1999.

Sánchez-Eppler, Karen. "Playing at Class." *The American Child: A Cultural Studies Reader,* edited by Caroline F. Levander and Carol J. Singley, Rutgers UP, 2003, pp. 40–62.

Sarris, Andrew. "Notes on the Auteur Theory in 1962." Mast and Cohen, pp. 650–65.

Schwebel, Sara. *Child-Sized History: Fictions of the Past in U.S. Classrooms.* Vanderbilt UP, 2011.

Sekora, John. "Black Message/White Envelope: Genre, Authenticity, and Authority in the Antebellum Slave Narrative." *Callaloo,* no. 32, 1987, pp. 482–515. *JSTOR,* www.jstor.org/stable/2930465.

Serwer, Adam. "The Fight Over the 1619 Project Is Not About the Facts." *The Atlantic,* 23 Dec. 2019, www.theatlantic.com/ideas/archive/2019/12/historians-clash-1619-project/604093/.

Shields, John. "Phillis Wheatley's Struggle for Freedom in Her Poetry and Prose." *The Collected Works of Phillis Wheatley,* edited by John Shields, Oxford UP, 1988, pp. 229–70.

Silverstein, Jake. "Why We Published *The 1619 Project.*" *The New York Times Magazine,* 20 Dec. 2019.

Sims, Rudine. *Shadow and Substance: Afro-American Experience in Contemporary Children's Fiction.* NCTE, 1982.

Smethurst, James Edward. *The Black Arts Movement: Literary Nationalism in the 1960s and 1970s.* U of North Carolina P, 2005.

Smith, Katharine Capshaw. *Children's Literature of the Harlem Renaissance.* Indiana UP, 2006.

Smitherman, Geneva. *Talkin and Testifyin: The Language of Black America.* Wayne State UP, 1977.

Sola, Michele, and Adrian Bennett. "The Struggle for Voice: Narrative, Literacy, and Consciousness in an East Harlem School." *Journal of Education,* vol. 167, no. 1, Mar. 1985, pp. 88–110.

Spaulding, A. Timothy. *Re-Forming the Past: History, the Fantastic, and the Postmodern Slave Narrative.* The Ohio State UP, 2005.

"Status and Trends in the Education of Racial and Ethnic Groups." *National Center for Education Statistics,* Feb. 2019, www.nces.ed.gov/programs/raceindicators/indicator_REE.asp.

Stevenson, Brenda E. "'Out of the Mouths of Ex-Slaves': Carter G. Woodson's *Journal of Negro History* 'Invents' the Study of Slavery." *Journal of African American History,* vol. 100, no. 4, 2015, pp. 698–720.

"The Story of the L.A. Rebellion." *UCLA Library Film and Television Archive,* www.cinema.ucla.edu/la-rebellion/story-la-rebellion.

Stuckey, Sterling. "A Last Stern Struggle: Henry Highland Garnet and Liberation Thinking." *Black Leaders of the Nineteenth Century,* edited by Leon Litwack and August Meier, U of Illinois P, 1988, pp. 128–47.

Szczesiul, Anthony. *The Southern Hospitality Myth: Ethics, Politics, Race and American Memory*. U of Georgia P, 2017.

Tate, Claudia. *Domestic Allegories of Political Desire*. Oxford UP, 1992.

Tettenborn, Éva. "'But what if I can't change?' Desire, Denial & Melancholia in Randall Kenan's *A Visitation of Spirits*." *Southern Literary Journal*, vol. 40, no. 2, 2008, pp. 249–66.

Thomas, Ebony Elizabeth. "The Shadow Book and Other Tales: Some Considerations of Racial Trauma in Children's Books." Scholar-in-Residence Presentation, Graduate Program in Children's Literature, 4 July 2022, Hollins University, Roanoke, VA.

Tolson, Nancy. "The Black Aesthetic within Children's Literature." *Exploring Culturally Diverse Literature for Children and Adolescents*, edited by Darwin L. Henderson and Jill P. May, Pearson Education, 2005, pp. 65–78.

Tolson, Nancy. *Black Children's Literature Got de Blues: The Creativity of Black Writers and Illustrators*. Peter Lang, 2008.

Toni Morrison: The Pieces I Am. Directed by Timothy Greenfield-Sanders, Perfect Day Films, 2019.

Tribunella, Eric. "Boyhood." Nel, Paul, and Christensen, pp. 34–37.

Trites, Roberta Seelinger. *Disturbing the Universe: Power and Repression in Adolescent Literature*. 2000.

Van Leer, David. "Reading Slavery: The Anxiety of Ethnicity in Douglass's Narrative." *Frederick Douglass: New Literary and Historical Essays*, edited by Eric Sundquist, Cambridge UP, 1990, pp. 118–40.

VanderHaagen, Sara C. "Black Heroes and 'The Jury': *The Brownies' Book* Biographies as Counter-Memory for Black Children." *A Centennial Celebration of The Brownies' Book*, edited by Dianne Johnson-Feelings and Jonda C. McNair, UP of Mississippi, 2022, pp. 56–77.

Vlach, John Michael. *The Afro-American Tradition in Decorative Arts*. U of Georgia P, 1990.

Voigt, Benjamin. "Marilyn Nelson 101." *Poetry Foundation*, 7 March 2019, www.poetryfoundation.org/articles/149830/marilyn-nelson-101.

Walker, Alice. "In Search of Our Mothers' Gardens." 1974. *In Search of Our Mothers' Gardens: Womanist Prose*. HBJ, 1983, pp. 199–243.

Walter, Mildred Pitts. Interview by David P. Cline. *Civil Rights History Project: Mildred Pitts Walter*, 1 Feb. 2013, www.loc.gov/item/afc2010039_crhp0059/.

Walter, Mildred Pitts. *Something Inside So Strong: Life in Pursuit of Choice, Courage, and Change*. UP of Mississippi, 2019.

Waniek, Marilyn Nelson. "Owning the Masters." *Gettysburg Review*, spring 1995, www.gettysburgreview.com/selections/detail.dot?inode=750c6431-75cf-422c-a3c2-e830e13afd8a.

Warner-Lewis, Maureen. "Africanisms in the New World." *The Oxford Encyclopedia of African Thought*. Vol. 1, edited by Abiola Irele and Biodun Jeyifo, Oxford UP, 2010, pp. 37–40.

West, Cornel. *Restoring Hope: Conversations on the Future of Black America*. Beacon, 1999.

West, E. James. Ebony *Magazine and Lerone Bennett, Jr.: Popular Black History in Postwar America*. U of Illinois P, 2020.

White, Deborah Gray. *Ar'n't I a Woman? Female Slaves in the Plantation South.* Norton, 1999.

White, Rachel E. "The Power of Play: A Research Summary on Play and Learning." *Minnesota Children's Museum,* www.childrensmuseums.org/images/MCMResearch Summary.pdf.

Wideman, John Edgar. "The Divisible Man." *Life Magazine,* vol. 11, no. 5, p. 116.

Wilcots, Barbara. "African American Folk Culture." *Companion to Southern Literature: Themes, Genres, Places, Movements, and Motifs,* edited by Joseph M. Flora, Lucinda Hardwick MacKethan, and Todd W. Taylor, Louisiana State UP, 2002, pp. 7–10.

Willis, John C. *Forgotten Time: The Yazoo-Mississippi Delta after the Civil War.* U of Virginia P, 2000.

Wilson, William Julius. "Why Both Social Structure and Culture Matter in a Holistic Analysis of Inner-City Poverty." *The Annals of the American Academy of Political and Social Science.* Vol. 629, May 2010, pp. 200–219.

Wohler, Kevin. "The Right to Letters: Shedding Light on America's Dark Past in *Nightjohn.*" *Filmguru,* 11 Feb. 2004, www.filmguru.net/essays/essay6.html.

Wright, Nazera Sadiq. *Black Girlhood in the Nineteenth Century.* U of Illinois P, 2016.

Yenika-Agnaw, Vivian. *Representing Africa in Children's Literature: Old and New Ways of Seeing.* Routledge, 2008.

Yetman, Norman, editor. *Voices from Slavery.* Holt, 1970.

Zinsser, William, editor. *Inventing the Truth.* Houghton Mifflin Harcourt, 1995.

INDEX

abolitionism: abolitionist literature, 12–13, 80; in *Elijah of Buxton* (Curtis), 131–33, 135; in *Home Is With Our Family* (Hansen), 163; in slave narratives, 117
activism, Black, 22, 28–29, 31, 52, 91, 102
Adventures of Pretty Pearl, The (Hamilton), 55
aesthetic movements, Afrocentric, 22, 34–35, 45–48, 101, 103, 201
Africa: Ashanti people, 53, 56, 57–61, 69; Dogon culture, 77–80, 81–84, 86–88, 92–93; East African cultures, 78; ethnic folkways, 57, 74–76; Ewe people/society, 56, 62, 63–64; Fulani traditions, 24; and gendered labor, 64, 68–69; idealization of African culture, 64; portrayals of in literature, 53, 55; Sierra Leone, 57–58; and spirits of past lives, 71–72, 78–86, 114–15, 193; views of, 38; West African folklore, 119–20
African American culture: aesthetic movements, 22, 34–35, 45–48, 101, 103, 201; alienation and nihilism, 18, 24, 67, 90; animal tales, 134, 156, 213n25; and assimilation, 48–49, 164, 198, 216n18; Black identity, 83–85, 93–99; communal aspects, 136; cross-class culture, 164, 165, 215n6; development of, 74–75; enslaved person's songs, 105, 110; folktales, 76–77, 121–25, 212n15; orality, 20–21, 35–36, 95, 98–99, 100–101, 116, 120, 177; Pan-Africanism, 53, 64, 78; representations of Black interiority, 10, 23, 34, 37, 39–40, 76, 166, 201; roots of, 33–34, 51–52; storytelling, 10, 20–21, 63, 68, 72, 76, 98–99, 120, 127, 177; in urban America, 165–79; visual culture, 86–91; voice, 97–98; worship, 118–19, 171, 210n12
African Americans: collectivity vs. individualism, 4, 25, 49, 53, 61 62, 85–86, 136, 179–80, 186, 188, 200; income/wealth gaps, 29, 190, 214n2; mortality and health statistics, 88, 208nn9–10; in public school systems, 29, 30; voice and expression, 41–42, 76, 96–98
agency: Black agency, 12–13, 16–17, 22–24, 37–39, 101–2; Black financial agency, 160, 162, 166, 168, 176; Black women, 97; play and children's agency, 126, 127, 129, 131, 211n5; in *Time's Memory* (Lester), 72–73, 84
Alexander, Kwame, 17, 51, 204n10
Alexander, Leslie, 165–66
Allen, Reniqua, 214n1
Amos Fortune, Free Man (Yates), 55, 65
Anderson, Carol, 30
Anderson, Melinda, 28
Argenti, Nicolas, 129, 211n6
Armstrong, William, 27
Ashanti people, 53, 56, 57–61, 69
Asim, Jabari, 122, 214n31
assimilation of African Americans, 48–49, 164, 198, 216n18
Associated Publishers, 47–48, 53–54
Astor, John Jacob, 169–70

Baker, Houston, 59
Batho, Nick, 39
Beloved (Morrison), 3
Bennett, Lerone, Jr., 41
Bernstein, Robin, 15, 144, 147, 156, 214n27
Bishop, Rudine Sims, 13, 22, 36–37, 77, 95
Black activism, 22, 28–29, 31, 52, 91, 102
Blackall, Sophie, 128
Black Arts Movement (BAM), 7, 22, 25–26, 32–39, 54, 95, 124
Black Folktales (Lester), 77
Black identity, 83–85, 93–99
Black Lives Matter movement, 10, 208n10
Black Man, The (Brown), 45
Black Nationalists and community, 161, 170–71
Black societal conditions: housing insecurity, 165, 176–77; land ownership and financial agency, 160–65, 190, 215n5; land ownership in postbellum South, 179–91, 193–94; land ownership in urban areas, 164, 176–79; North/South connections, 160, 163, 194–96; real estate ownership, 160–65
Black vernacular, 54, 112, 122–23, 149. *See also* trickster tales
Bontemps, Arna, 13, 41, 206n1
Botkin, B. A., 40
Bradford, Clare, 66
Brandt, Deborah, 104
Br'er Rabbit, 95, 148, 149–50, 156, 212n15
Brison, Susan J., 87
Brooks, Wanda, 11, 12
Brown, Anthony L., 28
Brown, William Wells, 45
Brownies' Book, The (magazine), 45, 46–47, 48, 53
Brown v. Topeka Board of Education, 30
Burnett, Charles, 3, 28, 100, 111, 112, 122–23
Butler, Octavia, 3, 13, 147–48

Cain, Bill, 112
capitalism, 156–57; and land ownership, 161–62; in New South, 164

Capshaw, Katharine, 13–14, 104. *See also* Smith, Katharine Capshaw
Captive, The (Hansen), 8, 13, 18, 31, 51–53, 56–62
Cary, Lorene, 13
Charles, Ray, 35
Cheng, Anne Anlin, 73
Cherokee community, 75
Chery, Marc Arthur, 136
Chesnut, Mary Boykin Miller, 119
childhood, Romantic concepts of, 111, 146–47, 157
Child Slavery before and after Emancipation (Duane), 73
Child's Story of the Negro, The (Shackelford), 47–48
Child Story of the Negro (Associated Publishers), 48
Chinese laborers in Reconstruction South, 145, 151, 153–55
Chinese monkey hero, 213n25
Christianity, 85–86, 92, 118–19, 207n7
Civil Rights Act (1964), 29
civil rights movement, 8, 22, 25–27, 192
Clark, P. Djèlí, 126
Clifton, Lucille, 4–5, 38
colonization: of Africa, 38; Spanish, in Florida, 68, 69
Coltrane, John, 35
Confessions of Nat Turner, The (Styron), 23
Congress of Racial Equality (CORE), 25, 26
Connolly, Paula, 12–13, 42, 43, 47, 71, 100, 131
Cooper, J. California, 13
Copper Sun (Draper), 8, 18, 51–53, 62–70
Corregidora (Jones), 38
Courlander, Harold, 115
Crawford, Margo Natalie, 26, 33, 37
Crisis, The (magazine), 45
crossover literature, 45, 205n21
Curtis, Christopher Paul, 6, 8, 28, 31, 126, 162

Dark-Thirty, The (McKissack), 123
Davis, Zeinabu irene, 9, 28, 31, 126, 136–43
Day of Tears (Lester), 39, 77

Dear America book series, 116–21
De Cunzo, Lu Ann, 156
Dessa Rose (Williams), 13
diaspora, African, 53–54, 56, 75, 80–83, 86–88, 94–97, 138, 149, 178
Diouf, Sylviane A., 74
Dixon, Melvin, 95
Dogon culture, 77–80, 81–84, 86–88, 92–93
doll play, 156, 214n27
domestic novels, 165, 172, 173–74, 216nn17–18
Door of No Return, The (Alexander), 17, 51
Douglass, Frederick, 104, 105–6, 110, 138–39, 148, 198, 200
Draper, Sharon, 8, 62–70
Duane, Anna Mae, 13–14, 104
Dubey, Madhu, 38
Du Bois, W. E. B., 33, 46, 114, 198
Dunbar, Paul Laurence, 33–34
DuVernay, Ava, 19

Easmon, Kathleen, 53
Ebony (magazine), 41–42
Elijah of Buxton (Curtis), 6, 8, 126, 130–36
Elliott, Zetta, 80
empathy, encouragement of readers', 16, 37
epistolary forms, 43, 116–18, 210n11
escape narratives, 5–6, 66–67, 73, 107, 144, 152–53
Essays (Plato), 45
Euro-American frameworks/values, 69, 80, 95, 117
Ewe people/society, 56, 62, 63–64
Ezra, Kate, 92

Family (Cooper), 13
Feelings, Muriel, 78
Feelings, Tom, 78
feminism, Black, 7, 38–39, 188
Ferguson, Katy, 46, 47
film: auteur theory, 10; impact on young viewers, 9–10. See also *Mother of the River* (film); *Nightjohn* (film)
Fine Dessert, A (Griffin and Blackall), 128
Five Slave Narratives (Katz), 41

Flake, Sharon, 14
Forty Acres and Maybe a Mule (Robinette), 162
Foster, Frances Smith, 106, 206n2, 209n7
Foster, Gwendolyn Audrey, 136–38, 212n10
Freedman's Third Reader, The (1865), 12
freedom: collective vs. individual struggle, 61–62; correlation with literacy, 104–5; history and meaning of word, 7–8; varying conceptions of, 25
Freedom Business, The (Nelson), 51
freedom narrative genre: African influences, 54; Black activism of writers, 28–29; Black activism's impact, 22; Black aesthetics, 45–48; Black agency, 16–17, 22–24, 37–38; Black Arts Movement's impact, 7, 22–23, 25–26, 32–39, 54, 78, 100, 124, 130, 177, 204n9, 215n13; Black creativity, 198–99; Black feminist critiques, 7; Black historical testimony, 39–45; Black land ownership, 160–65, 176–79; Black resistance, 200–202; challenges to simplistic historiography, 31–32; collectivity vs. individualism, 4, 25, 49, 53, 61–62, 85–86, 136, 179–80, 186, 188, 200; depictions of slavery, 17–19, 131–33; enslavement vs. freedom and social identity, 6–7; frameworks, culturally specific, of struggle/survival, 11, 14; frameworks for analysis, 48–50; overview, 4–6
Freedom to Remember, The (Mitchell), 13
Freeman, Elizabeth, 23–25, 44
Fugitive Slave Act, 176
fugitives from slavery, 115, 131–32, 133, 137, 143, 175
Fulani traditions, 24
Fuller, Hoyt, 34–35

Gates, Henry Louis, Jr., 96–97, 98, 104, 203n4
Gee, James Paul, 123
Genovese, Eugene, 138
Gilroy, Paul, 64
Giovanni, Nikki, 54

Giroux, Henry, 111
Givens, Jarvis R., 28, 201
Glory Field, The (Myers), 8, 121–22, 161, 191–98
Great Migration, 192, 196
Great Slave Narratives, The (Bontemps), 41
Griffin, Emily, 128
"group victimization," 4, 36, 37, 40, 107, 203n3
Gubar, Marah, 14–15, 146, 152

Hamilton, Virginia, 8, 16, 25, 80; Black perspectives in "liberation literature," 25–26; on cultural inheritance, 71; culturally specific frameworks of struggle/survival, 14; historical nonfiction, 34
Hansen, Joyce, 6, 8, 9, 31, 56–62, 100, 126
Harlem Renaissance, 43, 46
Harris, Joel Chandler, 95
Harris, Leslie M., 177
Harris, Violet, 11–12
Hate U Give, The (Thomas), 162
Heart Calls Home, The (Hansen), 43, 162
Her Stories (Hamilton), 8
history/historiography: Black agency, new perspectives, 27, 163; Black historical experience, synchronic vs. diachronic, 191–92; Black historical testimony, 39–45; Black history, contemporary approaches, 19–20; Black resistance, 200–201; commemorative projects, 200; insiders' accounts, 10; literary archeology, 43–44; of slavery, 107; superficial approaches to Black history, 27–28
Home Is With Our Family (Hansen), 6, 8–10, 19, 126, 160–61, 163, 165, 170–79
hooks, bell, 97
hospitality industry and Black labor, 196–97, 198
Hughes, Langston, 138

"I am accused of tending to the past" (Clifton), 4–5
Incidents in the Life of a Slave Girl (Jacobs), 13, 110, 174

individualism contrasted with collectivity, 4, 25, 49, 53, 61–62, 85–86, 136, 179–80, 186, 188, 200
interracial friendships, 127, 137, 141–42, 181, 189. See also *Sugar* (Rhodes)
I Thought My Soul Would Rise and Fly (Hansen), 8, 43, 100, 112, 116, 117–18

Jacobs, Harriet, 13, 110, 174
Jambo Means Hello (Feelings and Feelings), 78
Jirata, Tadese Jaleta, 129
Johnson, Dianne, 37, 42
Jones, Gayl, 38
Jordan, A. C., 140–41
Jordan, June, 38
Journey of Little Charlie, The (Curtis), 162

Katz, William Loren, 41
Keckley, Elizabeth, 69, 206n2
Keelan, Sarah Talbert, 53
Kelley, Robin D. G., 155
Killers of Sheep (film), 3
Kindred (Butler), 3, 13, 148–49
King, Debra, 188
King, LaGarrett, 27–28
King, Martin Luther, Jr., 26, 85–86, 169, 200
King, Wilma, 129
kinship systems: Fulani tradition, 24; kinship theory, 14–15

Land, The (Taylor), 8, 19, 43, 48–49, 161, 163–64, 179–91
Landers, Jane, 68
language: academic prose, 123; Black communication call and response, 195–96; Black vernacular, 54, 112; Black voices and expressions, 97–98; double-voicing, 105, 109; and empowerment, 138–39; linguistic acculturation, 59–60, 62, 65–66; mainstream American English vs. Black speech, 34–35; signifying, 177, 212n17; and storytelling, 95
L.A. Rebellion, 3, 10, 28–29, 130

INDEX

Lay My Burden Down (Botkin), 40
learning: and African literacy, 59–60; as creative interaction, 16. *See also* literacy
Legend, John, 19
Lesley, Naomi, 94, 134, 213n22
Lester, Julius, 8, 11, 16, 31, 39–41, 76–77; on writer's role, 93–94; *On Writing for Children and Other People*, 98
Let My People Go: Bible Stories Told by a Freeman of Color (McKissack and McKissack), 43
Levine, Robert S., 98
"liberation literature," 8, 25. *See also* freedom narrative genre
lieux de mémoire, 72, 94
literacy: background concerning Black community, 100–102; as cultural coping tool, 121–25; in Dear America book series, 116–21; and folklore, 102–3; idealist views of, 110–11; paradigm of young girls' power, 111–16; in Paulsen's *Nightjohn*, 106–9; resistance to, 103–4; in slave narratives, 104–11
Locke, Alain, 46
Loewen, James, 27, 41, 73, 205n12
Long Journey Home, The (Lester), 76
Look Out, Whitey! Black Power's Gon' Get Your Mama! (Lester), 39
L'Ouverture, Toussaint, 46

Magical Adventures of Pretty Pearl, The (Hamilton), 8, 74–76
Many Thousand Gone (Hamilton), 34
maroon societies, 74–75
Martin, Michelle H., 204n3, 206n23
masculinity, 38, 60–61
Masters, Edgar Lee, 166
May, Stephen, 31, 62, 179
McHenry, Elizabeth, 104
McKissack, Fredrick, 42–43
McKissack, Patricia, 8, 42–43, 100
McNair, Jonda C., 11, 12
Melamed, Jodi, 30–31, 49, 55–56, 164, 166, 192
Mellix, Barbara, 123

memory: and autonomy, 73; cultural memory, 74–76; fiction as preserver of, 72; memories of loss, 91–93; and visual culture, 86–91
middle-grade narratives, 8–9
Middle Passage: White Ships/Black Cargo (Feelings), 51
Mikkelsen, Nina, 76
Milliken v. Bradley, 30
Mirandy and Brother Wind (McKissack), 123
Mitchell, Angelyn, 13, 38, 117
Morrison, Toni, 3, 38, 43–44, 201
Mother of the River (film), 31, 126, 130, 136–43, 158
Moynihan, Daniel Patrick, 165
multiculturalism: *Amos Fortune, Free Man* (Yates), 55; critical, 31–32, 62, 160, 164, 191–92; failures of, 30–31
My Bondage and My Freedom (Douglass), 110
Myers, Christopher, 4
Myers, Walter Dean, 8, 121–22, 161
My Seneca Village (Nelson), 6, 9–10, 126, 160–63, 165–70

names, given, 24, 208n19
Narrative of the Life of Frederick Douglass, 105–6
Neal, Larry, 23, 45
"Negro Speaks of Rivers, The" (Hughes), 138
Nelson, Marilyn, 6, 9, 10, 51, 126, 215n8. *See also* Waniek, Marilyn Nelson
Nelson, Vaunda Micheaux, 14
neo-abolitionist literature, 12–13, 42
neoliberalism, 49–50, 136, 156–57, 197–98
neo-slave narratives, 13, 43, 72, 100, 112
New Negro Renaissance, 45–46, 47, 53
New York City: as Black urban mecca, 165–79; Central Park, 160–61. *See also* *Home Is With Our Family* (Hansen); *My Seneca Village* (Nelson)
Nightjohn (film), 3, 15, 35–36, 100, 111–16
Nightjohn (Paulsen), 3, 8, 103–4, 106–9
Noah, Trevor, 19
Nodelman, Perry, 133

Obama, Barack, 166, 169
Okpewho, Isidore, 138, 139
Old African, The (Lester), 77
On Writing for Children and Other People (Lester), 98
oral-based communal culture, 20–21, 35–36, 95, 98–99, 100–101, 116, 120, 177
Organization of Black American Culture, 34–35
Osofsky, Gilbert, 41
Our Nig (Wilson), 174
Out From This Place (Hansen), 8, 121

Pan-Africanism, 53, 64, 78
Parker, Charlie, 35
Patterson, Orlando, 24, 41, 67
Pattillo-McCoy, Mary, 164
Paul, Lissa, 111
Paulsen, Gary, 3, 8
persona poems, 10, 34, 162, 166. See also *My Seneca Village* (Nelson)
Picture of Freedom, A (McKissack), 8, 100, 112, 116, 120–21
Pinkney, Andrea Davis, 14
Plato, Ann, 45
play and leisure: freeing play in *Sugar* (Rhodes), 143–56; gendered aspects, 156–57; overview, 126–30, 211n5; portrayed in *Elijah of Buxton*, 130–36; and social justice, 156–59; wordplay, 133, 136–43, 177, 212n17
poems, persona. See persona poems
popular culture: Black agency, perspectives on, 27, 29; views on financial standing and poverty, 164–65; white cultural influences, 32–33
Pratt, Mary Louise, 66
Price, Danielle, 131–32
Price of a Child, The (Cary), 13
print culture: Black-owned presses and journals, 35–36; and orality in Black community, 101–2; white print culture, 96–97
Puttin' On Ole Massa (Osofsky), 41

racism: navigating constraints of, 191–92; in postbellum South, 48–49, 181–82, 183–84, 185–86; systemic, 30–31, 47, 189
Reagan, Ronald, 29
Reconstruction period, 18–19, 48, 102, 103, 117, 126, 161, 180, 190. See also *Land, The* (Taylor); *Sugar* (Rhodes)
Rhodes, Jewell Parker, 8, 28, 126, 143–56
Rice, Tamir, 128
riddles, 138–39. See also wordplay
Road to Freedom, The (Asim), 122
Roberts, John, 115, 134
Robinette, Harriette, 162
Roll of Thunder, Hear My Cry (Taylor), 180
Romantic concepts of childhood, 111, 146–47, 157
Royster, Jacqueline Jones, 124

San Antonio Independent School District v. Rodriguez, 30
Sanchez, Sonia, 54
Sánchez-Eppler, Karen, 126
schools: Black students in public school, 29, 30; curricular materials, 27–28
Schwebel, Sara, 31, 55, 62
Second Daughter (Walter), 6, 13, 23–25, 44, 126
segregation: housing, 30, 162; public school systems, 28, 30
Sekora, John, 97–98
self-determination vs. assimilation, 48–49. See also assimilation of African Americans
Seneca Village (New York City), 44, 163, 165. See also *Home Is With Our Family* (Hansen); *My Seneca Village* (Nelson)
Sent for You Yesterday (Wideman), 71
Shackelford, Janet Dabney, 47–48
Shange, Ntozake, 38
Sierra Leone, 57–58
signifying (wordplay), 177, 212n17
1619 Project, 20, 27
1619 Project, The (Hannah-Jones and Watson), 51
slave narratives, 40–44, 104–11, 138, 209n7

slavery: antislavery activism, 174–75, 176; enslaved children, 73; escape from, 67; legal challenges to, 23; Middle Passage, 51–52, 65; "natal alienation," 24; portrayal of in freedom narratives, 37–38; portrayed in Lester's work, 76–77; represented in children's literature, 17–19; resistance vs. acceptance, 66–67, 109, 140; "school of slavery," 56, 206n2; slave revolts, 92–93; "social death," 24, 56; stereotypes, 40; and survival, 82. See also *Captive, The* (Hansen); *Copper Sun* (Draper); *Elijah of Buxton* (Curtis); *Nightjohn* (film); *Nightjohn* (Paulsen); *Picture of Freedom, A* (McKissack); *Time's Memory* (Lester)
slave songs, 105, 110
Sleeter, Christine E., 31, 62, 179
Smethurst, James Edward, 35
Smith, Jean, 32–33
Smith, Katharine Capshaw, 45–46, 47–48, 53, 127. See also Capshaw, Katharine
Smitherman, Geneva, 212n17
social activism. *See* activism, Black
Song of the Trees (Taylor), 162, 180
songs, enslaved persons', 105, 110, 119
Sounder (Armstrong), 27
Southern Poverty Law Center (SPLC), 20, 27–28
Spaulding, A. Timothy, 80, 212n11
spirits of past lives, 71–72, 78–86, 114–15, 193
Spoon River Anthology (Masters), 166
Stepto, Robert, 104
stereotypes: of African Americans, 7, 144, 208n11; of African Americans' ability and achievement, 98–99, 209n4; African American slavery, 40; anti-intellectualism, 105; of Black children, 128, 146–47; of Chinese persons, 213n22; countering, 15, 103; noninnocence of Black children, 15; Sambo character, 128; slavery, 40
Stewart, Maria W., 170, 174
Still, William, 45
Story of the Negro (Bontemps), 206n1

storytelling, 10, 20–21, 63, 68, 72, 76, 98–99, 120, 127, 177, 189
Styron, William, 23
Sugar (Rhodes), 8, 15–16, 18–19, 126, 143–57
survival methods, culturally specific, 9, 14, 125
Sweet Whispers, Brother Rush (Hamilton), 71

"Tailypo" story, 173, 177–78
Tate, Claudia, 172, 174, 216nn17–18
Taylor, Mildred, 8, 43
Tettenborn, Éva, 90
Third Life of Grange Copeland, The (Walker), 38
This Side of Home (Watson), 162
This Strange New Feeling (Lester), 39, 77
Thomas, Angie, 162
Thomas, Ebony Elizabeth, 17, 25, 32
Time's Memory (Lester), 8, 11, 18, 31, 36, 39, 55, 71–74, 77–91, 99; and memories of loss, 91–93; writer's role and selfhood, 94–95
To Be a Slave (Lester), 16, 39–41, 76
Tolson, Nancy, 33
To Sleep with Anger (film), 3
trauma: childhood, 18, 157; racial, 90; recovery from, 87, 89; of slavery, 65, 67, 77, 79, 81
trickster tales, 16, 102–3, 105, 111, 114, 120, 133–34, 142, 144, 149
Trites, Roberta Seelinger, 179
Truth, Sojourner, 46, 174–75

Uncle Remus (Lester), 77, 95
Underground Railroad, 42, 120, 203n4
Underground Railroad, The (Still), 45

Vandervort-Cobb, Joy, 137
Van Leer, David, 105
Voices from Slavery (Yetman), 41

Walker, Alice, 38
Walter, Mildred Pitts, 6, 23–25, 44, 126; activism of, 26; on children's agency, 36–37

Waniek, Marilyn Nelson, 215n13. *See also* Nelson, Marilyn
Warner, Susan, 173
Warner-Lewis, Maureen, 58
Washington, Booker T., 69, 206n2
Watson, Renee, 162
Watsons Go to Birmingham-1963, The (Curtis), 31
Well, The (Taylor), 162
West, E. James, 41, 200
West, Kanyé, 19
Which Way Freedom? (Hansen), 8, 121
White, Deborah Gray, 107
White, Rachel, 129
white gaze, 136, 187, 204–05n8
white supremacy, 12, 28, 32–33, 59, 169–70, 180–83
Wide, Wide World, The (Warner), 173
Wideman, John Edgar, 71
Wilcot, Barbara, 88
Williams, Sherley Anne, 13
Williams-Garcia, Rita, 14

Willis, John C., 185
Wilson, Harriet, 174
Wilson, William Julius, 164–65
Woods, Brenda, 28, 211n5
Woodson, Carter G., 47–48, 53–54
Word Pictures of the Great (Associated Publishers), 48
wordplay, 133, 136–43, 177, 212n17
Wright, Nazera Sadiq, 174
Wright, Richard, 104
writers: Black activism of, 28–29; diary form for fiction, 117–20; Lester on writers' roles, 93–94; role in honoring past lives, 72
Wyeth, Sharon Dennis, 14

Yates, Elizabeth, 55, 65
Yenika-Agbaw, Vivian, 64
Yetman, Norman, 41
Your Legacy (Williams), 51

Zeely (Hamilton), 54
Zinn Education Project, 27

ABOUT THE AUTHOR

Karen Michele Chandler is an associate professor and the chair of the University of Louisville's Department of English. She is also a visiting associate professor in Hollins University's graduate program in Children's Literature and Illustration. A former president of the Children's Literature Association, she has published on African American children's literature and film and has coedited special issues of the journals *International Research in Children's Literature* and *Children's Literature Association Journal*.

www.ingramcontent.com/pod-product-compliance
Lightning Source LLC
Chambersburg PA
CBHW030619230426
43661CB00053B/2058